HISTORY OF THE HUTTERITE MENNONITES

Published in connection with the Centennial Observance of the coming of Hutterites to Dakota

The seal has been drawn to show that our history has been written with blood, sweat and tears. Down through the centuries the Hutterites have been severly persecuted. They were almost wiped out until they fled over the Carpathians into Romania. A moving people, because of their faith, they passed through several countries before they settled in Russia for approximately one hundred years. After homage was not granted for religious freedom, a big voyage across the ocean was necessary. Even when our forefathers came to America it meant much work as indicated by the man plowing on the South Dakota prairie.

Our forefathers gave worship of God first priority. Matt. 6:33 *"But seek ye first the kingdom of God, and his righteousness; and all these things shall be added unto you."*

We need to ponder and appreciate our heritage, a torch we did not light but was given to us by other hands. The torch is ours to keep burning brightly and ours to pass on to other generations.

Designed and written by Mrs. Jacob M. Stahl

WIPF & STOCK · Eugene, Oregon

Wipf and Stock Publishers
199 W 8th Ave, Suite 3
Eugene, OR 97401

History of the Hutterite Mennonites
By Hofer, Arnold and Hofer, Norman

ISBN 13: 978-1-61097-238-3
Publication date 7/1/2011
Previously published by Pine Hill Press, 1974

Table of Contents

Preface to the 2011 Reprint Edition

The History of the Hutterite Mennonites was first published in 1974 for the centennial celebration in Freeman, South Dakota commemorating the 100th anniversary of the migrations of the Hutterites and Prairieleut to Dakota Territory in 1874. Since that publication in 1974, the book was reprinted in 1975 and in 1986. It has been out of print for many years.

There has been such demand for it that the Hutterite Mennonite Centennial Committee has decided to reprint again. As a committee we have made certain that all the information in the original publication is included in the new edition.

All ship lists are exactly as the original publication, with the exception of the first Hutterite immigration ship, the Hammonia, coming to America in 1874. This ship list contains the Schmeidleut and Dariusleut Hutterites and the Hutterdorf "Prairieleut" church people. We are indebted to Anna Walter of Prairie Elk Colony, Wolf Point, Montana for updating this ship list for us and identifying many of the passengers.

Since 1974 over 23 books have been published about Hutterite and Hutterite Mennonite (Prairieleut) history. We have included an updated Bibliography in the reprint.

Thanks to William Schroeder and Helmut T. Huebert for permission to use a page from *Mennonite Historical Atlas* for the map of the Hutterite migrations in Europe and Ukraine.

The Hutterite Mennonite Centennial Committee has sponsored historical tours to Europe in 1993, 1998, and 2009 led by Gary Waltner of Weierhof, Germany, following the migrations of the Hutterites in Europe. Several study groups have been to Russia (Ukraine) studying the history of the Hutterites during their 100 year sojourn in Ukraine before their migration to America in 1874.

These historical tours have increased the knowledge of our history and migrations. In light of this additional information, we have asked Wesley Tschetter of Brookings, South Dakota to write a short history of the Hutterite sojourns in Europe and Ukraine. We are deeply indebted to Wesley for the history he has written and research he has done for this reprint.

Copies of this publication may be purchased from the committee.

Delmer Hofer, chairman
PO Box 476
1006 Stadium Drive
Freeman, South Dakota 57029

Vernon P. Hofer, treasurer
PO Box 688
1002 Stadium Drive
Freeman, South Dakota 57029

Norman Hofer, secretary
43439 279 th St
Freeman, South Dakota 57029

Foreword

Plans for a Centennial Commemoration of the coming to America of our forefathers were activated when a group of interested people met at the Bethany Church on March 12, 1973, and elected a Steering Committee for directing the event. The elected committee was as follows:

Arnold M. Hofer, Chairman
Kenneth Walter, Vice-Chairman
Joe D. M. Gross, Treasurer
David P. Gross, Secretary
Norman Hofer, Member

The need for a statement of purpose was sensed and the following was adopted. It is adapted from another group's statement.

Whereas the centennial (100 Year) of the arrival of the first of our Hutterite ancestors who came to America to make permanent homes will be upon us in the coming year and

Whereas there will be no more appropriate time in our life time to honor our ancestors who because of religious persecution suffered and died for centuries in foreign countries and finally through God's leading were able to find and settle in a free country (America) where they could live and worship according to the dictates of their conscience and

Whereas we are the descendants of these early pioneers who sacrificed and endured so much in order to leave us a rich heritage to enjoy and

Whereas it appears that nearly all of the early pioneers who were born in a foreign country have already gone to their eternal reward and

Whereas the old customs and traditions and our knowledge and appreciation of such are fast fading in our generation and

Whereas there appears to be considerable material of historic value such as Pioneer clothing, important documents, portraits, tools etc. in the community which should be preserved for future generations to appreciate and become a lasting monument and

Whereas there seems to be considerable interest in the community among our people to observe such a centennial in order to honor our ancestors and thank God for His wonderful leading and

Whereas other Mennonite groups are planning similar observations

We therefore designate Sunday, August 18, 1974, as the day for the commemoration of this event and to implement these purposes.

Further meetings resulted in the establishment of the following additional committees:

Program
Joe Hofman, Chairman
Mrs. Lloyd Hofer, Secretary
Rev. D. S. Wipf
Rev. Vernon Lohrentz
Jake Entz
Arnold M. Hofer

Memorial Committee
Ernest Tschetter
Derald Walter
Joe P. Hofer
Paul Stahl
Andrew J. Hofer
David P. Gross

Publications Committee
Mrs. Jacob M. Stahl
Mrs. Ernest J. Hofer
Ervin R. Gross
Mrs. John M. Stahl
Joe D. M. Gross
Kenneth J. Walter

Documents, Artifacts, and Clothing Committee
Mr. and Mrs. Joe G. Hofer
John M. Gross
Mrs. Jacob M. Stahl
Mr. and Mrs. John J. Walter
Mrs. Art (Justina) Guerkie
Norman Hofer

These committees have been active in the following ways:

THE MEMORIAL COMMITTEE represented the Hutterites in sponsoring and erecting the Centennial Marker on Highway 81, on Fensel's property, northeast of Freeman, which commemorates the coming of the three groups of Mennonites to the Freeman area starting in 1874—the Swiss, the Low-Germans and the Hutterites.

They are also in charge of erecting a marker which is to be placed in the cemetary of the Neu Hutterthal Church. This gives a brief history of the Hutterite people. It pays tribute to Paul and Lorentz Tschetter as leaders in the Migration. Also listed are all the churches founded by Hutterite Mennonites in the Freeman area.

Since Lorentz Tschetter's grave near Olivet is unmarked, the committee is placing a slab identifying the grave which is located on a hill about one mile east of Olivet.

THE PROGRAM COMMITTEE is responsible for the program on the commemorative day. It is printed in this publication.

THE DOCUMENTS, ARTIFACTS AND CLOTHING COMMITTEE will be in charge of displaying many items that were brought to America from Russia. The Hutterian Brethren are in possession of some very old original books, hand written, telling our history. An effort will be made to display as many of these as possible.

THE PUBLICATION COMMITTEE is in charge of publishing this book. Someone said recently that Hutterites are the most studied and most written about group of people for their number of any group existing. While this is probably true, we have access to material that is interesting and adds to the understanding of our history. On the part of some, there is increasing interest in our heritage and history, and this publication should help to add something to the excellent books already available. This is not an effort to produce something scholarly. It is merely an effort to give the people access to the information which is not readily available.

It is no doubt true that there is still much old, valuable, written or printed material in our homes which hasn't been recognized for its worth. Generally this is in the German language and individuals who can't read it often consider it of no value. Some of the material printed in this book was first discovered several months ago. We urge you not to destroy any material you cannot read which has been passed down to you, unless you have determined what it is. Old diaries, autobiographies or any writing coming from before the Migration should be carefully evaluated before being discarded.

In using and handling precious writings, the desire is strong to have a central archive where the items could be loaned or given for their proper care and preservation. Microfilms could be made available to interested persons to view. Do we have anyone among the Hutterian Brethren or the Hutterite Mennonites who would establish a Hutterite Archive Center?

The Steering Committee

Tribute

We thank and praise God for the faith and spiritual guidance given to our forefathers so that they boldly, in spite of much sacrifice, could live up to their convictions based on scripture.

We thank and praise God that they were willing to leave comfortable homes and prosperous economic circumstances because they believed in "Thou shalt not kill" and "Love your enemies" as a way of life.

We thank and praise God for their pioneering spirit. They were willing to brave the unknown. They left the sheltered community of the dorf and faced the open prairies with its fires, grasshoppers, drought and changeable climate.

We thank and praise God for their spiritual values and priorities. They believed in God and His guidance in their lives. They established places of worship for worshipping Him and for instructing believers.

We thank and praise God for the priority they gave to education. They petitioned the President for the right to have their own schools. They believed the three R's and that religious instruction was essential to their survival.

We thank and praise God for the fact that the convictions that brought our forefathers to America are still the convictions of some of their children's children. This is evidenced by the modern places of worship where the gospel is preached and where convictions such as nonresistance and not taking an oath still have support.

We thank and praise God for a country whose spirit and hospitality is evidenced by the inscription on the base of the Statute of Liberty, "Give me your poor, your tired masses longing to be free."

We thank and praise God for President Ulysses S. Grant for extending hospitality and interest to a strange people with rather special requests.

We thank and praise God for John L. Pennington of the Dakota Territory who saw in the Mennonites and the Hutterites, as well as other German Russians, a desirable class of people, and who implemented the erection of an immigrant reception house and the appropriation of funds to encourage immigrants to settle in Dakota Territory.

We thank and praise God that the landless and the poor had the new opportunity to become farmers, owning their own land because of the Homestead Act which granted them free land with the option to buy additional land reasonably.

We thank and praise God for a country that grants minority rights and privileges. Specifically we are thankful for its permitting Hutterite people to live in communities and colonies, for permitting the use of the German language, for exemption from military service, for being able to affirm in place of swearing an oath, for the privilege of parochial schools and for religious freedom.

We thank and praise God that throughout the last century, with a few tragic exceptions, the basic human rights and freedoms offered by this country have been upheld.

We thank and praise God that the Eastern Mennonites, specifically John F. Funk, showed concern and compassion for their brethren in Russia and were hospitable and accommodating to the delegates who came to view the land, for accommodating 32 Hutterites over the winter of 1874-1875, for assistance to Dakota Hutterites and Mennonites in the trying 1875-1880 period and for their visits to Dakota in the pioneer days with a special concern for their spiritual life.

We thank and praise God that the children's children of our migrating forefathers have gone beyond personal spiritual piety to an understanding of God's message in Christ, which includes witness and service, and love and care for all of God's children.

Rev. D. S. Wipf
John P. Kleinsasser
Paul G. Tschetter

A Tribute To Our Forefathers

Our forefathers came to America from South Russia with the hope that here they would be free from military service. Such freedom they believed was necessary for their survival as a people. The Czar had introduced military service thus, ending the favored status promised by Catherine the Great a century earlier. He had altered his position and offered forestry and other noncombatant assignments in lieu of army duty. But they were fearful for the future. Already some of their members including some of their leaders were hauling salt from the sea inland with their own horses and wagons to fulfill their military obligations. Would some future Czar fail to honor the compromise of the present ruler?

Their history gave ample proof that their fears were well founded. For 350 years the Hutterian Brethren named for their founder Jacob Hutter in 1528 had fled from country to country. First, from Morovia to Transylvania (1621) to Rumania (1767) to a province in Central Russia (1770) and then rescued from serdom by a Mennonite Johann Cornies and resettled to the South Russian Mennonite Colony in 1840. Would history repeat itself? No they would make their own choice and come to America.

But lets return once more to their leader Jacob Hutter. Like other Anabaptist leaders, he believed in separation of church and state, adult baptism upon personal confession of faith, non-resistance and non-swearing of oaths. However, he differed in that Acts 2:44 for him needed a literal intrepretation through a collective community sharing of material as well as spiritual gifts on scriptual not economic grounds. These collective communities known as Bruderhofs became easy targets for government, church and the general public both because they were easily identified by the strangeness of their practice. As a result they suffered more and greater persecution than any other Mennonite group. In America they hoped to find peace and rest.

In May 1873 two of their number landed in New York as a part of a twelve man delegation of Mennonites to explore the possibility of migration. Paul Tschetter a young minister of 31 and his uncle Lohrenz Tschetter were the Hutterian delegates. So intent were these two to gain some commitment from the United States government concerning freedom from military duty, that they received an audience with President Grant on August 8, 1873 at his summer home in Long Island. Their petition to him included, a request of exemption from military service and jury duty and the right to govern their own schools. Of this, Paul Tschetter, wrote in his diary, "the President received us in the most friendly manner and we presented our petition to him personally. After reading it very carefully the President replied that we must have patience to wait for an answer to our petition." The reply came on September 5, 1873 through Secretary of State, Hamilton Fish, who said in essence that such matters were the exclusive rights of state legislation and that the President had no assurance as to how states, where the immigrants might choose to live, would legislate.

The word Hutterian has both a religious and ethnic meaning. The religious meaning relates to collective communal living and was the exclusive mode of expression until their migration to America. The ethnic meaning relates to who they were and where they came from. Common Hutterian family names, such as, Hofer, Walter, Glanzer, Kleinsasser, Wipf, Tschetter, Mendel, Gross, Pullman, Wollman, Decker, Stahl, Wurz and others were added as they moved to new locations and local people accepted their beliefs and joined the Bruderhof. For instance, Abram Tschetter a Catholic priest was sent to convert the Hutterians but instead was converted and joined them. That was in 1760 in Hungary and the first appearance of this family name.

In America at migration only some of the Hutterian Brethren choose to live in Bruderhofs. The others choose to live as single family units. Thus, the Hutterian Brethren in America went in two directions; the "Bruderhof" people and the "Prairie" people. Both prospered and multiplied in their own right.

The number of Hutterian Brethren at any time prior to migration to America was always small, less than 300, and in 1767 the entire group numbered only 67 souls. Their coming to America had several unique features when compared with the general Mennonite migration. They all came between 1874 and 1880, there were about 1200 of them, they all came to South Dakota and they choose to continue or not continue the communal aspect of their religious belief.

These then are our forefathers. Unique in their religious concepts, driven across the eastern face of Europe seeking a home which would give them freedom to live according to their conscience, rescued from Russian serfdom by a Mennonite and resettled in South Russia to be reunited with the mainstream of Mennonites which had borne them in the early 16th century.

In 1974, the date of our centennial, we reflect and ask was it worth the effort? Is it to our gain or loss? In answer we respond, all of us, with A Tribute to Our Forefathers. This we do before God and man.

Let Us Give Tribute, to their basic concept of collective religious communal sharing which was their overriding conviction and kept them a viable spiritual community for 350 years before coming to America. Their willingness to suffer and die for their faith is the sole reason that any of us here today are Hutterians are here at all.

Let Us Give Tribute, to their willingness to leave comfortable homes and prosperous economic circumstances because they believed in "Thou shalt not kill'' and ''Love your enemies'' as a way of life which must be a part of each christian's personal testimony. They said so to Czar and President.

Let Us Give Tribute, to their pioneering spirit. They were willing to brave the unknown. They left the sheltered community of the ''drof'' and faced the open prairies with its fires, grasshoppers, drought, hot summers and cold snowy winters. They learned new ways of farming and housekeeping. Along with other pioneers of the west they adapted to and conquered their surroundings.

Let Us Give Tribute, to the way they adapted to their new environment. The German language had to be replaced with English. Their new neighbors were no longer the Russian natives in the next ''drof'' but prairie folk who were their equals. They learned new methods of doing business as they bought and sold. Government functioned differently from what they knew. They observed, learned and adapted to their choosen country's ways.

Let Us Give Tribute, to their priority for the need to educate their children. They had petitioned the President for the right to have their own schools. The educational system of the ''drof'' school is what they endorsed and wanted to continue. They found teachers from among their own and provided places for students to gather. They believed the 3 R's and religious instruction essential to their survival.

Finally, **Let Us Give Tribute**, to their spiritual values. They believed in God and His guidance in their lives. They believed in worshipping Him, first in their homes and then in church buildings. They believed in religious instruction for their children. They believed in being just and loving with their own and their neighbors. Their religion was real and demanded a spiritual walk examplary to christian and world alike.

And now what has happened in the century since their coming? We have gone from the village life style of Russia to the modern mechanized farm to the urban and suburban complexities of our modern cities. We have spread from the prairies of South Dakota to most of the states of the United States and the provinces of Canada and beyond these borders. We have come from the schools of the 3 R's to the colleges and universities of our land which in turn enabled us to enter the vast educational, professional and governmental arenas available to Americans. In spiritual matters, we have gone beyond personal spiritual piety to an understanding of God's message in Christ, which includes witness and service, love and care for all of God's children. *These, too, are tributes* to the children and Children's children of our migrating forefathers.

What about the next century? We will never again be the tightly knit group we once were. We will be assimilated into the general society around us and our characteristic identity will be more obscure. We can only hope that the heritage which is ours will continue to produce those virtues for good we know and discourage those which promote evil. If we continue to let God's Hand direct us, then history will honor our efforts and be kind to us. We have received much. Let us be responsible, each of us, and pass the gift on to our children.

Paul G. Tschetter
2494 South Cook Street
Denver, Colo. 80210

The following information placed by the Hutterite Centennial Committee is on a large stone marker at the Neu Hutterthaler Church, located 6 miles west and 6½ north of Freeman.

HUTTERITE MEMORIAL 1874-1974

In humble thanksgiving to Christ our Saviour, in grateful remembrance of our early church leaders, in deep appreciation of our Country America and as a challenge to our posterity, we dedicate this memorial. Jesus Christ the same yesterday and today and forever. Heb. 13:8.

The Hutterites, named after Jacob Hutter, an early church leader, are a branch of the Anabaptist Movement that began in Switzerland in 1525.

The Hutterite Church with the communal way of living began in Moravia, Austria in 1528.

After centuries of religious persecution in various parts of Europe God's providence through the leadership of Rev. Paul Tschetter 1842-1919 and Lorenz Tschetter 1819-1878 brought them to America between 1874-1879.

Rev. Paul Tschetter settled near this site and his grave is near by.

Lorenz Tschetter settled near Olivet, So. Dak. where a simple slab marks his grave on a lonely hill one mile Southeast of Olivet.

Two main branches of the Hutterites exist today:

Those who live in Bruderhofs and have all property in common and those who believe in individual ownership and identify with the Mennonites.

The latter, after meeting in private homes for worship and later in schoolhouses finally established the following churches in this area as listed on reverse side.

Hutterdorf Mennonite Church
First Building 1901
Location three miles South West of Freeman
First Minister, William Tschetter served 32 years
Rev. David Waldner
Dissolved in 1961

Hutterthal Mennonite Church
First Building in 1882
Location four miles North West of Freeman
Served by four Hutterite Ministers namely John Kleinsasser, John Waldner, Paul Hofer and John L. Wipf from 1879 for 19, 20, 29 and 30 years respectively

Neu Hutterthaler Mennonite Church
First Building in 1888
Location a few rods south of this site
First Minister Paul Tschetter 1874-1919

Salem Krimmer Mennonite Brethren Church
First Building in 1900 one mile South West of this site
First Minister Henry Goosen 1885-1899
First Hutterite Minister John Tschetter 1886-1908
Merged with M. B. Conference in 1960

Bethany Mennonite Church at Freeman
First Building 1898
Location on site of present Church Building
Served by various Ministers for many years
First Hutterite Minister Rev. P. P. Kleinsasser 1923-1924

Zion Mennonite Church
First Building 1913
Location three miles North East of Bridgewater
First Minister Michael J. Hofer served 1920-1950
Present Church Building in Bridgewater, So. Dak.

The following memorial is placed by the Hutterite, Swiss and Low-German groups combined, at the Fensel Motel, on Highway 81 east of Freeman.

MENNONITE AND HUTTERIAN IMMIGRATION MEMORIAL
1874—Centennial—1974

This marker commemorates the immigration of the first large groups of Swiss, Low German and Hutterian Brethern from Russia to Dakota Territory.

The first group of 15 families arrrived in Yankton on October 17, 1873. However a mass movement of several hundred families followed in 1874, with smaller groups arriving all through the 1870's. The Mennonites settled mainly in Hutchinson, Turner and Bon Homme counties.

The Mennonites and Hutterian Brethren have their origin in the Anabaptist wing of the Reformation which started in Central Europe. Their belief in separation of church and state and in nonresistance led to severe persecution for some three centuries. Hounded from country to country in Europe, God's providence finally led them to America for asylum.

The first years of severe winters, grasshoppers, prairie fires and drought threatened their survival. However, hard work, an unwavering faith in God and financial aid from the Eastern Mennonite Organizations carried them through these critical years.

To commemorate the hardships they endured, the sacrifices they made and the rich heritage they left for us, we dedicate this monument. May their positive Christian living challenge us to rededicate ourselves to a more humble and closer walk with our Creator.

"For other foundation can no man lay than that is laid, which is Jesus Christ." I Cor. 3:11.

Due to the demand of this publication The Hutterite Mennonite Centennial Steering Committee decided to have a second edition printed. Several corrections were brought to our attention. They are listed below. Also added were available pictures of the Centennial and Memorial Program.

Additions are found on Pages 2a, 2b, 3a, 3b, 61, and 168.

A map on page 24 of Russia was incorrect and is eliminated.

On page 96 find an explanation under the map.

On page 65, second column first sentence is corrected.

On page 76, corrected passengers No. 241 and 254.

On page 77, corrected passengers No. 71.

On page 79, corrected passengers No. 99.

On page 88, corrected passengers No. 96 with an addition.

On page 102 corrected explanation on top picture.

On page 105 corrected explanation of lower right picture.

On page 110 corrected explanation on both top pictures.

HUTTERITE MENNONITE CENTENNIAL SPEAKERS

August 18, 1974

Dr. John Hostetler

Arnold M. Hofer

Rev. Paul S. Gross

Dr. Bernie Wiebe

Hutterite Mennonite Centennial Choir, Aug. 18, 1974

'O God Our Help In Ages Past'

2:30 P.M.

Chairman .... Mr. Joe T. Hofman

Prelude

General Song

Welcome

Devotional .... Rev. LaVerne Hofer

Centennial Choir .... *For All The Saints*

Hutterites in Europe ....*Dr. John Hostetler
"1528-1874"

Music .... The Harmony Hofers

The Migration Story .... Mrs. John M. Stahl

Centennial Choir .... *Ein Auswanderungs Lied*

A Century of Change .... Mr. Arnold M. Hofer
"The Prairieleut 1874-1974"

Acknowledgements and Announcements

Offering

Closing

*Professor of Anthropology and Sociology at Temple University, Philadelphia

'Our Hope For Years To Come'

7:30 P.M.

Chairman .... Mr. Norman Hofer

Prelude

Devotional .... Rev. P. P. Tschetter

Welcome

Centennial Choir .... *O God Our Help In Ages Past*

Hutterian Brethren ....*Rev. Paul S. Gross
"The Challenge After a Century in America"

Music .... James Valley Christian H. S.

God With Us ....*Dr. Bernie Wiebe
"Past, Present, Future"

Centennial Choir .... *Grosser Gott Wir Loben Dich*

Tribute .... Rev. D. S. Wipf

Acknowledgements and Announcements

Offering

Closing

*Minister at Espanola Hutterite Colony in the state of Washington.
* *President of Freeman Junior College

Music Director—Mr. James Glanzer
Organist—Mrs. Orville Wipf
Pianist—Mrs. Harold Hofer

Mennonite Centennial Memorial Marker Unveiling

and Dedication Program

Sunday, September 22, 1974

(Weather Permitting)

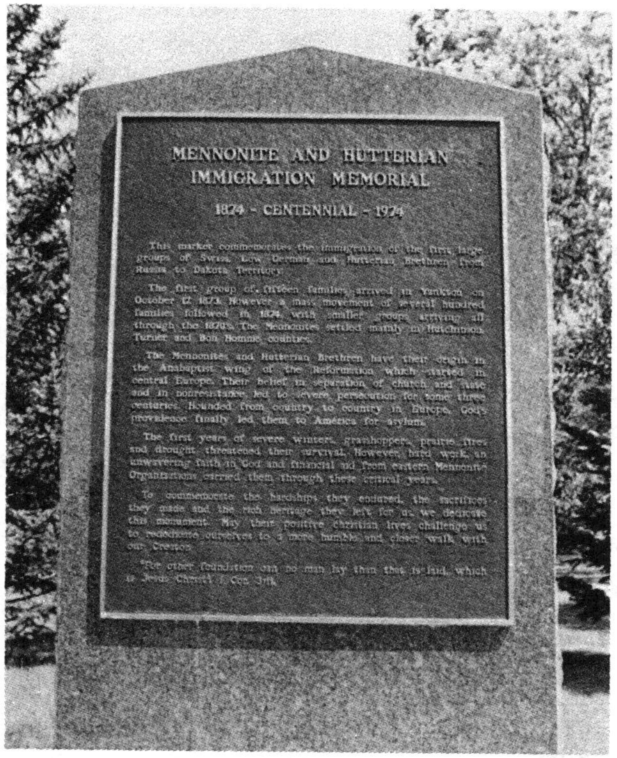

Centennial Memorial Marker Erected Jointly by the Swiss, Low-German, and Hutterite Mennonite Churches Located on Highway 81 on the Northeast Edge of Freeman, South Dakota

The Public is Invited to Attend Any or All of The Following Open Air Program

Four Stops Will Be Made at Four Different Sites, Respectively

1. The first stop will be at Fensel's Motel Driveway, where a Centennial Memorial Marker has been erected jointly by the Swiss, Low German and Hutterite Churches.

PROGRAM AT 1:30 P.M.

Music .... Freeman Junior College
Topic The Pilgrimage of Faith, Heb. 11:13,16 Dr. Bernie Wiebe
Unveiling of Memorial Marker
Dedicatory Prayer .... Dr. Bernie Wiebe

2. Next stop will be at the Schartner Cemetery 5 miles North, 2 miles East and 1½ miles North at the site where a Centennial Memorial Marker has been erected by the Low German Mennonite Churches.

PROGRAM AT 2:30 P.M.

Welcome and Prayer .... Rev. Paul Kroeker
Song *Men's Glory* Jake Becker
Remembering The Past .... Rev. August Ewert
Tribute to Elder Tobias Unruh .... Dave Becker
Unveiling of Marker
Dedicatory Prayer .... Rev. John Kliewer
Closing Prayer .... Rev. Elden Classen

3. The third stop will be ½ mile North, 2 miles West, then 7 miles West on the Clayton Road and ½ mile North to the Neu Hutterthaler Cemetery where the Hutterite Mennonite Churches have errected a Hutterite Memorial.

PROGRAM AT 3:30 P.M.

Invocation .... Rev. Paul Kliewer
Song .... Neu Hutterthal Church
Tribute .... Wesley Tschetter
Unveiling of Marker
Dedicatory Prayer .... Rev. Arlie Rauch

4. The last stop will be ½ mile South, 1 mile West then 14 miles South to Highway 18 at Menno, then 4 miles West on Highway 18 to the site of Delegate Lorenz Tschetter's grave.

PROGRAM AT 4:30 P.M.

Tribute .... David P. Gross
Thanksgiving Prayer .... Rev. Vernon Lorentz

The time for each stop is approximate.

The Memorial Committee

Hutterite Memorials

Front Side of Memorial Located at the Neu Hutterthaler Church

Back Side of Memorial Located at the Neu Hutterthaler Church

Marker Placed on Grave of Lorenz Tschetter, Delegate to America in 1874, Located 1½ Mile East of Olivet

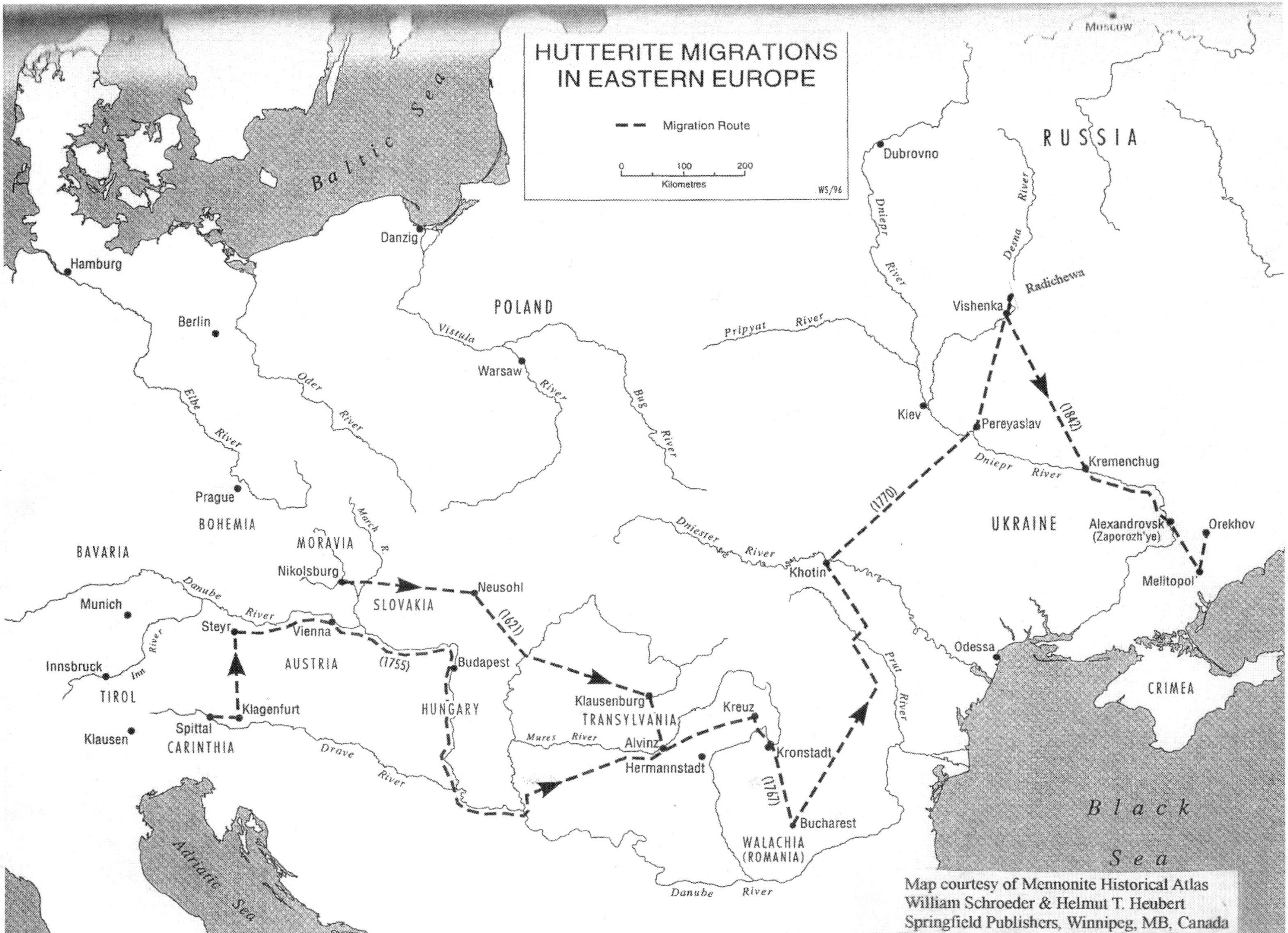

Map courtesy of Mennonite Historical Atlas
William Schroeder & Helmut T. Heubert
Springfield Publishers, Winnipeg, MB, Canada

Chapter 1
European History

O. T.	3½ yrs.	30 A.D. Holy Spirit Comes	100 A.D.	325 A.D. lull	590 A.D.	1517	1525
	Christ Preaching	Pentecost (Birthday of Church)	persecution anti-Nicene	post Nicene	Medieval Period		

Two thousand years ago Jesus Christ came from heaven to earth, to be the Saviour of the world. He showed us how to be obedient to the will of God, even to the death on the cross. Christ established His church and gave it the great commission to go into all parts of the world and preach the Gospel to every creature. Mark 16:15 - 16. He enriched the church by sending the Holy Spirit on the day of Pentecost 30 A.D. so that His disciples were given power to preach His gospel.

We are the heirs of the faith of this church. The Anabaptists hold to these truths of simple faith and purity of life which is taught in the New Testament.

It is necessary to go back and look at the development of the early church. It spread rapidly, as persecution set in against the Christians, to Europe beyond Rome, to Persia, to Egypt and all along the coast of the Mediterrean Sea. Most church members were from the lower class of people. Thus the state of the church had no temporal advantage such as wealth or material things. This did not hinder the early Christians, they wrote many devotional material, creeds and essays on the defense of the faith. The pagan rulers made their governments enforce extreme persecution, on these Christians from 250-310 A.D., until in 311 A.D. Christianity was legalized by the Roman Emperor Constantine. The church then became a state religion which meant each citizen automatically became a member. Thus the church was no longer composed of persons who had repented of their sins and had been born again by the Spirit of God.

Many changes began to take place, one being the development of the hierarchy. Also there was much interest in historical and devotional literature. Men worked on Bible translations such as: O.T. Hebrew, LXX Greek, New Testament Greek and in 400 A.D. the Vulgate.

This now brings us to the Medievel Period on the time line. The pope (that word means father) had become so powerful that he had absolute reign and everyone had to bow to him. He then decided to build in Rome a huge new cathedral and for this he needed lots of money to pay for the materials and workers. He sent a monk named Tetzel to Central Europe to sell papers called "Indulgences." These papers stated that in return for a certain sum of money, a certain number of sins were forgiven, and the buyer of the paper was excused from a certain number of years in Purgatory.

All of this might have worked in 1517 if the printing press had not been invented. One of the first items Johann Gutenburg printed on his press was indulgence blanks. But another thing was being printed: The Holy Bible. This became a revival for learning as Christian reading material was widespread. People began to read, study and learn of Jesus' life and teachings, and these teachings of Jesus were far different from the teachings of the Catholic church.

Catholic	Lutheran	Presbyterian & Reformed &	Anabaptists
	Luther	Zwingli	

One man named Martin Luther objected to the sale of indulgences and hoped to correct the Catholic church of some of its wrongs. The greedy men in the church refused to allow any change in church teaching, so on the eve of October 31, 1517 as Martin Luther nailed 95 thesis on the church door at Wittenburg, Germany, the Protestant church was born. Luther and his followers formed a separate church which we know today as the Lutheran church. They were persecuted by the Catholic church but soon they became too strong to be destroyed. In the German states where Luther's teachings were followed, all citizens had to be members of the Lutheran church.

Calvin and Zwingli from Switzerland also broke away from the Catholic church. Now known as the Reformed and Presbyterian churches, respectively, they insisted that people must belong to the ruling church and must bring their babies to be baptized into the new church.

Some of the men who worked with Zwingli were dissatisfied and felt the need for a free voluntary church. They met in homes for many years and it was during one of these Bible Study meetings that George Blaurock asked Conrad Grebel to baptize him and he in turn baptized others present in the room. They were called Anabaptists (re baptizers) because they could not recognize infant baptism.

January 17, 1525 Zwingli and his followers called a public debate with the Anabaptist leaders. The date of this public debate is known as the birthday of the Anabaptist church. The Anabaptist leaders held fast to the Gospel which taught:

1. The word of God as a standard for being a Christian, (not those who were baptized as infants and attended mass).
2. The Church was separate from the State. (They did not like government appointed ministers and government paying expenses of the church.)
3. They believed in baptism upon confession of faith.
4. They believed in the way of love instead of war, strife and violence.

Zwingli, Calvin, Luther and other "State" church leaders did not agree with this teaching and joined forces with the Catholics in an attempt to kill the movement. Today many of the convictions for which these men died are accepted by all Christians, but it was the Anabaptists who were ahead of their time by several centuries in thought and theology.

Some of the early leaders of the Anabaptist movement were: Conrad Grebel, George Blaurock, Felix Manz, Balthasar Hubmaier, Menno Simon, and Jacob Hutter. These men were highly educated, intelligent men many of whom were ex-monks or Hebrew scholars.

Persecution set in immediately directed against the leaders. This drove many preachers from Switzerland to South Germany and Austria.

Smith's *Story of the Mennonites* tells that in July 1526 Dr. Balthasar Hubmaier organized at Nikolsburg in Moravia a church of over 6,000 members. Their basic principles were the following:

1. Adult baptism upon confession of faith
2. The Lord's Supper as a memorial feast
3. Non-resistance
4. Opposition to the oath and swearing
5. Separation from the world
6. The ban to be used in church discipline

These members came from all over Switzerland, South Germany, The Tyrol, Schleswig, and Upper Austria to escape persecution. But at this time the turks were threatening war on Moravia and the government asked them to bear arms. This caused a split in the church, in which the conservative group (which was the smaller) believed that under no circumstances can a follower of Christ bear arms and in Chapter Two of Acts the only Christian way to live is the one which the early church in Jerusalem followed by having all things in common. Jacob Wiedeman, who was the leader of this group, left Nikolsburg in 1528 with his followers and traveled to Austerlitz to seek refuge on the Kaunitz estates. On their way they stopped at Bogenitz where they spread a cloak on the ground and all members placed their material possessions on it. This was the beginning of the religious community way of life which is still practiced among the Hutterites of South Dakota and Canada.

Wiedeman and his followers were warmly welcomed by the four Kaunitz brothers and on their estates they built the first household or Bruderhof.

Jacob Wiedeman lacked only one thing, the ability in leadership. He appealed to Jacob Hutter known as Jacob of Welfsberg, a Tyrolian, who by trade was a hat maker, to assist him. Hutter, who was a believer in the community way of life, sent the persecuted from other countries to Austerlitz from 1528 to 1533. Then in 1533 he along with a large group of Tyrolians joined the group at Austerlitz. Soon because of his strict discipline and ability as an organizer Hutter became leader of this congregation, which has remained unchanged for more than four centuries.

In 1536 persecution set in and Hutter was burned at the stake. The Hutterites, as they are called after their leader Jacob Hutter, have a history of almost continuous persecution. They paid the ultimate price for their faith. Some were left to rot in prison, while others were broken on the rock, thrown into rivers, burned at the stake, sold as galley slaves, beheaded or buried alive.

The Moravian nobles took a stand against the Imperial orders who were persecuting their good farmers. The Hutterite chronicles report that between 1550 until King Ferdinand's death in 1564 was "the time of the great persecution." During this time 16 colonies were destroyed, 81 members murdered and 140 sold into slavery to Turkey.

The chronicles also report that "the good time of the church" was during the reign of Maximillian II (1564-1576) and the first half of the next monarchi reign (1576-1612). Even so, soldiers would come to the Bruderhofs to steal and harass the believers. During this time their bruderhofs prospered under their Moravian nobles. It has been estimated that there were eighty-six Hutterite bruderhofs in Moravia and Hungary. The population of each of these bruderhofs was between three to four hundred.

These bruderhofs were mostly agricultural and flour mills, and large herds of cattle and fine breeds of horses. They also manufactured cutlery and pottery. Their nobles employed them as administrators of mills and farms. In 1581 one of their physicians was called upon by Emperor Rudolph II after other physicians from as far as Italy and Spain could not help him. The doctor was able to help the Emperor.

Everyone did what he was best suited for and the profits from the different trades were put into the communal treasury. Food, clothing and expenses were taken from the treasury. Widows, orphans and the old were taken care of and no one was in want.

Then a religious war broke out called the Thirty Years War (1618-1648). Many armies marched through the country and plundered down on the Hutterite Bruderhofs since they had large amounts of food and other materials. These soldiers stole from their granaries and tortured and killed Hutterite men.

On page 54 *The Hutterian Brethren* which gets its account from the *Geschechtbuch* p. 565, describes the cruelty of the armies as follows:

"It was stated above that the year 1621 began with much tribulation. The robbing, plundering, and burning of houses carried on by the soldiers continued throughout this and the following year. Altogether it was a very fearsome, miserable, and evil time. It is impossible to write or tell of all the great and inhuman cruelties which were inflicted upon us and others in this godless, accursed, and devilish war at the hands of the Spanish, Walloon, Polish and German Imperial forces. I cannot tell what awful devilish things were perpetrated on many good, pious and honorable sisters who had loved sobriety and purity from their youth, yea, on children, both boys and girls. Women with child and mothers on their deathbed as well as virgins were most outrageously attacked. The men were burned with glowing irons and red-hot pans; Their feet were held in the fire until their toes were burned off; wounds were cut, into which powder was poured and set afire; fingers and ears were cut off, eyes forced out by inhuman torture; men were hung up by the neck like thieves; all sorts of such diabolical brutality and unheard of godlessness were committed, half the shame of which is not to be written. Such things were openly practices by the imperial soldiers who believed themselves to be the best of Christians. It would be impossible for one who had not himself seen and witnessed it to believe that a human being could conduct himself as did these demon possessed men. It would have been no wonder had the heavens turned pale, the earth shaken and all the elements trembled; yea, one would suppose that the devil himself would have been more fearful of the might, power, glory and majesty of God than these shameless men. May God lead them to realize it, to whom and to whose righteous judgment we commit everything."

Many congregations fled to Bruderhofs in more remote areas. The Austrian government issued a decree in September 22, 1622 that all Hutterites were to leave Moravia in not less than four weeks or they would be put to death.

There were many sick and aged and winter was coming. The Chronicles of the Hutterites report that they had to leave twenty-four bruderhofs that were filled with barley, wheat and oats, 130 head of cattle, 150 horses, 70 oxen, 655 hogs, 300 barrels of wine, cloth, linen, salt, lard, wool, copper and tools in the shops. This was estimated to be $367,000 in value.

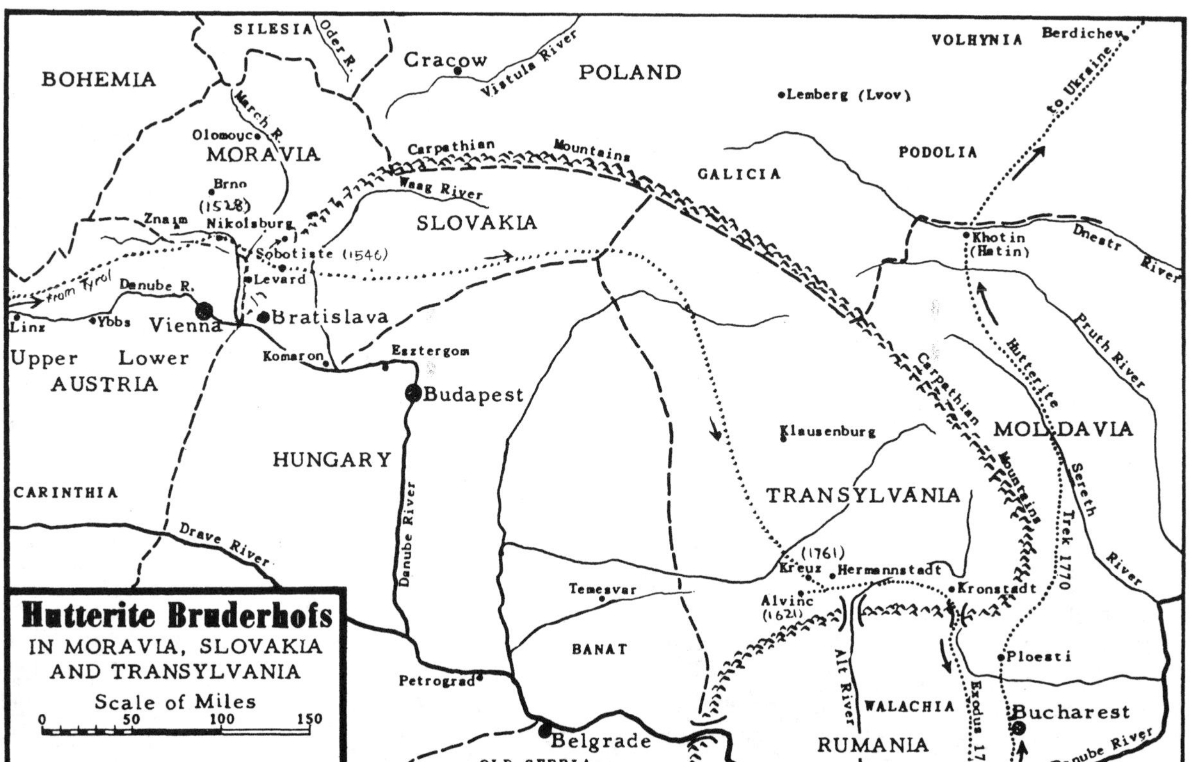

Hutterite Wanderings in the Wilderness of This World

The persecuted Hutterites who had been driven from Moravia fled over the Hungarian mountains and came to seek refuge among their brethren in Hungary. The following three bruderhofs were established: Sabotisch, Protska, and Lewar. It was hard for these bruderhofs to help these empty handed newcomers. Sabotisch, the smallest bruderhof, had 3,000 refugees for the winter. Many of the younger men sought employment from the Hungarian nobles in order to buy food supplies.

The Turkish wars followed the Thirty Years War and once again the Hutterites were subjected to the ruthlessness of the invaders. The Turkish armies carried off the rich spoils from their storehouses and livestock. This was all taken easily for the brethren were believers in non-resistance.

The Hutterites were reduced to poverty so in 1665 they sent representatives to Holland to beg aid from the Mennonites and it was given to them. The Hutterites decided to abandon their community way of life in 1686. Their large supplies of food and other essentials in one place seemed unwise because of the repeated raids by the Turks. Everyone returned to private ownership after the property was divided.

The Hutterites during the eighteenth century had a tremendous struggle for survival. Because of persecution they were forced several times to switch from community living to private ownership and back again. The repeated raids by the Turks and persecution by the Catholics dropped their membership.

In 1760 the Jesuits received from Maria Theresa permission to force the Hutterites to convert to Catholicism. Hutterite homes were searched and their religious material that was found was burned. The Hutterite ministers were put into prison and were promised freedom only if they became Catholic. They closed their churches and opened Catholic churches instead. Hutterite families were not left alone for soldiers slept and ate in their homes.

After awhile the Hutterites were allowed to have their own church services, own teachers, own ministers and be exempted from military service provided they become Catholic. Many accepted this offer probably afraid and tired of going through more persecution. These Catholic Hutterites were known as Habaner. The word Habaner in the slavonic language means an awkward person. The Hutterite way is to die for principles of faith instead of recanting. A small group of Habaner exist yet today in Slovakia. They were once great tradesmen in pottery called Habaner ceramics. Now hardly anyone knows about these people while their brethren who continued to be true to the faith and the Christian fundamentals of love and the cross prosper here in America.

The Chronicles report that by 1760 terrible persecution reduced the number of Hutterites to sixteen. The ones named were: Andreas Wurz, Johann Kleinsasser, George Waldner (father of the Chronicles), Peter and Joseph Mueller, Christian Glanzer and Johannes Stahl. Johannes Stahl described in appearance as small, swarthy with curly hair and Lohrenz Tschetter were thrown into prison. The Jesuits took the children and had them baptized in the Catholic faith. When he saw he had no method to convert these imprisoned men he banished them from the country with Joseph Kuhr (Chur). Johannes Stahl had to leave behind his wife and four children not knowing if he'd ever see them again. These two men wandered into Wallachia (Rumania). There they found prosperous people who were given religious freedom. The country looked promising for agricultural purposes. They returned and informed their brethren that they had found a place to live.

This mere handful of brave and God-fearing people (who were members of the congregation in Alwintz) along with a large number of Lutheran exiles from Carinthia, who had accepted the Hutterian way of life, fled Maria Theresa's Empire and crossed the Carpathians into Rumania. They left all their possessions and avoided well traveled roads so they wouldn't be found. At first they took wagons but when they reached the Carpathian Mountain range their guides told them to pack necessary things on four horses and leave the wagons behind. The Hutterian Brethren on page 105 explains, "The escorts took us on untrodden ways through the underbrush and wilderness, where they knew that we were safe and without danger, for they knew all the secret ways and paths of the mountains. At many places we had to climb up on hands and feet. Everyone took care to follow closely so that he would not be left behind. At several places the loaded pack-horses were brought up only with great difficulty. So we struggled on during the entire night. Each one can best imagine for himself what a difficult and tedious journey that was, with bag and baggage and little ones on the back, to climb the high mountains, with young and old and weak ones, and that at night. The border was at the very top of the mountain.

Having crossed the border we were safe. We travelled slower a distance on the yonder side of the mountain until daybreak. Then we halted at the side of a brook and had a season of united prayer and thanksgiving."

The Hutterites rented lands from Rumanian noblemen. A Bruderhof was established not far from the capital of Rumania which was Bucharest. Around 1767 some Habaner came and joined the brethren.

A year later war broke out between Turkey and Russia. Turkish raids again swept down on the Hutterites. Sämetin, a Russian general, and his army were camped near the Hutterite Bruderhof. This general told the brethren that Czarina Catharine the Great of Russia, who herself was German, welcomed German farmers to her country. She had large areas of unimproved lands that needed to be developed. He was sure that they would be granted exemption from military service, be given control over their own schools and their own local self-government such as had been already granted to other

Germans including Mennonites. The Hutterites also learned that a Russian nobleman Field Marshal Count Romanov had large areas of land and he needed good farmers.

General Semetin helped Hutterite representatives with passports so they could negotiate with Count Romanzov. Count Romanzov offered one of his manors at Wischinka on the Desna River in the province Tscherinogov.

The Count and the Hutterites drew up the following agreement, freedom of religion, their own schools, no one forced to take oath, exemption from military service, no interference with community living and own local self-government.

The Hutterite representatives went back to the brethren to tell them the good news. The Count sent money, also a sergeant and ten cassocks along to give protection as they journeyed from Rumania to Wischinka. August 1, 1770 they arrived to establish a new Bruderhof. The count gave them a loan to start building. They built barns, houses for winter was coming on. When spring arrived the farmers started working in the fields and the tradesmen started their industries such as pottery, weaving and metal.

And so they settled down enjoying the time of opportunity which had come. The Hutterites were excellent wheat growers and industrialists and soon their Bruderhofs became wealthy.

The Hutterites haven was short lived even though the terms on the contract with the Russian seal beautifully stated from "eternity to eternity to eternity."

Mrs. Jacob M. Stahl

The following transcript was discovered in late June, just before the publication deadline of this book, in the papers of David J. Mendel. It was felt to be of importance because of details not found elsewhere. The origin of the paper is not sure. At the beginning of the transcript is written "David J. Mendel 1892." His daughter, Mrs. Joe G. Hofer was kind enough to translate this immediately so it could be published here. We apologize, as we realize that portions may have been repeated in the preceding story.

THE ESTABLISHMENT OF THE HUTTERTHAL COLONY IN PROVINCE TAURIEN, SOUTH RUSSIA

In 1843 the Hutterthal Colony was established. Because of the mild winter, plowing started in February. In April mud houses were constructed for occupancy during the summer months until the building of dwelling houses could be completed. However, this plan was not accomplished because of heavy rains. Although sixteen houses were erected and covered, none were finished enough to be liveable. As a result the winter was spent in the above mentioned mud houses. Not until 1844 were all houses finished and occupied.

This colony was close to Taschenak River, 18 werst from Kreizstadt, Melitopal (2/3 mile equals 1 werst). The land was level prairie and along the river were fertile meadows. These fertile lowlands provided good nourishment so that the horses, stock cows and sheep soon were in good condition. Both penetrating and heavy rains were necessary for prairie hay and a crop. There were no rock or stone bridges. The necessary rocks or stones were brought from 60 werst away. Soon, however, the newly established brick yards provided durable bricks, making stone and rock unnecessary. Although there were no forests, there was a small wooded area where approximately 1200 trees thrived with much care. There also were a few spots of (Saltpeter) gumbo which were very noticeable during the dry years.

The Honorable Bishop Johann Kornies named the colony Hutterthal in memory of our Reformer Jacob Hutter, who was born in Mesz one-half mile from Bräunchken, Pusterthal. In 1529 Jacob Hutter came to Grafschaft, Tyrol, to the colony after leaving the Catholic church. He was a talented, educated, and highly respected individual and was soon recognized as such by the colony. Soon he was appointed as a teacher. He was instrumental in uniting the church at Austerlitz, Tyrol, with his church at Grafschaft, Tyrol, in Mähren. More churches were organized with the result that new managers had to be elected. The evil one was successful in sowing his seed among the Elders of this congregation. Jacob Hutter had great struggles with these Elders. However, he remained true to his faith. Soon it was revealed that these Elders did not stay with the true gospel. Investigations were made to determine whether some of the members of the colony had become selfish with the colony's profit. Consequently, some of the Elders were found guilty of embezzlement even as Ananias had been. Because Hutter was faithful, the whole congregation accepted him with love. From that time on they were called the Hutterian Brethren. At the same time other congregations were separated and dispersed during the Catholic persecutions.

In 1535 someone betrayed Jacob Hutter; he was arrested because of his staunch faith. He was mistreated unmercifully, and soon after dreadfully martyred. The wounds of his severe torture were filled with alcohol and set on fire. During all this he did not renounce his faith but instead remained steadfast. Although sentenced to be burned alive, he remained true. These events happened March 3, 1536. Even during his torture Hutter called to his persecutors, "Let us try our faith by fire, for this fire cannot damage my soul any more than the hot furnace hurt Shadrack, Meshach, and Abednego."

In this Bruderhof of Hutterthal lived 69 families consisting of 205 males and 210 females. Historians consider theirs to be one of the great emigrations.

In 1753 an awakening came to Ertzherzogth, Körnthen, through the reading of Luther's writings. At this time no religion other than Catholic was permitted. The reading of Christian books enlightened many people. Such books and meetings were kept as secret as possible. Nevertheless soon sermons were given in the Catholic church against these books and teachings. When the sermons alone did not succeed in keeping the people from reading the forbidden books and meeting, public persecutions were begun. Government officials had instructions to make a clean house of the Lutherans and to consider them non-resident citizens. Only two alternatives were given—to make confession to the priest or to leave the country.

Many feared the decree and turned back while others remained steadfast in their newfound faith. This strong faith even separated many families. Among these faithful were several of our forefathers, namely John Kleinsasser, George Waldner, Peter Müller, Andrew Wurz, Christian Glanzen (Glanzer), John Hofer and Joseph Müller. Because he had no sons, Joseph Müller's name was not carried on. These and many others were arrested and taken to Klagenfürth to the city of Ybbs along the Danube River. Here they waited two months until others joined them. In all there were approximately 270 souls.

In 1755 they journeyed to Transylvania (Siebenburger). Here a government official and a Lutheran minister offered them freedom of religion. The Empress offered to finance their transportation, to build homes for them and to help them with land and farming necessities but in return they were required to take the Oath. Since this requirement was contrary to their convictions according to Matthew 5 and James 5, they did not accept the offer. Then new difficulties started. These people had to look for work and eventually came to the Hutterish Brethren at Alwintz. After studying the teachings and doctrines of this congregation, they found them to be more accurate than those of the Lutherans even though this brotherhood was not at it's best since many had left the communal way of life and were on their own. However, they all had agreed to refuse to take the Oath, to accept the doctrine of non-resistance, and to reject infant baptism. The newcomers were ready to join these brethren. Unfortunately the government was notified and upon investigation refused to allow them to join. Finally, a Catholic priest from Alwintz, who was an agricultural man, called Elder Joseph Kuhr, telling him that his people would no longer be tolerated and that there was no work available for them.

In October of 1756 this group was taken to Groszpolndorf of Transylvania (Siebenbürger). Here they were told that they would receive newly built homes, each family having its own land and meadows, if they would return to the Lutheran faith.

In 1757 more people came to Alwintz. Among them was a certain Mathias Hofer. Hofer and others were arrested and taken to the Hermanstadt prison. Hofer was a writer and a poet. The following poem was written by him.

1.

Man hat uns genommen von der Christlichen gemein
Gebunden und geführt Hermanstadt ein.
Da Haben wir gelitten viel Schmachwort und Pein.
Das tun wir dir klagen O Herr unser Gott.

2.

Man hat uns gesperet ins Zuchthaus wie ich sag
Da haben wir müssen arbeiten ein Jahr und viel Tag
Man gab uns ein gröfl und ein Brot auf ein Tag
Gott hat uns gesegnet wir haben kein Klag.

3.

Wir haben müssen arbeiten in Wolle und Decken
In die Woche siebezig Pfund Reisen oder 100 Pfund Flechen
Sonst hat uns gegeben fur 1 Pfund ein Streich
Man hat uns gescholten für foul und für weich.

Hofer spent 16 years in prison. Upon his release he went to Wischinka, Russia. He had peculiar ideas that he expected the congregation to adopt. One idea was that they should eat only twice daily at noon and evening because the scriptures do not record that Christ ate more often than that. Another was that prayers should be audible and that every silent prayer was a demon offering. After much consultation, the congregation could not convince him of his error. He than left the congregation, separated from his wife and went to Prussia (Preusen). He spent the rest of his life in Elbing, Etterward, with a Mennonite minister Gerhart Wiebe.

The exiled people in Poland did not attend the church services of the Lutherans or Catholics. Therefore, the government decided to scatter them so that they would have no knowledge of each others whereabouts. Families were put on ordered wagons and drivers took them to different places.

John Kleinsasser arrived at Kreuzdorf, George Waldner at Schluszburgen Stuhl, Christian Glanzer at Steindorf. Within ten days they all knew where each one was located. Instead of destroying the congregation, new ones were formed and sprouted at different places. For needed counsel they went to Alwinz. John Kleinsasser was baptized and ordained as Elder. This strengthened the Brotherhood.

In September of 1763 Elder John Kleinsasser went to Hermanstadt to visit his brethren and sisters in prison. Upon his return, he reported that the "government made certain decisions against the anabaptists (Wiedertäufer)." The King of Prussia and Empress (Kaiserin) Maria Theresa had made a peace treaty after seven years of war. Together they planned to cleanse the land of heresy (Ketzer). If the Lutheran ministers were unsuccessful with their admonishment, then Catholic priests were to take over. If these also failed, the people were to be considered heretics and to be forever banished from the land. This report brought great sorrow to all churches.

Many earnest prayers were said. With confidence and faith, they submitted to God's will.

The Catholic church received both instructions and power to convert heretics to Catholism. In Ungarn were three churches—Sabatisch, Levar and Schutzen. The persecutions started here. Some were beaten and some were imprisoned. The persecutions at Alwinz followed. Jesuit Delphini came to Alwinz trying to convince the brethren, but he was unsuccessful, even though he had even invited them to his services. He preached on John 16 proclaiming that the Catholic faith is the true faith. He also claimed to have healing power and to be able to remove mountains. At this time Roth and Kuhr were the Elders of the Brotherhood. Joseph Kuhr challenged Delphini by saying, "What you read from the Bible is well known to me and is true, but the miracles you tell of are lies. The Lord did not command nor give power to his disciples to remove God's created mountains. They still remain. Whoever wants to stay with his faith should follow me." He went out but nobody followed him, not even his own son.

Kuhr was a very wealthy man and respected by the world because he helped the poor and loaned them money. He was the owner of a large orchard and vineyard. Everyone thought it would be hard for him to leave all this behind, but nothing held him.

Roth was a comfortable, wealthy man and was unwilling to surrender. He became a backslider. Kuhr was arrested and taken to capital Kassenburg where he spent three years in prison. A grandchild of Kuhr is living with us and is the last of his descendants. Kuhr himself had an unfortunate marriage.

The people at Alwintz did not accept the Catholic faith so they fled to Kreutz. The government repeatedly returned them. Among these were Johann Stahl (his descendants are the Stahl families) and Lorenz Tschetter. Both were imprisoned at Klassenburg. The Catholic priest asked Kuhr, "Do you know Zacharius Walter at Sabatisch? He's an intelligent man and has accepted our faith." Kuhr answered, "I know him well but do not consider him an intelligent man because he denied his faith." The Walters are descendants from this Walter. Kuhr and Stahl were exiled but Tschetter was kept back because he was quite young and the priest hoped to persuade him, although he also wanted to go with Kuhr and Stahl. These two were escorted across the border by Commissars to a great wilderness with a script stating that "they were banished from Transylvania (Siebenburger)." Both knelt to praise God for their release from prison. After a three day journey they arrived at a marketplace. This happened in 1766. In that same year in November Tschetter was released and joined the Kreutz brotherhood.

Kuhr and Stahl continued their journey, crossing the frozen Nister River by Selischeck on Nicholaus (Christmas) Day. Here they worked during the winter and earned enough money to continue their journey.

On May 15, 1767 they started again from Selischeck and came to Moldau and Walachen unto Bucharest. Here they discovered the possibility of freedom of religion. They decided to notify the Brotherhood of the possibilities of settling here. They asked a farmer by Walachen to guide them secretly at night across the mountains to Alwinz. They arrived at Kuhr's son's place. Because the son had returned to the Catholic faith and Stahl's wife had fled to Kreuz, they continued the same night. On the way they escaped several dangers and arrived safely at Kreuz.

Let us consider the church or Brotherhood at Kreuz. After Delphini had finished his work at Alwinz he came to Kreuz. He found the people to be very sincere and withdrawn because they had detected his cruel plans. He did not rest but traveled to Vienna (Wien) and conferred with Countess Maria Theresa to gain permission to torment these people until they forsook their faith. He returned with authority and power to order government officials to help him carry out his plans. He ordered that the small children of the brotherhood be placed in an orphanage under Catholic supervision and that the old people be distributed to different prisons. The Brotherhood lived in great fear and anxiety. At this time Kuhr and Stahl came with the message. The brethren were assured that God had answered their prayers.

On October 3, 1767, at 10 a.m. 76 souls left Kreuz. The local citizens were glad to see them go because they too lived in fear.

At Alwinz was a widow with two daughters and three sons—Elias, Johann, and Samuel Wipf. From this family the Wipfs originate.

On this journey the people came to Reges at the river Alt. They had no passports. Discouragement was at a peak. The following day wagons and canoes were hired to help them across at night. They continued across the mountains traveling only at night. They passed Kronstadt. The next day as they were hiding in a heavy forest, a hunter found them during the day. They asked for mercy but he told them that he had sworn to report everybody he saw and didn't promise that he would not do so. Evidently he didn't because nothing happened. As they came to the mountains, wagons were left behind. The journey was very troublesome. Everyone carried his own bundle and a small child. The sixteen year olds also had to help in carrying their share of the load. Four and five year olds had to run along side. The hired Walachen took them through heavily wooded areas. The mountains were so steep at places that they had to climb on hands and knees, especially where there were washouts and gullies. One can hardly imagine what it meant to travel with children, weak ones, and old people. When they came over the mountain peak, it was announced that "we are across the border." The congregation offered a prayer of gratitude and continued with God's blessing.

They then came to Tschakerlein. Kuhr and Kleinsasser continued to try to find a suitable place for the congregation to locate. At Bukarest they met Jacob

Fredrick Wolfe, a German. He was the servant of the Prince. They told him of their predicament and mission. He willingly showed them to places where they might have possibilities of settlement if they found them suitable for their situation. One place was by a brook Krabäch (Ravenbrook). That same year on November 16, they moved to this place. In a short time five to six mud houses were ready for occupancy during the winter months. Each one started his own handicraft and made fairly good progress. All were happy and content even though poverty and persecution were continually their partners. They were poor but could live in peace.

Before long their good fortune changed and a dark cloud came. During the summer an epidemic broke out. On some days 16 to 18 people were bedfast. Many in the congregation died. It was especially sad when some of the honorable, industrious, religious leaders died. The dark clouds became darker, for soon they discovered that this was not a peaceful place. In 1768 war broke out between Russia and Turkey. The Walachens were of the Greek orthodox religion and, therefore, joined the Russians in driving out the Turks.

On November 24, 1769, an army—really a group of robbers—came to the Bruderhof and demanded money. They tried to force the brethren to give them money. They tortured them with beatings and when that was not enough irons were heated which they used to burn the brethren. At the same time they cried, "Money, money." Glanzer softened when they took off his shirt and were about to burn him with hot plow lays as they asked for two gulden. Glanzer went to Elder Johann Kleinsasser who was sick in bed. The robbers went along. When the robbers saw the money, they took all of it and kicked Kleinsasser out in the yard and beat him unmercifully because they thought he had some more money. Johann Kuhr had to suffer the most because he spoke and understood the Walachen language. Two Germans in the group witnessed all of this and they took Kuhr and hung him by his legs so high that he could barely touch the ground with his fingertips. Still they demanded money. Torture continued by starting a fire under Kuhr, singeing his hair and beard. This was a pitiful sight. Finally he was released. Next they put all brethren and sisters in one room and asked for money. They threatened to burn the house. The captain of the robbers had requested that fire be brought. The brethren tried to reason with them in all kindness telling them that they had come into this country as very poor people, had relocated before this, and had no money, not even a groshen (penny). Then the robbers went from room to room, took whatever they wanted and broke or tore up whatever they did not want. This frightening terror lasted from early morning till late at night.

Later the brethren were told that these robbers were killed in the war against the Turks. Wandering robbers were continually around us. The week after New Year many left for the forests with women, children, and cattle, even though it was winter. Seven or eight men stayed with the houses to protect them from fires started by mobs.

On March 27, 1770, new peril appeared. Two thousand Turks, who had ridden on horseback all night, crossed the Danube and arrived around 7 o'clock. They dismounted and took four brethren and one sister with them. When they were told who we were, they released us and said, "Don't be afraid. Germans shall not get hurt." But we didn't trust them and went to our families in the woods. We soon heard and saw that these Turks accomplished great robberies. There were pitiful cries but there was no mercy. When these Turks came to our yard, they found our houses empty so they left. We thanked God for such gracious deliverance. We knew we couldn't stay here very much longer, because even in times of peace, these people had the robbing spirit. The above mentioned robbers came to Dschurschu where the previous day Turkish merchants had come. Misery and afflication increased and some surrendered to slavery. The stronger men were sold for 70 to 90 Leu (1 leu equals 18 4/5¢). The older men were a little cheaper. These facts were related to us by a Walachen who also was a prisoner and had had three different owners. He escaped and fled at night to arrive in his homeland. We knew that we weren't safe here either.

We were willing to move—but where to? We shared our plight with General Semetin, who was sympathetic to us. He was a Russian general fighting in Walachia against the Turks. He advised that we move to Russia (Klein-Russia) and assured us that we would have religious freedom there. After prayerful consideration, we accepted this as God's will.

General Semetin gave us a pair of oxen and a wagon to continue our journey. He also gave us the proper credentials to pass into Russia. On April 10, 1770, our little group started again. However, we all returned to our houses once more to be sure that nothing was left behind. Nature was at its best. The flowers in full bloom, the tall green grass, and the cheerful music of the birds gave us a heartbreaking farewell. We had lived 2½ years at Walachia. Even here our happy days were few in number. General Semetin suggested that we contact the Field Marshall Romanzof and accept his help and suggestions. We traveled with five wagons with a pair of oxen, for each wagon also had cows and sheep. We passed Bucharest around sunrise. After six days of travel we arrived at the city of Busau.

The citizens in this city lived in great fear because of the soldiers. News had been spread that the Turks were coming back. Within four days they did return. Villages were surrounded and the inhabitants were taken prisoner. When we received the message we took to the mountains and hid in a valley two days until the terror was over. We thanked God for His protection.

Discomfort and hardships were continually with us on this journey. Oft times nights were spent out in the open during rains and storms. Our diet consisted of Pautuas (dried fish) and sweet milk provided for us by our cows and sheep. They were most beneficial to have along. To eat bread was unthinkable because there was none to be gotten. We were glad to get millet (hirse) and Turkish wheat (mais). We often said, "If only the time would come when we could eat as much bread as we want, how happy and thankful we would be."

When we came to the Polish border at Hottin, we met the already mentioned Romanzof with a Russian nobleman. This nobleman suggested that we move on his property in Klein-Russia. He promised to advance or loan the use of his lands and meadows. We were to pay a certain tribute. He drew up a contract and after thorough and prayerful consideration, we accepted the contract.

(The following translation of the contract itself is taken from *Banished for Faith* by Emil J. Waltner, page 64).

Privileges to be granted to the colonists who intend to settle at Wischinka:

1. Their full and free religious practices; neither shall they be required in court or elsewhere to give an oath.
2. Shall not be required to render military service.
3. In their congregation they shall not be molested by anyone. Shall be permitted to work as a community and pay taxes.
4. Three years of exemption shall be granted.
5. Immediate necessities shall be advanced to them, and for the whole congregation one bushel of flour daily.
6. For the journey thirty rubles shall be advanced, and on arrival other necessities. In addition money and lumber shall be advanced for homes.
7. For the land for farming, hay and gardens, they shall pay a definite price after three years.
8. Each shall be allowed to practice his trade; they shall not enter into the liquor business; they shall be permitted to sell articles which they manufacture.
9. Their freedom shall in no wise be taken away. They shall be permitted to leave if it is not agreeable to them to stay, but must refund the amounts advanced to them plus ten percent of their increase.
10. After the time of exemption they shall pay taxes per acre and on the dwellings in cash.
11. For haymaking they shall have 80 loads of hay for their cattle.
12. Since they cannot get buildings done before winter, they shall be provided for.

—In camp at Pruth eit Rabog, June, 1770

After this contract was signed Romanzof sent a guard of ten Cossacks to guide and protect us through Poland until we came to his land. Whenever we were close to a village, two Cossacks would be sent ahead to notify the villagers that the Fieldmarshall's people were coming and that they should prepare meals and a night's lodging for us. The authorities supplied us faithfully. When we arrived, the bread and hot meals were ready.

On August 1, 1770, we came to the river Desna. Here the Okonomia (stewards) gave us everything as the contract stated. Winter grain was sown and hay was made. The same year land was shown to us where we could settle down and start housekeeping and farming. A house and cattlebarn were started, but not finished so we had to winter in the nobleman's homes.

On July 20, 1771, the whole congregation moved on their own property. On July 24 the first church preaching service was conducted in the new house. On April 16, 1772, we observed our first communion service in two years, since the unrest had prevented us from regular service.

In 1772 Paul Glanzer went back to Hermanstadt to inform those that were left behind where the congregation had settled. He could not appear in public in any way because of fear that he would be imprisoned. His wife, daughter, and brother and many others were held as prisoners here. He said farewell to all and set out to go back to Wischinka by traveling through Walachen past Bukarest. Here two women who had been released followed him. The three made a safe trip to their home. This seemed to be the Lord's guidance, for these women had been imprisoned a long time. It was the desire of the Empress (Kaiserin) that the prisoners would become her servants. Glanzer's wife received her belongings after her release. She gave it to the brotherhood and they in turn applied it to the debt which had been made December, 1772.

From 1772 to 1779 they were prosperous in that they started weaving and pottery of which Stahl was the master. Handicrafts or trades of shoemakers (cobblers), blacksmiths, hat-makers, and tanners started here. With these handicrafts they were kept occupied. In 1776 the count (a government official) gave them permission to build a watermill, and in 1777 they built a windmill. These industries brought gain. Knowledge of their useful and beautiful products spread. The Brotherhood was flourishing because every member lived a God-fearing life. The Lord blessed these industrious and ambitious brethren. Their reputation in the community and country was such that noblemen, princes, and lords came to observe their arrangement. Everyone praised the work. Often five to six coaches were on the yard with government officials, princes, noblemen, and women (damen) who were touring the workshops, the school, gebet house (sanctuary), dining room, nursery and dispensary (drug room) with great amazement and satisfaction. Some even attended the worship service. Their products were gladly bought and praised. Even graff Romanzof was enthused at how this Brotherhood progressed on his property. He proudly talked about his Germans.

Their dress was very simple. The men wore short black trousers, and the women had blue dresses and white caps. Whenever they were out haying, the groups in such apparel looked very neat. All travelers were amazed and astonished at this group.

The Brotherhood was well organized. After a mother had taken care of her child for 1½ years, it was placed in the nursery where different women took care of them and gave them their meals. Two carefully chosen women were responsible for night duty. At the age of three the children were placed in the Kindergarten school. Here they were given spiritual instructions as much as children can comprehend at that age. At the age of six they were promoted to the regular school.

The congregation had their daily scheduled morning and evening communal devotions. Worship services were held every Sunday and on church holidays. A young boy would run to the workshops and homes to announce "zum gebet" (to prayer meeting).

In 1781 Andrew Gross came to this congregation from Ungarn. All Grosses are his descendants. The older people were joyfully reminiscing about the prosperous good times they had had. But it caused grief and heartaches to see the congregation dispersed.

In 1780 Roman Empress Maria Theresa died. Her son Joseph II became the ruler. He permitted freedom of religion. He banished the Jesuits and destroyed the cloisters. Many brethren wrote from Wischenka to Kärthen, Siebenburger and Ungarn. The circumstances created a new desire among these to return to their fathers' faith especially since they had become dissatisfied with the Catholic faith.

In 1781 two brethren were sent by the Brotherhood from Wischenka to Ungarn to bring some back, but they returned unsuccessful on December 2 of the same year. Some had left the Catholic church at Sabatisch. Six brethren were arrested and imprisoned. Appointed men went to Kaiser Joseph and asked for their release. The Catholic priests tried to convince them with threats to accept their faith. Jacob Walter, son of Zacharias Walter, was firm but had to flee. He left his wife and child.

After a troublesome journey, Walter arrived safely at Wischinka. He received a Russian pass from Count Romanzof and returned to Ungarn. There he was reunited with his family and then returned to the Brotherhood. His oldest daughter who was married to a Catholic did not come because her husband refused to leave the Catholic faith. But later they too joined the church. The separation of parents and daughter was heartbreaking.

At Sabatisch two ambitious and energetic young men, namely Wollman and Tittel, decided to go to Russia. Paul Mändel, who was in the workshop with them escorted them. Mändel was a native Bohemian. On the way they persuaded him to go along to Russia and so he continued with them in his working clothes without notifying his employer or parents of his whereabouts. They safely arrived at Wischinka. Mändel died in 1846 in the Hutterthal colony and left behind a grandson and great-grandson to carry on his name. Wollman's descendants carry his name to this day; however, Tittel had no male descendants to perpetuate his name.

On March 4, 1784 Johann Waldner and Jacob Walter were sent to Ungarn. They traveled through Prussia and arrived at Franzthaldorf near Drissen, a Mennonite community. Jacob Walter met his daughter Susan with her husband, Tobias Pohlman. This meeting was unexpected, and, needless to say, a joyful reunion. The Pohlmans decided to wait there until Walter and Waldner came through on their return trip. The two men then continued their journey through Schlesien.

Near Gnadenfeld, Waldner became ill. Walter stayed with him because he didn't want to leave Waldner alone among strangers. Walter sent a messenger to Sabatisch telling them that whoever was willing to go along to Russia should come as soon as possible and join the Brotherhood in Russia.

The messenger returned to report that many were willing to go but could not get ready to leave so soon. They asked for a delay. Waldner and Walter did not appreciate this; they decided to return to Prussia. A few started from Sabatisch by way of Schlesien to Gnadenfeld. Hernhutter (Moravian brethren) lived here at this time. But the two brethren had already left, causing a great disappointment to the others. Soon these learned that the brethren were waiting for them in Prussia. There was a gathering of 47 souls. Among the group were yet another Wollman and Pohlman whose descendants (erben) are still alive. Because a number of the brethren had no male descendants, their names were not carried on.

In 1785 Joseph Müller and Christian Hofer were sent to Sabatisch because of a quarrel which arose among the backsliding brethren. To their great disappointment they learned that all had left the faith with the exception of the before mentioned Jacob Walter. Müller and Hofer continued their journey to Wien where they appeared before Emperor Joseph and requested their remaining property (hinterbleibenes Erbgut). The Emperor was very friendly and inquired of them how, why and when they had left the country, and if the persecutor's name had been Delphini. They related to him in detail where they lived, what kind of homes they had and the conditions of the contract. He encouraged them to return, but they answered "We weren't only suppressed but persecuted." He asked with violence, "Where?" Hofer related the incident of the imprisonment of the six men. Then the Emperor calmed down and remarked, "You must have a stronger religious faith than the Catholics, Lutherans, Calvinists or Greek Orthodox Catholic." In great humility they pleaded for their property. He didn't promise them any assistance. However, the Hermanstadt Brotherhood's property (or money) was sent to Wien. It amounted to 2151 Florin, but who received it no one knows because the Brotherhood never got any of it.

The two brethren returned to Wischinka, going through Prussia where several Mennonites joined them. All returned except two widows who remained—Mrs. Decker with three sons and two daughters from whom the present day Deckers descend and Mrs. Knels with one son and one daughter from whom the Knels descend.

—o—

This is the history and origin of our ancestors, the Hutterthal colony and the lineage of each name. However, we would like to mention a few experiences that took place in later years.

In 1786 the colony chose Christian Wurz, a young man, to become a medical doctor to meet the colony's needs. He was sent to be trained by the personal doctor of Count Franzian. Wurz was of good testimony and was respected by the brethren; nevertheless, he received strict instructions to remain in the simplicity and true faith of the fathers. He promised. For a time he seemed to be true to his promise, but finally he conformed to the world with his clothing and beard cutting. He started to wear braids and scorned the faith of his fathers. The church dealt with him, but his love for worldly pleasures won his heart, and thus he was excommunicated. At the age of 26 years he left the colony, his wife and three children. He died at Moscow. All this grieved the colony, for they were very sympathetic with him because of his waywardness.

Later another young man, Samuel Wipf, was appointed to become a medical doctor to be educated by the same Count Franzian. He remained true to his faith and became a skilled doctor, a very valuable asset to the colony.

The colony lived in contentment and peace. But this was of short duration. Russia and the Turks were at war. In 1787 a law was passed and enforced which included all land owners. They were to contribute a certain amount of money and flour for the war. The colony was included in this. The brethren refused to pay such a tribute because it was against their conscience and against the contract. This developed into a scandal. They were threatened with imprisonment and openly were pronounced to be "stubborn." They were accused of setting a bad example for the other people of the land. The manager of Count Romanzof was embittered and provoked because the brethren made reference to the contract. He said, "It (the law) was the demand of the crown (krone) and the law of the land and not his."

The brethren were firm and said, "We do not plan nor expect to meet the demand regardless of what the verdict will be."

The same year on October 23, the Elders decided at a business meeting that "We will rather leave houses and land before we sear our conscience." All members agreed. Two brethren took this decision to the count who was a friend of the colony and didn't want them to move away. He requested that they appear later. Then he made them a different offer. "Because the war tax is against your faith and conscience, you could give a certain amount of money yearly to the count." The brethren agreed to this. Added to the yearly payment of 104 rubles and 95 kopek (ruble = 100 kopek = ½¢), were 150 rubles. The Emperor received information of this transaction and was well satisfied. The Brotherhood thanked God for such definite guidance and an answer to prayer.

On June 21, 1794, at 10 p.m. a fire broke out in a Russian dorf (village). Our dorf was in great danger because the wind blew directly toward our yard. With God's help and the strenuous labor of the brethren, we were spared.

On May 18, 1796, Jacob Müller, a teacher, Jacob Bergthold, and three other families from Galizien were sent by their congregation to investigate and study our way of living. If they found it satisfactory, they would join us. The agreement in its entirety could not be met. During this meeting three other families came and were sorry that the union had not been completed. They were indeed sorry. They felt that they had been too fast in selling their property. These families stayed for a time but were never truly united with us, for they differed in many views. The church did not intend to leave the faith of their fathers. Since these families differed in their way of thinking, before long they left us.

In December, 1796, the Count Romanzof died. Three brethren were sent to the funeral and to contact the young counts who were at their father's funeral. These brethren were to receive assurances from these young counts from Petersburg of the same protection and peace we had had during their father's reign.

The brethren were cordially received and were told by the counts, "We will do the best we can for you, as much as is in our power." In that same year Prince Karakov came from Petersburg with the instruction that all property must be shown to him. He also stated that the counts had traded their property for some of his. A discussion followed upon which we showed him the contract that we were a free people and as such could move whenever we wished. He answered, "You still have time—before we close the deal."

Immediately two brethren went to Petersburg to have the contract renewed. After reading this contract, the count said, "I cannot differentiate between you and my people. You cannot expect that from me, for you are sensible and honorable people." They answered, "We do not expect that of you but we are a free people and may go whenever we wish." He replied, "You are a good people but haven't you been recorded the second time as required in the revision? You have paid a head tax." They were not aware of the true meaning of this statement. It seemed that according to the Count, they were not exempt nor a free people. Greatly discouraged, they wrote a petition and sent it to Emperor (Kaiser) Paul.

The Brotherhood called on the Mennonites who by this time had come to Russia and had full freedom of revision and a statement from the Emperor.

> Because the petitioners belong to a property owner they may not enjoy the same privileges as those who are located on Crown lands. Their petition can therefore not be granted, but they should remain for the future in the same conditions as they had under the Count Field Marshall.

The message just quoted from Waltner's book *Banished for Faith,* page 92, was the one the brethren returned with from the Emperor in answer to their petition. Discouragement was high, for all felt that their freedom and that of their descendants had been taken from them. In addition the government added another 150 rubles to their annual payment of 150 rubles. Although they were reluctant to pay, after consultation with other noblemen who were doubtful of their release, they too became doubtful and resigned themselves to the payment.

In 1800 Count Sergei Petrovitsch Romanzof came to his estate. He had a writing stating that since we were not registered in the revision during his reign and had only been registered during his father's reign, we must help support the Rekruten (recruits) or military service. We replied that we would not pay such support. We also noted that if they forced us, that point nine on the contract would be void and that we would then appear before the Emperor ourselves.

Two brethren brought this message to the Count. He was very cordial and requested them to have patience. He was about to go to Germany and he promised that upon his return he would discuss this matter with the Emperor himself in order to lighten their consciences. But when he returned in fall, they received no reply.

The brethren then selected two brethren, namely Johann Waldner and Jacob Walter, to go to Petersburg. Prayers followed these men, and they left with God's will and blessing. They started on February 19, 1801, and safely arrived at Petersburg on March 9. They acquainted the Count with their mission. On the twelfth of March great changes took place in the government. Emperor Paul died and his son Alexander came to the throne. The Court suggested that they go home because it was not adviseable to make proper agreements during this change. He said that he would do all he could for the colony, but they didn't trust his honesty any more. Their petition was to have crownland assigned to them. They were directed to Count Ekatharinoslav, who declared them a free people. The brethren came home with this resolution. Everybody was joyful that they weren't under the bondage of serfdom.

The land near Raditschewa was considered for settlement. The Count instructed his officers to put pressure on the brethren to move off the presently occupied property within three months.

On March 20, 1802, we started to dismantle our houses and journeyed to Raditschewa which was 15 werst from Wischinka. By the fifteenth of July the last group had left Wischinka, leaving behind three brick houses. We also left a beautiful orchard, for which we received nothing. The Count's generosity did permit us to cut and keep the winter rye crop. Under such circumstances we left Wischinka and were released from the Count.

We had lived in Wischinka 32 years minus 36 days. One hundred and seventy-two souls had died here.

The Dorf Reditschewa was close to the river Desna. Soon five large, strong brick houses were built. Underneath two of these houses were strong cellars in which the bricks were laid in a corrugated fashion.

This newly established Bruderhof had a square or courtyard of 70 Faden (1 faden equals 1 fathom equals 6 feet). It had a large entrance gate which was securely locked every night. The yard was under close guard. Every profession had its workshop in the house on the main floor. Every family had an unheated, small bedroom on the second floor. The furniture consisted of a bed, one table and two chairs. At childbirth the mother could go to the children's room which usually was heated.

Every man had to learn a trade in which he was capable or qualified. All men had to spend a certain length of time working in the barn annually as Stahlknecht (barn-servant). The Brotherhood was short on finances for completion of the building project. However, the Crown (government) advanced them 4000 rubles which they were to pay in ten years. Twelve brethren gave their signature. And when the paid note was returned, none of the original signers were alive.

The Brotherhood was quite successful, but they never regained the prosperity which they had had at Wischinka. The older ones died, and the new generation could not appreciate the hard labor and thriftiness of the older people. They wanted more freedom and became selfish and dishonest. Of course, this does not work in communal life. The rules were that every profession had a manager, who assigned the work. It was also his duty to sell finished products and turn in the money made to the steward of the colony. In turn finances for raw material was supplied by the steward. For such offices only faithful, dependable, honest, and worthy men were carefully appointed. In Reditschewa, however, this arrangement was neglected. Every worker wanted to be a manager, to see the finished product and to buy the needed tools and material for his own handicraft for himself. They became very selfish. Instead of bringing the money to the steward, only the balance account sheet was presented. Money was kept for themselves to provide better food and more drink. With such dishonest deeds occurring, discontentment, jealousy and quarrels made great headways to destroy the unity. It grieved the brethren that some sought their own comforts.

A disagreement between Johannes Waldner and Jacob Walter, both ministers or elders, was a great hindrance to the Brotherhood. Walter with his brothers and sisters was the first to move away. He built a house in a nearby valley. Before long, half of the colony became his followers. The rift grew. Finally, they called on Count Ekatharinoslav (government official) to help them in their dispute. They sought to continue Christian fellowship, thereby, trying to motivate reconciliation and more peace. However, hatred and envy ruled the camp. "A divided house cannot stand" was a proven statement within the Brotherhood.

In 1818 one half of the colony moved to Chortiz, a Mennonite settlement. In 1819 the whole Raditschof dorf burned, including houses, barns, and equipment. Elderly people still talk about this tragedy and of the separation with aching hearts. But they also recall the fortune and blessings. It was hard to understand how all could vanish so fast.

In 1820 the group which had gone to Chortiz returned and divided the leftover livestock and land among the fifty families. They started two small villages (dorfs) near the banks of the Desna River. However, they never regained the original prosperity.

Very soon many noticed that they could not thrive spiritually or physically under such circumstances. Their land was scattered in 43 places within a radius of 20 Werst. The congregation asked the government for permission to move elsewhere. In 1842 the delayed answer came that they may move to Molotschna in Province Taurien. It was impossible for all to leave at the same time; therefore, they divided themselves into five groups, the older brethren being the leaders. In the fall of 1842 they proceeded to South Russia with a government guide. Here in Province Taurien in the Melitopol they established the Hutterthal Colony as mentioned in the beginning of this writing.

In 1853 Johannasruh started to build three werst north of Hutterthal. By 1857, 38 farmyards (Höfe) were finished. It was a beautiful village with houses of masonry and barns built with burnt bricks and decorated with built on gutters. Fences of masonry were built along the streets and ash trees beautified the avenues.

In 1857 some more land was bought in the same Province from Oreckov, 20 werst away and the new dorf Hutterdorf was established. In this dorf a small Bruderhof was organized and was very prosperous. A second Bruderhof was organized.

In 1864 a few members at Johannasruh started communal living. However, within two years they had discontinued. The improper arrangement of their homes and other buildings seemed to be a hindrance to their success.

In 1868 more land was bought in the Province Ekatharinoslav, and a fourth colony was established named Neu Hutterthal.

In 1874 the government started the conscription law. The Hutterites were given a choice—either to serve the Russian army or to leave Russia. They chose the latter.

They migrated to America, coming to South Dakota. The Hutterdorf people were the first to leave. The two colonies which had lived in communal life for 15 years came to South Dakota and established Bon Homme along the Missouri River and Wolfcreek colony near the James River not far from the Wolf Creek stream in Hutchinson county. The Neu Hutterthal were the next group that emigrated but most of them went on their own farms.

In 1877 some more came from Hutterthal and Johannasruh. Some chose to go on their own farms while the others started a third colony along the James River in Hutchinson County. In 1878 and 1879 all the rest from Hutterthal and Johannasruh came and only a few chose to join the communal living. Most of them settled on their own farms.

This wedding dress is believed to have been worn in Russia, by Anna Pollman when she married Josua Hofer, on Nov. 7, 1826, in Reditschewa. They are the parents of Michael R. Hofer (Rutschield). It is also said that the dress was worn by Justina Hofer (Josuas daughter) when she married Joseph Pollman, on June 21, 1853.

Dress is shown by Mrs. Sharon Schrader, a great great granddaughter of Anna.

This is a wedding letter of 1868 for the marriage of Rev. Johann L. Wipf and Katharina Kleinsasser, including a list of those invited. This was to be forwarded in the order of names listed. Wedding letters of this sort were used in America into the 1920's.

Esteemed Friends,

According to the wise guidance of God, we plan to enter the bonds of holy matrimony with the blessings of the officiating minister. The nuptial service will be held next Sunday, the 13th of this month. We therefore extend our cordial invitation to all here named friends, asking that they show us their love by being our guests on the aforesaid day. The marriage ceremony is to take place at the Johannesruh schoolhouse in the forenoon. Together, in the fellowship of our friends, we will entreat our heavenly father to bless our marriage.

At the conclusion of the church services our friends will please assemble at our parental—the Johann Kleinsasser—home. There we will serve them a well-meant wedding meal.

With mutual love and respect,
Bridegroom, Johann Wipf
Bride, Katarina Kleinsasser

Friends are requested to forward this in the order of the names listed.

Johannesruh
October 12, 1868

(First to the Esteemed Elias Wipf in Hutterthal. 1868)

Esteemed Elias Wipf
Honorable Michel Stahl
Esteemed Andreas Müller
Esteemed Benjamin Stahl
Esteemed Johann Stahl
Esteemed Peter Hofer, Andreas Hofer
Esteemed Samuel Glanzer
Esteemed Mathias Kleinsasser
Esteemed Michel Hofer
Esteemed Josua Wollman
Widow Wollman
Widow Michel Wollman
Widow Samuel Kleinsasser
Honorable Johann Waldner
Esteemed Zacharias Wipf
Esteemed Andreas Wollman
Esteemed Jakob Gross
Esteemed Joseph Polman
Esteemed Wilhelm Martens, Wilhelm
Esteemed Paul Tschetter
Esteemed Peter Enz
Esteemed Peter Ens
Esteemed Elias Wipf, Elias
Esteemed Susanna Wipf
Esteemed Samuel Kleinsasser
Esteemed Jakob Walter
Esteemed Joseph Hofer
Esteemed Samuel Glanzer
Esteemed Michel Hofer
Esteemed Peter Tschetter
Esteemed Johann Wipf
Esteemed Michel Hofer, Michel
Esteemed Andreas Wipf
Esteemed David Glanzer
Esteemed Joseph Wipf
Widow Hester, Elizabeth

Historical account of where our ancestors came from and the villages they established

By Wesley G Tschetter

During the 1750's when Catholicism was the state religion in Austria, other religious materials were furtively brought into the country, and secret meetings were held where people accepted beliefs of the Lutheran faith. These new Protestants resorted to holding religious meetings deep in the forests and mountains to escape detection. In an effort to suppress other religions, homes were searched, and Bibles and books were confiscated. Only Catholic Church sanctioned literature was allowed. Fines were levied and Lutheran converts were threatened, whipped, and imprisoned. Austrian Empress Maria Teresa gave Jesuit priests and local authorities permission to pursue and drive out Austrian citizens who followed Lutheran teachings rather than attend the Catholic church.

Kleinsasserhof, overlooking the Drau River Valley.

View of Drau River Valley, taken from Kleinsasserhof, showing villages of St. Peter and Unter Amlach

The former Andreas Wurtz house at St. Peter, Austria

The former Johann Hofer farm house in St. Peter, Austria.

Former Glanzer farm house, now used as storage and wine cellar in St. Peter, Austria.

Former Jerg Waldner farm house in Unteramlach, Austria.

Those who refused to recant were placed on trial and "banished" from the communities along the Drau River valley in the Carinthian province near the present day city of Spittal, Austria. Over time, 689 adults plus an uncounted number of children were evicted from their homes and imprisoned. In 1755 a large group was deported by boat on the Danube River to an area near Alwinz, Transylvania, in what today is Austria. Among a group of 104 Lutherans evicted on September 10, 1755, were families with the surnames of Kleinsasser, Hofer, Glanzer, Wurtz, Miller and Waldner plus other family names no longer associated with the Hutterites and Mennonites. Ironically, two decades later these hundreds of deportees were granted permission to return to Austria.

Once resettled in Transylvania, these former Austrian people openly followed their Lutheran religion. They made the acquaintance of a small group of about 20 Hutterite Brethren who practiced community of goods according to the Biblical account found in Acts chapters two and four. This Hutterite group had been banished from Moravia, what is today Slovakia and the Czech Republic, in years following 1620 as they too had not been willing to accept the Catholic faith. They and their ancestors had come from the villages near modern day Seneca, Slovakia, including many from Sabatisch, Slovakia and Velke Levare, Czech.

The Austrian group renounced their Lutheran religion and joined the small group of Hutterites who were practicing community of goods. Not only was the Catholic church unhappy with this decision, but the Lutheran ministers were also unhappy because they were obligated to pursue these new converts to the Hutterite ways. Those who did not recant their Hutterite beliefs and attend the Catholic church were always under the threat of imprisonment. Upon hearing about the Catholic church's plan to remove their children from their homes if they did not return to the Catholic church, the Hutterites and former Austrians together hired a guide to lead them south over the Carpathian mountains and out of the Austrian Hungarian Empire.

By 1769 this combined group who had come from Austria and Slovakia was near the present day city of Budapest, Romania, then called Moldovia, where the group reestablished homes and a new means of livelihood. However, with this move into present day Romania, they found themselves in the midst of the lawless situation prompted by a war between Russia and Turkey. To avoid getting caught in the midst of the Russian-Turkish war and the possibility of being taken as Turkish hostages and slaves, the group was forced to again leave their homes and live under the cover of a nearby forest during the winter of 1769-1770. During this grim winter season, the community was robbed; men were beaten, tortured, and robbed again by transient groups who thought the community had money.

How they got to South Russia—now the Ukraine

While hiding in the forest, they saw and heard of horrors imposed by bandits, misfits, and the Turkish army. A Russian military officer, Count Rumiantsev, saw their plight of being caught between two fighting units and offered them refuge on his personal estate in what is now the Ukraine, then called South Russia. This estate was hundreds of miles northeast at the village Wischenka, which is along the Desna River about 120 miles northeast of Kiev. The Community had few options but to accept this offer of refuge and move still further northeast into Russia. The trip from Moldovia to Wischenka was about 940 miles. The group embarked on April 10, 1770, escorted by Russian horsemen and arrived without incident on August 1, 1770. The community picked a favorable site along a creek and bridge "between the old church site and the new village (Russian Orthodox) church." (Source: The Hutterite Chronicle, volume II, page 457.)

Group settles and establishes homes in Wischenka:

There were about 120 persons who came in this first group that had originated by way of Hungary. Upon finding out that there was an opportunity for religious tolerance in South Russia, between 1771 and 1795 several groups totaling 56 persons came directly from Sabatisch, Slovakia and Velke Levare, Czech. Although they are in two different countries today (Czech and Slovakia), these two communities are near each other, are still called that, and are about one hour north, northeast of present day capitol city Bratislava, Slovakia. The family names of Tschetter (Czetterle), Pullman (Bolman), Wollman (Waleman), Walter and Mendel came from these communities. Additionally the Stahl family came via this route, even though it did not originate from these two communities. (Chronicle, Volume II, page 535)

Over the 32 years from 1770 to 1802, the Community was very successful in reestablishing community of goods with the community income at Wischenka being dependent upon the production of its industries such as pottery, bricks, weaving, tanning, and wood products, but not necessarily the production of agriculture goods. While farming existed, it was supplemental and more for the production of food for the community's use. The group established a water powered mill, built a distillery and brick factory, and established homes and industry. They quickly earned the respect of the Russian nobility for their hard work and industrious production methods.

Wischenka, meaning "sour or small cherry" in Ukrainian language, has a nearby sister village two miles east called Chereskenka, meaning "sweet cherry". The Count had his personal residence and sugar plantation and production headquarters in this nearby village that still has at least one large, unused brick building and a walkway that dates back to the 1700's. According to the Chronicle, during this 32 year period (August 1770 to June 1802), the remains of 172 people were buried at Wischenka. There is no record or visible evidence of a cemetery from this era.

The Russian Count Ruminatsev's death in December 1796 resulted in a very uncertain future for the Community. While always wary of the taxes and fees they paid, they nevertheless had confidence in the Ruminatsev family. Time proved otherwise. The Community's situation, i.e. their freedom, was in a precarious situation. The son Sergei Petrovitch von Rumiantsev, who lived in St. Petersburg and was a Russian official, inherited the estate and as the new Count, he considered the Community to be his property even to the point of being serfs since they had been registered twice through a census and had paid a head tax to his father, Count Rumiantsev, their original benefactor. The head tax was interpreted by the Count's son as a payment in lieu of military service.

The Community had not fully realized that through registration (census), payment of head tax and the decree of the previous czar, the Community had lost its freedom. However, their future was a matter of prayer and continuous efforts to state their case that they were a free people. Emissary trips were made to the regional officials at Chernigov and to the Russian capital of St. Petersburg. In 1797, Russian Czar Paul I rejected the Community's petition that the contract be interpreted as exempting them from military service as a matter of faith and conscience and stated "Inasmuch as the petitioners belong to a propertied lord, they cannot enjoy the same rights and privileges as settlers on state land." The Community had a very insecure feeling regarding the future. (The Chronicle Vol. II, pages 569 and 570).

With the assassination of Czar Paul I on March 12, 1801, his son the new Czar Alexander I ascended to the throne. Two community representatives, Johannes Waldner and Jacob Walter, were in St. Petersburg at that time and finally had an opportunity to meet the Czar. In the meantime, the Community, which then consisted of 44 families, took the matter to prayer that God would work things out in a favorable way for their future. Within three weeks the Czar ordered the investigation of the Community's situation and subsequently, on May 22, 1801, decided that the Community members were free people—thus ruling in the favor of the Community. The Czar signed the decree that allowed the Community to leave the Count's property and move to leased crown (government) lands.

Most certainly, Count Rumiantsev was not pleased that he was losing the Community. Nevertheless, the decision restored the freedom to leave the Count's property and settle on already rented crown lands. In May and June, 1802, the group moved once more, this time to Raditschewa, also along the Desna River, about 10 miles by river route northwest. Wooden buildings were disassembled and moved, but three brick buildings were left standing in Wischenka. One brick building with parallel (or double) vaulted cellars extending the entire length of the building is still standing at the present time (2010). This building measures about 30 feet by 60 feet, with ample space for small living quarters in the attic. It is likely that this was built in 1780's. Today this remodeled building with its domed shaped (vaulted) ceiling cellars (still in place but not used) is used as a vacation home by a family who lives in the city. It is the only reminder of the 32 years of Hutterite residence.

Wischenka brick building built in 1780's, still in use today

Also remaining at Wischenka today and situated only 200 yards from the former Hutterite settlement is a poorly maintained white washed "castle" built during the 1780's. During the Community's stay in Wischenka, the Russian government constructed a very large edifice from 1784 to 1786, about 200 yards west and across the dry creek bed from the Community with the intended use as a hotel "and stop over" for Russian dignitaries who traveled from Moscow and St. Petersburg south to the Crimea. It was built with bricks, and since the Community had a brick factory, it is reasonable to conclude that they made at least some of the bricks for this "castle." The Russian Czarina, Catherine the Great, stayed at this "castle" once in 1787. When she left, Count Ruminatsev accompanied her, and he never returned to his estate before he died in December, 1796. (Source: As stated by the archivist and historian OlgaIvanovna Maltchukova, from the neighboring village of Chereskenky on June 14, 2005, to Wesley G. Tschetter). The small museum and archive have records of the small German community that once lived in Wischenka). Today, about one

Count Rumiantsev Castle at Wischenka overlooking the Desna River

third of this castle looking building is still in use to house a summer camp for disadvantaged children.

Castle at Wishenka. Note dry creek and bridge in foreground referenced in Hutterite Chronicle II

Wischenka village continues as a small, farming based community that surprisingly has a very small Baptist church that was established in the early 20th century. It also has a Russian Orthodox church.

In Raditschewa—1802 to 1842 (Village presently named Raditschewa)

In May and June 1802, the group moved once more, this time to Raditschewa, also along the Desna River, about 10 miles by river route northwest. The following is quoted from the Chronicle, Volume II:

"On June 15, 1802, the last brothers and sisters left Wischenka. Building up a new community at Radicheva began in May, the place allotted by the government and situated on the River Desna about 10 miles [16 km] from Wischenka. Bricks were fired and lime burned for the purpose and soon five brick buildings and a number of wooden ones were erected. The community buildings formed a square measuring 490 feet each way, with a large entrance gate which was locked and watched at night. The workshops for the different trades were on the ground floor, and on the upper story every family had a small room called their "little place," with a bed, a table, and two chairs.

Two schools, for the older and the younger children respectively, each with classrooms, were built on the old, well-proved plan, and workrooms were soon set up for weaving, pottery, tailoring, shoemaking, turning, hat making, tanning, spinning, and broom binding. A smithy, a washhouse, and a bakery were finished, as well as a dining room and a mothers' and babies' room.

Ten miles [16 km] away, on a river called the Jessman, they had a water mill which the government allowed them to run for their own profit. They had a big windmill, too, which they themselves had built on the hill on our place, for they were experienced in such undertakings."

They also owned a distillery in the fir woods (forest) on the others side of the Desna, where there was a fine big fish pond, connected to the river and well-stocked with fish. It had been given them by the government."

Raft crossing Desna River near Raditschewa. This is very likely the location of the tragic drowning of two Hutterite girls crossing from Raditschewa to Neudorf in 1824

Although the Desna River has a major dam that maintains a high water mark, a wide view of the river still shows evidence of the fish ponds. The site of the water mill and an island used for pasture and hay is now covered with water. There are still several brick buildings in the area occupied by the Hutterite Community with at least two vaulted cellars still in existence, easily accessible, and usable by the owners. A panoramic view of the area occupied by the 490 square foot community is shown in the picture (calculates to 5.5 acres). In the background is a destroyed Russian Orthodox church. Note the close proximity to the Desna River in the background.

Raditschewa Note Desna River in background

There were several significant events that occurred during the forty year period of 1802-1842. First, disagreements among the ministers prompted the establishment of a second, sister community across the Desna river, called Neudorf, that never flourished. Today nothing remains of this second village location which is across the Desna. Secondly, a fire in 1819 completely destroyed the 490 foot square building site. The fire was caused by a newly made barrel when with its "hot" hoop rolled out the door and touched the thatched roofing materials which hung over the doorway. The community was already experiencing dissention on the matter of communal ownership, and there were financial problems. The effects of the fire resulted to the discontinuance of "community of goods" as well as the cessation of many trades such as pottery and weaving, which meant that families had to then rely almost exclusively on agriculture production for income.

In a 2007 visit to Raditschewa, the author found that the 1819 fire is still a part of the history of the existing community as evidenced by a 1999 Raditschewa publication that references a major 19th century fire. The historical account also states that a German group lived at Raditschewa during the 19th century. A Street (more like an alley) where the community was built is today named "German" street.

There was not enough land to support the increasing numbers persons in the community and the land was too dispersed in location for the efficient use by the individual family units. Eventually the standard of living diminished to the extent that they no longer had a school and stopped providing an education for the children. Over the next twenty years the government and the Mennonite groups in the southern part of what is present-day Ukraine recognized the financial and social plight of the group at Raditchewa.

Realizing their plight, the Hutterite leadership made a request to the Russian authorities to move to where other German speaking communities were in southern Ukraine. They made multiple inquiries and petitions with the Guardian's Committee for Foreign Colonists in Odessa, but the appeals were denied. Years passed, and the financial situation for the community become worse. The community decided to send two men and a driver to make another "in person" appeal at Odessa with this same Guardian's Committee for Foreign Colonists. The petition was again denied. On their return trip the men decided to go to Johann Cornies and present the community's desperate situation. Cornies, an industrious Mennonite agricultural leader, was a member of the Supervisory Council for Government Lands and had a good working relationship with the Russian authorities. He lived in the area that the group would eventually move to near present day Melitopol. With Cornies personal guarantee that the Hutterite community would be successful, in 1842 the Community was allowed to move once again.

1842—the move south to the Molotschna near the present day city of Melitopol, Ukraine

Recognizing their similarity to other German speaking residents 400 miles to the south, the entire group was moved in the fall of 1842. Mennonites had already established many successful communities in the early 1800's as a part of the Russian invitation to German settlers. This region had numerous Mennonite, Catholic, Reformed and Lutheran communities that had a common bond of special privileges from the Russian government, which were extended to only German people who resettled in Russia.

The first community, named Hutterthal, was built about 12 miles southwest of present day city of Melitopol. All the residents from Raditschewa made the move to Hutterthal. Ten years later another sister community, named Johannesruh in honor of than deceased Johann Cornies, was built. Hutterthal and Johannesruh were about two miles apart and established with private ownership of property. These two communities plus another three constructed in later years were to be the homes until 1879 when the immigration to the United States was complete.

Hutterthal was a well-planned community designed by Johann Cornies and featured very wide streets and a school, similar to the Mennonite villages established in that era. Two-story house/barn structures were designed as two family homes (duplexes) with a central hall perpendicular to the longer side of the house. The top floor was generally used for storage for items such as sacked grain and equipment. The central hall doorways were aligned in such a matter that one could see to the other end of the village via the open doorways. This same design was used in many of the first homes and barns built in America.

House in village of Hutterthal

The census of 1843 listed 316 residents living at Hutterthal (153 males, 163 females). In the last census before immigration; taken in 1864, Hutterthal had 368 residents (192 males, 176 females). In 1879, most of the last group of immigrants came from Hutterthal. (Source: Archival search conducted by Maxim Kuleshoff, Kiev)

Hutterthal had a nearby brick factory that was later owned privately by Isaac Mathew Wollman. (ibid) Of interest is that the author found that the bricks used at Hutterthal had the same dimensions (4 inches by 10 inches) as used in Wischenka and Raditschewa.

The former village of Hutterthal still exists as a very small community of homes, farmsteads, and orchards. Some of the homes constructed by our ancestors were divided to create single family dwellings, but they retain the unique appearance as constructed during the 19th century. Steep pitched roofs and window frames and doorways retain the historic appearance. One such home that still exists is only half the size of the original, with the other half moved to another lot across the street. Even the remaining portion has been further divided into two separate living quarters. As a result, the distinctively constructed vaulted cellar is no longer under the home but in the back yard where the other half of the house once set. Interestingly, the cellar still remains in use. There are no persons with German background living in these now Ukrainian villages.

Entrance to underground cellar in village of Hutterthal.

Hutterite house in Johannesruh

Domed cellar in former village of Hutterthal, still used today.

The village of Johannesruh, named in honor of Mennonite Johann Cornies, their benefactor, was constructed in 1852 with a layout similar to Hutterthal. Today it is much larger than Hutterthal and has many of the features of the original village including the long wide street, a major cross street and many original buildings and cellars. These high pitched buildings are used for homes and storage.

Johannesruh village view

The Establishment of Hutterdorf (Kutcheva)

Of the three additional villages established during this same time period, one was named Hutterdorf, also called Kutcheva, built in 1857, and the other was Scheromet, built in 1868.

Due to the growth in population, on March 1, 1857, 33 families who lived in Hutterthal and Johannesruh sold their possessions to relatives and moved to a newly acquired 4,000 acres plot purchased for 21,000 rubles from a woman named Kutcheva. So after nearly 40 years of private ownership, this group reestablished and practiced community of goods since the issue of communal ownership had not been settled due to the reading of sermons which presented communal ownership as an ideal Christian life, even to the point that one could hardly be a Christian without it. Within the first year disagreements caused two separate communal groups to emerge, one on each end of the village and a third group in the middle of the village retained private ownership. There remains a very large abandoned cellar at the edge of this village.

This village was about 80 miles north east of Hutterthal and Johannesruh and some homes constructed in this 1850's time period remain. On the outskirts of the village there remains a cellar, although its entrance is barred with a large slab of concrete.

Village of Hutterdorf in 2002

In 1868 the followers of Michael Waldner on one end of the village sold out and formed the village of Scheromet about 10 miles away. There is no evidence of this village today. This was the last bruderhof built in the Ukraine but the first group to immigrate to America. After six years in this village, the group immigrated in 1874. This group of 109 people established Bon Homme Colony near Tabor, South Dakota. They were known as "Schmeidleut."

The followers of Darius Walter on the other end of the village also continued living communally until the migration to America in 1874. They established Wolf Creek Colony, nine miles west of Freeman, South Dakota. They were known as "Dariusleut." (Note: The present day Wolf Creek colony are "Schmeidleut" as the original "Dariusleut" moved to Canada.)

Those in private ownership remained as such and established the Hutterdorf Church west of Freeman which no longer exists. These Hutterdorf families constituted the greatest part of the move to Langham, Saskatchewan, area in the early 1900's.

Neu Hutterthal, also known as Dabritscha—1868

By 1868, the need at Hutterthal and Johannesruh for expansion was anticipated. Several thousand destines (2.6 acres to one destine) of land was secured about 120 miles north of Hutterthal, near the present day city of Zaporozhe, Ukraine. Neu Hutterthal consisted of twenty farmsteads with ten on each side of the three quarter mile street, all in private ownership. Since this village's minister, Rev. Paul Tschetter, had been a delegate to America in 1873, and a favorable report of conditions in America was given, this group voted unanimously in 1874 to move to America. A nobleman bought out everything for 150,000 rubles. Nothing of Neu Hutterthal remains today, and it is generally thought that it was destroyed during the 1917-1920 Revolution.

Source Material:

The Chronicle of Hutterian Brethren, Volume II. This was written on a contemporary basis throughout the history. Volume II deals with historical events and the families that came from Austria and from Slovakia.

Banished for Faith was written by Emil J Waltner in 1968 by using the Chronicle as a source.

History of Hutterthal Mennonite Church, Freeman, SD—Introduction article by Norman Hofer

Summary of Villages, unpublished material by Arnold M Hofer

Additional Source material including pictures acquired and in possession of Wesley G Tschetter

Background & Author's note of visits to these former Hutterite villages. The villages were visited by Rev. D. M. Hofer during his 1922-1924 Mennonite aid work to Russia as recorded in his book "My trip around the world and the famine in Russia." The book is written in German.

In 1976 a tour group of 44 persons including 13 with Hutterite heritage sponsored by Menno Travel Service and led by Gerhardt Lorenz were given Soviet Union permission to visit the villages established after 1842, so the visit did not include Wischenka and Raditschewa. The visits to villages were in a single afternoon, were very brief and did not allow for any research or inquiry.

In the mid 1980's Galen Hofer, son of Norman Hofer, was the first person to visit these two villages and relied on maps that Arnold M Hofer faxed to him. These maps were German maps from WWII that Arnold had acquired from John Hostettler of Temple University. Galen took many pictures.

The real opportunity to visit these places came in the 1990's through Gordon Schmidt, president and founder of York Manufacturing in Nebraska who had grain storage business trips to the Ukraine. He knew enough history to realize that he would be traveling and working near the locations of Wischenka and Raditschewa. His visits to these villages led to a group of 13 "Prairieleut" people visiting these two villages in fall of 2002. The trip was a Part of Mennonite Heritage Cruise and visits to Wischenka and Raditschewa were coordinated by Pam Mendel of Doland, SD, who was then in Christian service work in the Ukraine.

Arnold M. Hofer was a part of the 1976 and 2002 visiting groups. Arnold, the author, Wesley G. Tschetter, and Pam Mendel took a "research" trip to these two villages in May 2003 and established some personal connections with these villagers. At Wischenka, an original Hutterite brick building with double, arched cellars and thought to have been built in the mid 1780's, was discovered. This building has since been renovated into a summer villa for a wealthy Ukrainian businessman. A second trip by Wesley G. Tschetter, Don Mendel, and Pam Mendel in June 2005 to all of the still existing Hutterite villages verified the existence of original Hutterite cellars and buildings.

Chapter 2

THE DIARY OF PAUL TSCHETTER, 1873

I

Translated and Edited by J. M. Hofer

PAUL TSCHETTER
Born Oct. 5, 1842. Died Nov. 17, 1919.
Minister for 53 years.

LORENZ TSCHETTER
Born Jan. 16, 1819. Died Dec. 8, 1878.

A BRIEF BIOGRAPHY OF PAUL TSCHETTER, 1842-1919

By his son, Joseph W. Tschetter
Written in 1931

My dear father was born October 5, 1842, in the village of Blumenort, Molotschna, South Russia. His parents were Jacob and Barbara Tschetter, members of the Hutterite Church. The old church book shows that the name "Tschetter" was formerly written "Zetterle." Soon after he was born, his parents moved to the village of Hutterthal, where he was reared and attended the village school. In the spring of 1860 he was baptized and received into the Hutterite church at that place. In the same year, 1860, November 27, he was married to Maria Walter. In the year 1866 he was ordained to the ministry by Rev. Peter Wedel. In the year 1868, together with several families, he founded the village of Neu Hutterthal.

In the year 1874, he and his family, with four more families, left Russia for America and settled forty-five miles northwest of Yankton, South Dakota. About five years later the whole church came across and settled in the same neighborhood.

On January 28, 1883, he was ordained as an Elder of the church by Rev. Friederich Schartner. On December 21, 1915, the Lord took our dear mother from his side. On November 17, 1919, our dear father died of a stroke of paralysis. His age was 77 years, 1 month, and 10 days. Father and mother lived in holy matrimony for 55 years and 10 days. Their union was blessed by the Lord with five sons and five daughters. One son six years old died in Russia while father was on the trip to America, and one daughter aged eight years was killed by a threshing machine in the next year, when they came to America. The other sons, Paul, Jacob, Joseph, and David, and daughters, Mrs. Susanna Decker, Mrs. Maria Hofer, Mrs. Barbara Stahl, and Mrs. Justina Hofman are still living. He had served his church for 53 years as a minister. He was buried November 19, 1919, in the Neu Hutterthal cemetery that is located on the old homestead that he took when he came to America.

As a minister of the Gospel he was very simple and calm. In his sermons he laid much emphasis on being honest and upright and walking the narrow way that Jesus taught and walked while on earth. He lived out his convictions. He was firm in his belief and creed. He was very slow to accept some new teaching even though the Bible did not oppose it. He advocated farm life, for he thought it was the most honest occupation for a child of God.

My father's career will be better understood if I give a few words of explanation about the Hutterian Brethren. The name derives from Jacob Hutter, who was born about 1496 at the village of Moos in Pusterthal, Tyrol, and who early became a leader of the Anabaptists in Moravia, in particular of the branch which adopted communism according to Acts 2. Jacob Hutter was burned to death as a martyr February 25, 1536. After much persecution lasting over two hundred years, sixty-seven souls escaped to Rumania and in 1770 into Russia. First they lived for seventy-two years about six hundred miles north of the Mennonite settlement in the Molotschna. They lived in a Bruderhof, holding all properties in common, until in 1819. At that time each family moved on its own land, although the name Hutterian Brethren was retained.

In the year 1842 (the year that my father was born) the Russian government moved them (at that time 50 families) about six hundred miles south to the Mennonite Colony of Molotschna, because the government thought they had about the same belief as the Mennonites, especially on the military question. Here for the first time the Hutterites came in close contact with the Mennonites. From that time on the word Hutterian or Hutterite was applied to their language or dialect, as well as to their religion, in order to distinguish from the "platt-deutsch" of the Mennonites. Here the church was organized according to Mennonite principles. In 1857 a minister by the name of Darius Walter organized a communistic Bruderhof again, although not all the Hutterites entered the Bruderhof. When all Hutterites in 1874 and 1879 moved to America and settled down in South Dakota about half settled down in the Bruderhof and the other half settled down on individual farms, each family holding its own land and property. The non-Bruderhof people organized their local churches according to the principles of the Mennonite faith either as they had it in Russia already, or as a new adoption in America. Both groups kept the name Hutterite, although this referred to their dialect more than their religious views. Those that lived in Bruderhofs preferred to be called "Hutterian Brethren."

About 40 years ago some of Hutterite Mennonites living outside the Bruderhofs joined the Krimmer Mennonite Brethren Conference and established their local churches. These churches baptize by immersion and observe feet washing as an ordinance according to John 13. So among the descendants of the Hutterites there are three groups; the Bruderhof group who live in communistic colonies, having all property in common, the General Conference Mennonites, and the Krimmer Mennonite Brethren. My father never lived in a Bruderhof, nor did I ever hear him advocate joining the Bruderhof, although he was in a good standing with the brethren in the Bruderhof. He was a leader in the group which joined the Krimmer Mennonite Brethren Conference. Chicago, Ill.

Introduction

When it was decreed in 1870 by the Russian government that there was to be universal military training in that country in the future, there was great uneasiness among certain groups who believed in nonresistance. Among these were the Hutterites who at that time numbered about one hundred families and lived in the government of Jekaterinoslav, South Russia. They had four main settlements: Hutterthal, Neu Hutterthal, Hutterdorf and Johannesruh. Thirty-two of these families lived in two communistic colonies while others lived as private owners in villages as was then customary in that country. Under Czar Paul I, the Hutterites (as also the Mennonites) had secured a privelegium which guaranteed to them exemption from military training. This exemption was now seemingly withdrawn by Alexander II, and so a delegation composed of Rev. Paul Tschetter, than a young minister, twenty-nine years of age, Michael Stahl and a number of other brethren were sent to St. Petersburg in January, 1873, to investigate whether this privelegium would be valid in the future or not. The best that the Russian authorities would grant was noncombatant service. This was unsatisfactory to the Hutterian Brethren and so they decided to send a delegation to America to learn whether more favorable terms could be secured here in regard to military service. This delegation was composed of the same Rev. Paul Tschetter, and his uncle Lorenz Tschetter, both of Hutterthal. They journeyed together with ten Mennonites, delegates also from Russia, who came to America for the same purpose. On this journey to America the diary which follows and which is the subject of this article was written. It was written in the German language and very likely was recorded from day to day, or as it seems sometimes, a day or two afterwards. The writer was a keen observer of farming conditions, amount of rainfall, fertility of soil, temperature, crops, water supply, etc. But he felt his responsibility not only in this respect, but also in the matter of securing possible exemption from military service for his brethren. He appeared before President Grant and pleaded his case. President Grant replied: "It would be unfair to favor one group of people more than another, but the constitution of the United States," he said, "guarantees religious liberty." To that extent the President was willing to meet their demands. This manuscript, which is the original, written by Rev. Tschetter on this journey, was put into my hands in 1921 when I first became interested in Hutterian history, by the Rev. Joseph W. Tschetter of Chicago, a son of the writer of the diary. Recently the idea came upon me to publish it, because it would probably prove of interest to others. The editor of the MENNONITE QUARTERLY REVIEW was enthusiastic about it and so with immense pleasure and interest I have translated it and put it into its present form.

Description of a Journey to America, April 14, 1873, with Lorenz Tschetter, Accurately Recorded from Day to Day

Saturday, April 14. I began my momentous journey to America taking leave of my wife and dear children with a heavy heart and also took leave of all my brothers and sisters. Due to circumstances my brother Joseph Tschetter and my sister-in-law could not be present although they had planned to accompany me as far as Nikopol. Their son had taken sick at Hutterdorf[1] and they wished to visit him there. There were two brethren visiting at our home at the time, i.e. George Hofer and Joseph Hofer and of these I also took leave. Love obliged my dear mother and father to accompany me as far as Nikopol and so we left with a sad and troubled heart, only God knowing if I should ever see my loved ones again. I put all my trust in the Lord that He might send His angels to guide and protect me.

There were also three brethren from Hutterthal[2] at our home, i.e. Peter Tschetter, Peter Mendel and Christian Hofer, who accompanied us as far as Nikopol for it seemed the will of the Lord to have a number of our brethren present when we departed. At five p.m. we arrived at Nikopol. We immediately went to see the steamship and purchased our tickets to Cherson, second class, costing three ruble, sixty kopeck.[3]

Sunday, April 15. Early Sunday morning we all boarded the steamship which was named Listalscha. At six o'clock I took leave of my dear father and mother who embraced me and wept bitterly. So also Lorenz's daughter wept loudly and embraced her father. After this, we departed in God's name arriving safely at Cherson before evening.[4] We remained for the night at a European hotel. Cherson is a large city, well-built, and has paved streets.

Monday, April 16. After awaking all well, praise the Lord, we went to our steamship at eight o'clock and purchased tickets to Odessa, second class, and paid two ruble, forty kopeck. The name of the ship was Gibson (Giessen). There was quite a wind, but the ship did not rock much until we came upon the Black Sea. Here the wind became stronger, the waves rolled furiously, and the ship swayed violently to and fro. Lorenz went to the upper deck, but soon returned and said that the ship was very unsteady and the waves high. I also went on deck but soon began to feel bad since I was not accustomed to traveling on the sea. After a short while I returned to our cabin below. Then I again went to the upper deck for better air, as I had a severe headache. I remained there until we arrived at Odessa at five o'clock in the afternoon. Odessa is a large city, and we made our headquarters at the Maiback Nerro Lazar Hotel.

Klassen and myself called upon Toews[5] to get information in regard to our journey. He greeted us very cordially. Since it was late in the evening, he asked us to come again and see him early the next morning for further information.

Tuesday, April 17. In the morning after giving thanks to the Lord for His protection we called on Toews at nine o'clock and he went with us to the Exchange Bank of Odessa. He assisted us as much as possible. We exchanged only fifty-two ruble and fifty kopeck, one part into Austrian florins (gold) and the other part into francs. A florin is worth seventy kopeck silver, and a franc five ruble and ninety-three kopeck. He gave us letters of introduction to Trütschler in Berlin, and Maier in Hamburg.[6] We asked him whether it would be necessary

---

1 Hutterdorf was a Hutterian village.

2 Also a Hutterian village.

3 A ruble was a Russian silver coin worth 51½ cents and a kopeck was worth about the 100th part of a ruble.

4 There were two Hutterian representatives, Rev. Paul Tschetter and his uncle Lorenz Tschetter, both from Neu Hutterthal. At Cherson they were joined in their journey to America by ten Mennonite brethren making an entire delegation of twelve.

5 Evidently Toews was in charge of the travelers information bureau at Odessa, and was in touch with the German Immigration offices in Berlin and Hamburg.

6 Trütschler was connected with the German steamship line and accommodated strangers on their way to Hamburg. Maier was a reliable hotel owner in Hamburg where they were to lodge while in the city.

to secure a different pass and he informed us that we might possibly have to exchange it for another in Hamburg and, if not, the pass we possessed now was good clear to America, for the Russian authorities do not favor exchanging their passes in Germany. We thanked him for his assistance and left. That same evening at eight o'clock we arrived at Wolotschisk on the Austrian boundary line. We traveled throughout the night, third class with a mixed crowd of Jews, women and children. The train was so crowded that we were obliged to sit up all night and were unable to sleep much.

Wednesday, April 18. After traveling across long stretches of plains, hills, and valleys at a tremendous speed, we arrived at Wolotschisk at six o'clock in the evening. This city is on the boundary line between Austria and Russia. Our passes were examined here and our baggage inspected. We purchased a ticket to Podwotoczyska, costing ten kopeck[7] and from there another ticket to Oswiecim on the Prussian boundary line, for which we paid nineteen gulden and eleven kreutzer.[8] The Russian language became useless because no one understood it or could speak it. Most of the people spoke the Austrian language and some the German. This country is known as Galicia or Austrian Poland and is mostly woodland.

Thursday, April 19. At nine o'clock in the morning we arrived at Lemberg, the chief city of Galicia, where we changed cars and at seven in the evening came to Oswiecim. Here we purchased a ticket for Myslowitz, a short distance from Oswiecim, and remained for the night. We were tired from the journey for one cannot very well sleep on the train. We had a quiet room.

Friday, April 20. In the morning after we had praised and thanked the Lord for His protection, we departed for the station to proceed on our journey. We purchased tickets as far as Kassel and left at five o'clock in the morning from Myslowitz and came to Breslau, the chief city of Silesia. At Breslau we purchased tickets for Berlin, the chief city and capital of Prussia. We arrived in Berlin at eight o'clock in the evening in a large railroad station such as I had never seen in my life. This railroad station was even larger and more magnificent than the one at St. Petersburg. The railroad was crowded with thousands of people and there was great noise and bustle in and about the same. It was night and we were strangers in a city where, no doubt, plenty of wicked people can be found. Soon a man approached us, saying that he had quarters for us for the night nearby, and we entrusted ourselves to this stranger although with certain fear and distrust. We followed him rather reluctantly, into the basement of a large five story structure, where we found great crowds of people and here he showed us a dingy, little room with four bedsteads and one window, where we were to spend the night.

The room did not particularly appeal to any of us, but being unable to find a better one, we decided to remain there for the night. The manager and his wife seemed to be respectable and honest people. We locked the doors and prayed to God that He might protect us during the night. We retired and slept well.

Saturday, April 21. After morning prayer, we called at the Hamburg railroad station about two verst distant,[9] for Trütschler was to assist us in the matter of exchanging our money. We did not find him at the office and waited for him two hours. When he arrived he greeted us cordially and exchanged for each of us seven hundred ruble into American money. For the seven hundred ruble we received six hundred twenty American gold dollars. He advised us to again change these American silver dollars to American paper money and gain a further premium which we did. We purchased third class tickets from Berlin to Hamburg, but secured them at the fourth-class rate. The distance from Berlin to Hamburg is one hundred thirty-seven miles. We left Berlin at ten a.m. by train and arrived at Hamburg at seven in the morning. The country between Berlin and Hamburg is very low and woody, so low in fact, that drainage-canals around the fields are necessary and by means of windmills the water is drained from the fields. When we arrived at the Hamburg railway station, we again found the same noise and bustle that we had already experienced in Berlin. One cried, "Come to my quarters," another, "I have a room for you" etc. All of a sudden we heard someone's voice above all the rest, "Klassen, Toews, Tschetter, come to me." We were surprised to hear our names in a strange place like Hamburg but were informed that he represented the German Company and had orders to accommodate us. We entered a spacious hall in a five story building, where boys and girls were dancing. I was almost terrified and shrank back. The man said, "Follow me, I will give you a room where you shall be undisturbed." This was true. I inquired of him as to who these people were who found so much pleasure in dancing, upon which he answered that they also expect to sail for America on April 24. I said, "They should rather pray than dance." "Yes," he said, "but we cannot always pray; we must enjoy ourselves." That is the way of the wicked world. We then went to our room and retired for the night.

Sunday, April 22. I remained in my room until noon, read the Word of God and meditated. In the afternoon we

---

7 A gulden was worth 48.2 cents and a kreutzer about one-half cent.

8 Wolotschisk and Podwotoczyska are located on opposite sides of the river.

9 A verst is a Russian measure of distance, approximately 3500 feet in length.

called upon the agent August Bolten and presented to him our letter of introduction from Toews of Odessa. After he had read the letter, he said that he would do everything possible to accommodate us. We purchased second-class return tickets from him, two hundred dollars each, and he promised to ask the captain on the ship to give us a good cabin. We thanked him for his kind assistance and returned to our lodging place. The immigration building on one side faces the water front and rests upon strong piers.

Monday, April 23. During the night shortly before daybreak many more emigrants arrived, mostly German, Mecklenburgers from Prussia, with women and children, numbering more than five hundred souls. They were emigrating for various reasons. Here at the immigration building all ate at one table and at a regular hour. Breakfast was served at seven in the morning and consisted of a large cup of coffee and white bread. At noon, soup, meat and potatoes and in the evening a cup of coffee.[10] The board was good.

In the afternoon I went out sight-seeing in the city and among other places I drifted into a bookstore, where I purchased a little book on Menno Simmons. I walked through the city and observed the hustle and bustle of the city, for Hamburg is a great business and commercial center with many canals and bridges, large warehouses and an excellent harbor in which many ships were anchored. The people of Hamburg are mostly Lutherans. The city has large buildings, five, six, and seven stories in height. Most of the buildings face a water front and rest on piers. In the evening I again returned to my room and retired for the night.

Tuesday, April 24. I remained in my room practically the entire day, writing letters, and spent some time buying the necessities for the ocean voyage. I was also invited to visit Rev. Rosen,[11] but feared that I might get into an argument with him, for I knew that he was an unsound Mennonite. The Apostle warns us to "avoid those who may harm our souls."

Wednesday, April 25. In the morning we left our lodging place and drove to the ship which was harbored in the Elbe about two verst away. Here our passes were examined and we entered the ship with sighs and prayers to God, trusting our all in Him that He might guide and protect us on the wide and angry ocean. We departed at eight o'clock in the morning in a small ship and after sailing for two hours we came to a very large ship which we entered and were assigned to our cabins. There were six beds in the cabin and, since there were only four of us, two friends joined our company and shared the sleeping room with us. For a dining room and a sitting room there was a large hall. There was always plenty to eat, such as soup, meat, fish, cheese, butter, plums, cherries, nuts, apples, and many other things, the names of which I did not know. Meals were served four times daily, one hundred eating at each board. Words fail me to express the table manners and courtesy of both waiters and patrons. From the Elbe we sailed the first day into the North Sea. The sea was calm all day and we slept soundly that night.

Thursday, April 26. The sea was clam until ten o'clock in the morning, then the wind increased and the ship commenced to sway back and forth. I began to have a severe headache, but was able to partake of a good dinner. Some people had to leave the dinner table, and still others did not leave their cabins. Of our companions, Toews did not eat a morsel all day. I was also able to eat lunch and supper. As our ship sailed into the English Channel, shortly before evening, the wind increased so that we were unable to sleep very much. I began to feel so bad that I had to go on deck to get better air. As I watched the rolling waves and the ship plowing through huge mountains of water, my spirit went up to God to Whose care we had entrusted ourselves. The godless were little disturbed by the great storm. They continued dancing and were merry. After a while I returned to our cabin and retired for the night.

Friday, April 27. When I awoke Friday morning it was day and the ship stood still. I thanked my heavenly Father for His protection for another day and night. I went on deck and in the distance could see Havre, France, a beautiful city with a fine harbor in which many ships were anchored. At Havre we were detained for twenty-four hours, and spent the time sight-seeing in the city. During this time our ship was loaded with a supply of coal and water. Around the city of Havre several fortresses are located.

Saturday, April 28. At eight o'clock in the morning we steamed out of the harbor of Havre. Our hearts went up to God, that He might protect us on our voyage and send His angels to guide us on the wide ocean. After a lapse of two hours we lost sight of all land and now only the blue heavens and the deep ocean could be seen. The ship moved along smoothly that day. The frivolous and gay crowd was happy and paraded up and down the deck, a thing I abhorred. I thought it would have been more appropriate to pray to God for His protection, but they had not the slightest thought of this. I went to bed and slept well that night.

10 In the language of the Hutterians "a cup of coffee" was symbolic of the evening meal because coffee was not used for the midday meal. Altho spoken of only as "a cup of coffee" it included a full meal of bread, butter, meat, potatoes, etc.

11 Berend Karl Roosen, pastor of the Mennonite Church at Hamburg, Altona.

Sunday, April 29. Awoke all well and thanked my Lord for His Fatherly protection. The ship sailed on smooth seas until ten o'clock in the morning when a storm arose which rocked the ship to and fro so that many of the passengers began to feel sick. Only those who were used to traveling on the sea and those who possessed a strong constitution were not affected. I, being frequently bothered with headaches, was also forced to retire to my room, although I was able to partake of a light dinner, lunch and also supper. Many left the table while others did not even appear at meal-time. I thought and remarked to some of the people, "Yesterday you were so jolly and gay and today you look so sad."

Monday, April 30. Did not feel well all day. Remained in bed most of the day without eating much.

Tuesday, May 1. Rained in the morning. Felt good so that I could eat well. Had rain and storm in the evening so that the ship rocked considerably, but I was already getting accustomed to this.

Wednesday, May 2. The ocean was more calm than any day since our departure. The people recovered their former health, but at the same time became more godless. In the evening the wind became stronger.

Thursday, May 3. The sea was quiet. One of our brethren, Toews, had been in bed for eight days and during that time had hardly eaten anything. The other brother, Klassen, was not seasick at all.

Friday, May 4. Rain and storm to-day. The waves were so high that they seemed as mountains and the ship at times seemed to be moving between two walls. It was nearly impossible to eat for the tables were very unsteady. Many again became seasick, but I was not materially affected for I was already used to sea travel. The storm raged far into the night.

Saturday, May 5. Rain in the morning and the ocean was more calm. The wind blew from the east. The sails were put up and this greatly increased the speed of the ship so that we sailed three hundred forty miles in twenty-four hours, as formerly we made only two hundred ninety-eight to three hundred fifteen miles per day. The weather became colder for we began to approach the icebergs near Iceland.

Sunday, May 6. This was a beautiful Sunday morning. The sea was quiet. In the morning the pastor delivered a sermon on Psalm L, 14.[12] The prayer which he offered was reverent and effective, but the sermon seemed much too mild for such godless rabble as that on the ship. His object in the sermon seemed merely to entertain the audience. At dinner an offering was taken for a family, whose father and husband had died on the voyage and who were in meager circumstances. I also gave a small donation. The orphans were four children, most of them already grown, the youngest being nine years old. At eleven o'clock in the night the corpse was lowered into the depths of the sea and buried beneath the waves. The burial was not public so as not to frighten the people on board the ship.

Monday, May 7. In the morning at ten o'clock the flag was raised and we met a small ship from New York which escorted our ship back to the city. Oh how the people all rejoiced that land was finally to be in sight soon. The pastor sang a song of Thanksgiving with a group of men and women in which I heartily joined. It gave me great joy to know that there were at least some on board the ship, who thought of praising God for His guidance and protection during our long voyage.

Tuesday, May 8. Early in the morning, we sighted land toward the north after wandering on the large and stormy ocean for thirteen days. We all rejoiced at the sight of land. It was not until eleven o'clock that the magnificent "Silesia" stopped and we were all transferred to a smaller steamship and after steaming past more than one hundred ships in one hour we landed at Hoboken. At noon we left the ship, went to the city and found a lodging place in the Karles Unrein Hotel where we had dinner. During the afternoon and evening until twelve o'clock I wrote letters and then retired for the night in God's name.

Wednesday, May 9. After breakfast, at ten o'clock we called on Pastor Neumondt, crossing a small body of water in a steamboat in order to get to his house to get some information and advice. He greeted us cordially, but his advice according to my opinion was too excessive. He spoke too much and acted too wise. He asked us to call again in the afternoon, when he would give us references and advise us as to exchanging our money. Klassen and Toews went, but Lorenz and myself did not and exchanged our money without his assistance. For three hundred dollars in gold we received three hundred fifty dollars in paper money. New York is a magnificent and beautiful city with many large ships in the harbor and is very populous. The railroads run double-deck,[13] supported by steel pullars. In the evening at eight o'clock we departed from Hoboken by train for Elkhart, Indiana. We passed through a tunnel two versts in length. Throughout the entire night we traveled through a mountainous region.

---

12 "Offer unto God Thanksgiving and pay thy vows unto the most High." Psalm L. 14.

13 Here the writer refers to the elevated trains which he for the first time saw in New York City.

Thursday, May 10. At eight o'clock in the morning the locomotive suddenly lost the rest of the train but returned to pick us up. Throughout the day we again traveled a country with lofty mountains, some as high as six hundred feet. The mountains are rocky and are covered with trees. People are found living at the foot of the mountains, plowing such small patches as they have cleared. On the mountain sides there seem to be springs that develop into small rivulets flowing down the steep grades. The soil is chiefly of a yellowish color. The country with its many green trees seems not a bad region, very beautiful but probably not so suitable for agricultural purposes. That same midnight we arrived at Domkirch (Dunkirk) where we remained for the night. We had a good night's rest. The lady at the hotel could speak German but in general the people were English speaking.

Friday, May 11. At nine o'clock in the morning we departed from Domkirch. Domkirch is near a large lake (Lake Ontario) and the country is quite level with many orchards. The trees were in full bloom. At three o'clock we came near the lake and passed through the city of Ziehago[14] in which there were many steel factories and foundries. At three in the morning we arrived at Elkhart and remained in the station until morning. We could sleep little for there was much noise caused by steam engines. From New York we traveled to Elkhart in forty-six hours.

Saturday, May 12. In the morning we called at the home of John Funk, a minister of the Old Mennonite Church. He was not at home, but we were cordially greeted by members of his family and given breakfast. The Old Mennonites have beards and shave around the mouth. They rather speak English than German. After breakfast we called at the Funk publishing house. I was given a little book and also purchased a song book. In the afternoon there was a street parade in Elkhart. Thirty-four wagons in which were all kinds of animals passed through the streets. Seven teams of horses were hitched to the first wagon. All the men and horses were decorated with plumes of red, white, and green colors. The wagon was as if of gold and seated upon it were musicians and comedians who played tunes.[15] The other wagons were all drawn by two and three teams. I have never seen such things in all my life. In the afternoon there was a circus. I did not attend for I considered it a sin to witness such devilish things. I was glad that I had been relieved of the godless rabble with whom I was obliged to spend such a long time on the ocean. In the afternoon many Mennonites came to Elkhart and a man named Isaac became acquainted with us and took us to his home. We wished to attend church services the next day and the church was not far away from Isaac's home.[16] They do not live in villages like we do.[17] Every one has his own piece of land which is fenced. Isaac's land is seven miles from the church. We arrived at his home just at sunset and were warmly welcomed. Isaac has a farm of two hundred acres of which one hundred acres is woodland. He also has a fine orchard.

Sunday, May 13. Awoke all well and gave praise to God for it. At nine o'clock we drove to church with Isaac where many people had already assembled. They gave me a seat among the ministers. It happened incidentally that an infant had recently died and so the funeral services commenced. Songs were sung for the opening, the first one in German and then another one in English. The first sermon was in German on the text Corinthians, 1, 15. Then followed an English sermon of which I understood nothing. Prayers were said aloud and the people knelt, although some remained seated. After this another song was sung and then the child was carried out and buried. While the child was being buried, the congregation sang another song.

The style of dress among the men is conservative. Their coats are somewhat short with buttons on the trousers and vests.[18] The young men are well dressed, wearing breast shirts with green or blue neckties. They part their hair in the middle like we do and some part their hair on the side. Most of the men have beards. The women are dressed in a variety of styles and colors. Some wear white knitted caps with lace in front. Others wear hats of various colors. Girls wear straw hats with long ribbons. Some are dressed in white, others in blue, black, red, etc.[19] The small children are also taken to church services, some sitting on their mother's lap while others walk around. After the services were over, one of the women repented for her sins. The minister then made a few remarks. The Old Mennonites address each other as "brethren" and "sisters." The ministers are elected, just as we do, and are finally chosen by lot.[20] The Lord's Supper is taken twice a year, not at a definite time and not

---

14 The name of this town seems to be misspelled.

15 The writer was all his life opposed to instrumental music and did not permit the members of his church to have any musical instruments in their home.

16 Isaac Gelert (df diary entry for July 12). The church was that known as the Yellow Creek congregation.

17 In Russia the Hutterians lived in villages although under private ownership, with the exception of two communistic colonies at Hutterdorf. All the Hutterians formerly lived under communism but many had since 1819 changed to private ownership.

18 This fact is mentioned because hooks and eyes were used among the Hutterians instead of buttons.

19 Hutterian women were not permitted to wear hats or gay-colored dresses. They wore shawls and the older generation does so to this day, although the younger people are becoming more Americanized.

20 Several candidates are first nominated and the final choice is made by drawing lots according to the Scriptures (Acts 1, 26).

for the forgiveness of sins, but in memory of the suffering and death of Christ. They baptize when an applicant calls for baptism.[21] The ministers do not marry couples in case one is a member of the church and the other is not. Some marry couples if both are non-members and when they are later baptized they are accepted into the membership of the church and become brethren and sisters of the same. The ban is enforced as in our church. If the accused repents and confesses, he is again taken into the church.

There was one thing which I did not approve and that was the fact that some of the women smoked and chewed tobacco. They spoke mostly the English for that is the language they study in school. They can speak only a broken German, even one of the ministers was unable to speak in German. We again went to the home of Isaac and a certain Armendiener[22] went with us. I inquired of him why it was that they preach in the English language; whether it was against the law to preach in German. He said, "No, the government does not object, neither does the government care what one preaches. The chief reason is that so few of the people understand the German language." I asked him why. He told me, "Most of the people come from Holland and England and therefore know no German." I wondered whether these people realize how much they have lost by giving up their mother tongue. For dinner we were at Isaac's, fifteen in number. At three o'clock we again assembled at the church, where I preached a sermon on the text, I John V, 14 "For whosoever is born of God overcometh the world." I preached according to our custom because the ministers wished it that way. According to our custom I dictated the songs.[23] After the services, one of the ministers, Daniel Brennemann invited me to his home. All the meals, breakfast, dinner and supper were the same: coffee, ham, butter, white bread, syrup, apple sauce, cherry cakes and blackberries. Prayer is said before meal-time, but not after. After supper we sang a song, had a brief prayer service and then retired for the night.

Monday, May 14. In the morning after we had risen, Daniel led in prayer and then we had breakfast. After supper he took us to Isaac, who lived four miles away. The people in the community have good horses and strong harnesses, but the wagons are not so very good and convenient. The wagon boxes are long and look like a trough. The wheels have wooden axles and are very high, with only a little iron used as rims. The people have good cows which cost about forty dollars per head, also fine hogs, which, as a rule, are fat. They feed them corn. Only a few sheep can be seen and these are not very good. Most of the money is made on cattle and wheat. I also inquired about the matter of military service. The ministers said that their young men were exempt but during the last war they had to pay three hundred dollars for every young man who was drafted.[24] I asked about those who were unable to pay, and they said that the churches assisted those who were unable to pay that amount. During times of peace these three hundred dollars need not be paid. In America so far, I have seen very few soldiers. They are stationed only near the boundary lines to protect the country against the Indians. A murderer in America is punished by hanging, if found guilty. A thief is imprisoned in a penitentiary for a time. I inquired if Mennonites bring suits into the courts and if they are required to vote. I was told that the Mennonites do not go to court, and the matter of voting is voluntary. In regard to taxes I was informed that a person's property is first assessed and then he pays according to the amount of property possessed, so much per one hundred dollars. Isaac said that he owns one hundred forty-five acres of land and paid forty last year, payable to the county or district wherein one resides. I also asked in regard to insects that may prove injurious to the crops. He said that there were potato bugs, which he also showed to us. They were black and had white strips with yellow heads and were about the size of a bean. They were first seen years ago and unless they are picked off, there is no potato crop. These bugs are very poisonous, but they are not injurious to wheat.[25] In the afternoon Isaac took us to Elkhart, but Funk was not at home. As a matter of pastime I went to see his press. The machinery and the speed with which it works is a marvel. I have never seen anything like it. At ten o'clock the same evening, Funk came home.

Tuesday, May 15. In the morning Funk told us that Suderman of Berdjansk and Buller of Alexanderwohl[26] had telegraphed that their ship would arrive in New York Wednesday and he advised us to wait until they had arrived and thus work with them together in our appeals to the government. Funk said that he would accompany us since we were unacquainted with the English language. In the evening two ministers and two other brethren from Pennsylvania came to Funk's house for the purpose of uniting the different churches in the community.[27] In the

21 The Hutterian method of baptism is by sprinkling, after a period of instruction in the Bible under the direction of a minister.

22 Armendiener, German title for deacon, probably not recognized as such by Tschetter.

23 In the Hutterian Church services the sermons are read from manuscript and the songs are dictated by a minister. A stanza or part of a stanza is read at a time and then sung by the congregation and that continuing until the song is ended. No songbooks are used by the congregation.

24 American Civil War.

25 The Hutterians were interested in wheat-raising and cattle-raising, as may be inferred from the diary. Those were their chief occupations in Russia.

26 Berdjansk and Alexanderwohl were Mennonite Settlements in South Russia not far from where the Hutterians lived.

27 Probably a committee called in to deal with the Whisler difficulty.

morning these brethren led in the morning worship and prayer and after breakfast at eight we left, ten of us on two wagons to go out into the country a distance of ten miles to attend church services. One of the ministers of Pennsylvania preached a sermon. Then I followed with an extemporaneous sermon, as much as the Lord gave me grace, for it is customary here in America to preach from memory. After the sermons, Funk gave the following report of what had been decided at the Conference.[28] 1. That they should not chew tobacco during church services because spitting is obnoxious. 2. Not to run back and forth so much during the services and keep from vain talk. 3. Everyone should act as is fitting for a Christian. 4. Parents should raise their children in the fear of the Lord. 5. A minister should be elected and the brethren should pray so that the Lord may show whom to choose. Brother Funk, four people from Pennsylvania and four of us were invited to dinner by one of the brethren. At three o'clock we again went to a church six miles away, where services were conducted and in the evening we had supper at the home of a man named Holdemann. There were nine of us at the table. In the evening we again went to church where I preached the first sermon, followed by the two Pennsylvania ministers. One of these ministers did not appeal to me because he smoked and as a whole seemed a rather cold Christian. We spent the night at Joseph Holdemann's.

Wednesday, May 16. In the morning after breakfast, David,[29] one of the Old Mennonites, took us to the Amish Mennonites who live six miles away, and left us at the home of a minister named Mosi, where we had dinner and supper. After supper Mosi took us to another minister where we remained for the night. The Amish Mennonites are more plain in their style of dress as well as in their homes in comparison with the Old Mennonites. They are not permitted to wear loud-colored clothes or to dye anything in a gay color. Their clothes must be of one color. They use hooks and eyes instead of buttons except on trousers. The men must wear hats instead of caps. Their trousers are of a blue color and have a tight fit. The slit in the trousers is on the side instead of in front. They are not permitted to cut their beards around the mouth. The hair is worn long. Girls and women must cover their heads with a white hood. In their style of clothes the Amish Mennonites agree with our Hutterites. They have no church buildings but have their church services in the different homes.[30] The man in whose house the services are held must then furnish dinner for the entire group. Visiting ministers may not preach in their services.[31] The Old Mennonites are more hospitable to visitors than the Amish Mennonites but they also have their dark sides. The minister at whose home I stayed had three guns in his house and everyone in the house smoked, even the women. What is worst among the Old Mennonites, is that even the ministers smoke.

The country in this community is very prosperous with fine orchards and pastures and beautiful fields of grain. The people seem pale and not very healthy. They have plenty to eat and in my opinion they eat too much, especially of sweets and fruits. If they would eat more sour foods, they would look more healthy. They do most of the work themselves for I did not see many hired men and maids.

Thursday, May 17. In the morning after I had arisen from my bed and as I walked out into the yard I heard someone shooting. Who would be shooting so early in the morning I thought, and just then a gray-haired old minister emerged from the woods, gun in hand. I did not know what to think and much less what to say. What a fine example of a non-resistant Mennonite. We had breakfast at his house and I purchased from him a Martyr's Song-Book for one dollar.[32] After that he accompanied us to Elder David. Both David and his wife smoked. Here we had dinner and in the afternoon David took us to one of the Old Mennonites, a certain John Kreider, who was a very friendly man and he and his wife showed us great hospitality. Here we had supper and after that attended evening services in the church, where I preached the sermon. No other minister was present. After the services we again returned to the home of Kreider where we remained for the night. They had a large house. Most of the houses in the community are wooden, two-story structures. The upper story is used for bedrooms for visitors and the floors are covered with red and checked rugs. Many of the rooms have mirrors and the walls are papered.

Friday, May 18. In the morning we arose, all well, praise God for it. After breakfast John Kreider took us to Joseph Holdemann, six miles away where we had dinner and after that Kreider took us to Elkhart to Funk, where we remained for the night.

Saturday, May 19. To-day I remained in my room the entire day and wrote a letter home.

Sunday, May 20. To-day I felt somewhat ill. Immediately after breakfast I called on a certain Brennemann and went to church with him for this was Pentecost Sunday. I preached on Acts 2. After the sermon there was

28 The Mennonite Annual Conference.

29 Possibly David Burkholder. He took them to the Amish community near Nappanee.

30 Communistic Hutterians to this day do not have a church building. Services are held in the school house.

31 Only on very rare occasions were visiting ministers permitted to preach in Hutterian church services.

32 The Ausbund.

a short business meeting which dealt with two brethren, who had trouble amongst themselves. They said, however, that they had no differences and were ready to partake of the Lord's Supper. With this the meeting was dismissed, and we went home with Rev. Daniel Brennemann together with a large number of other guests. After returning to my room at Funk's house in the city, I attended evening services at the Evangelical Church which was located next to Funk's house. The Evangelicals differ from the Lutherans somewhat in their form of baptism. They do not emphasize infant baptism so much. The pastor spoke on "Cast thy burden on the Lord and he shall sustain thee: he shall never suffer the righteous to be moved. But thou, O God, shalt bring them down into the pit of destruction." (Psalm LV, 22-23). The minister began to speak louder and louder and as I sat near the pulpit I was greatly bewildered; in fact I felt like running from the church. He marched back and forth behind the pulpit, once to this side and then to the other as if he were insane. He hammered on the pulpit with his fist, and pointing to his heart he cried: "Herein must the Lord live." At times he pointed toward heaven and then again down to hell, shouting like a mad man, for only a mad man could act like he did. His actions were not those of a minister of the Gospel but those of a general. Sometimes he praised everyone into heaven and then again he damned us all into hell. It is not in my power to describe this and my readers will doubt my statements, but it remains true nevertheless. I have been in many churches but have never witnessed the like. A comedy could hardly offer more entertainment. He preached the truth, but with great indiscretion and lack of judgment.

Monday, May 21. As I awoke to-day I felt a headache and stomach pains. I praised the Lord for His protection and guidance. I feared a fever, because of the many places where one eats in traveling. After breakfast I went to a druggist for some medicine. The doctor said that I had quite a high fever but after taking the medicine I felt much better. In the afternoon I visited a paper mill. The paper is made of all sorts of old rags. At first the rags are moistened and then stuffed into a large container where they must remain for a time. It is then cut fine, run through rollers, and finally becomes paper.

The Old Mennonites permit their people to have instrumental music. Last Sunday, when we visited at Brenneman's, who is overseer of the poor,[33] he asked us if we enjoyed music. We said, "No." He had a music box in his house and he began to play the instrument. After he had played several pieces, I remarked to him that the Apostle said, "Speak to yourselves in Psalms and hymns and spiritual songs, singing and making melody in your heart to the Lord" (Eph. V. 19).[34] He said that the Psalmist David also played on his harp and I replied that David was also a warrior and had shed much blood. Thereupon he became silent and did not say another word.

Tuesday, May 22. As we did not know the brethren who had shortly arrived from Russia, we proceeded on our journey alone with John Funk. We boarded the train at Elkhart at four-thirty in the morning and at eight we arrived in Chicago which is one hundred two miles from Elkhart. The city is located on Lake Michigan, and has a large navigable canal. This city was nearly all burned to the ground one and one-half years ago. The people say that since the creation of the world there never has been a fire like that. The loss of the fire was estimated at $200,000,000. Many people lost their lives. By this time large portions of the city have already been rebuilt. There are buildings from seven to eight stories in height. We went through many long and crowded streets and came into Chicago by a subway such as they have in Berlin. This passes under the Chicago River. It was a fathom high and one and one-half fathoms wide with an arched ceiling laid out with brick, like a cellar. The inside was cool. The street cars passed through the tunnel while over it passed boats and steamships. It took us fifteen minutes to walk through it. One's mind can hardly comprehend what man is able to construct. According to all these things the end of the world must be nigh. Since I was very tired and did not feel well we went to a hotel to rest. Later in the day we went to the city to look for the brethren but could not find them. We then looked up the railroad station agent and inquired about the land and then returned to our room. On our return from the station we saw in a tent on the street two wild and uncivilized men from a distant island, caged up. They were over 50 years old, very small, with long hair and short beards. The structure of their frames was as slight as that of a child of five years. I was much astonished when I saw one of these men raise up another man of at least thirty-six "pud" weight.[35] The thought came to me, as I looked upon these poor creatures, whether God would also demand an account of them on the judgment day. We remained that day and the following one in our rooms surrounded by so much noise and tumult that my head ached. How much relieved I would be if I were once again in my home, where everything is quiet and peaceful.

Wednesday, May 23. Since there was no hope of meeting the brethren in the city, we boarded the train at ten in the morning for St. Paul. This city lies in the state of Minnesota, four hundred eight miles from Chicago. We traveled through all kinds of territory. At first the land was beautiful and level with plenty of water and good

---

33 Deacon Henry Brenneman, Elkhart, Indiana.

34 German version says, "Singet und spielet dem Herrn in euren Herzen." Eph. V, 19.

35 A pud is 8 pounds.

thick woods. Then we came to a hilly region with many bridges over streams and then more level country. After twenty-one hours we arrived at St. Paul.

Thursday, May 24. At seven o'clock this morning we arrived at St. Paul and went to the business section of the city. We made our headquarters at a hotel. The hotelkeeper's name was Wildenjäger. In the forenoon we went to the courthouse to inquire for information. They treated us courteously, asked for our names and said that in the afternoon we could meet a man who had also lived in Russia. He would explain to us in regard to the different land, here in America, for there are railroad lands, government lands, and school lands. He said that he would see us in our rooms at two o'clock in the afternoon. At that time the man came to our room and gave us much information in regard to the land. He took us to the railroad agent who also has millions of acres to sell at reasonable prices. We received telegraphic information that Suderman and Buller were also on their way to St. Paul. This city was founded sixteen years ago. It is not a very large city, but has fine buildings and quite an important trade and commerce. One can buy everything that is needed. In the evening the Bergthaler deputies, Jacob Peters, the village mayor (Oberschulz), Henry Wiebe, a minister, and Cornelius Boer came to our room.[36] Oh how glad we were to see them. It seemed to me that they were of my own. They had already visited many parts of the country, but as yet had not found homes. They had been in the South in the state of Texas and informed us that people in that state were already harvesting wheat, but they did not like that country. After talking over many matters, we retired to our rooms for the night.

Friday, May 25. Arose well, thanks only to God, the Almighty for His Fatherly protection and guidance. The Bergthaler brethren came to our room. We asked them to travel with us, but they said that they had already promised to join the Molotschna brethren who were to meet them in the city.[37] In the morning we proceeded to the station, Wiebe helping me to carry my baggage. On the way we talked about non-resistance and how he liked the country here. He said the country did not appeal much to him and that after all the question of military service is the most important. He thought that it would not be possible to secure total exemption from military service in the United States but that the English government would be more liberal and grant a Charter guaranteeing exemption from military service which was better than what this country could offer. He spoke very sensibly, so that I immediately learned to love him. He said that one should not only consider the land question but also not forget the matter of freedom, for that is the reason why we came to this country and are making this long journey. Then we took leave, boarded the train and left St. Paul. The city lies on the Mississippi River and a long bridge several fathoms high spans the river at this point. Our destination was Duluth. At first the country was quite level but somewhat woody and then came many rocky cliffs. We crossed five different bridges, so high that one became dizzy when looking into the deep below. I estimated the height over one hundred feet and the stream was so swift that it had the force of fifteen thousand horsepower. The name of the river was St. Louis. At four-thirty we arrived at Duluth. The city is located on a lake, which was full of floating ice. The city is only small, having been founded only four years ago. On one side the city lies on a high hill with many trees. The city is one hundred fifty-six miles north of St. Paul. Due to the ice, it was quite cold. We remained in the city for the night. There is also a large immigration house here, built by the railroad company for the welfare and comfort of the immigrants as well as for their own interest and profit.

Saturday, May 26. At seven in the morning we again took the train, traveling toward the southwest, because the country here seemed too cold to us and grain was planted too late in the season. We journeyed through level plains of woodland with many lakes. Here and there one could see a miserable hut inhabited by Indians. These Indians are quite civilized and would not hurt anyone. At two o'clock in the afternoon we arrived at the city of Bremont which was founded only two years ago. The town is only small and we had dinner. The woodland became thinner here and finally the land seemed clear altogether. The land at times was level and then again slightly hilly. The hilly land seemed to me the more fertile of the two. Here and there one could see a settlement of white people and small fields of grain. The wheat was yet very small. At eight o'clock in the evening we arrived at Glyndon, where a large immigration hall is located, built by the railroad company. We decided to remain here over Sunday because lodging is free and meals could be secured at very reasonable rates. The land around Glyndon is very level. It is probably too wet most of the year and that is a great drawback in spring plowing. Several people have already settled here. The distance from Duluth to Glyndon is two hundred fifty-eight miles and it took us thirteen hours to travel the distance by train. In the evening there was a great thunderstorm accompanied by rain and wind.

---

36 They were deputies from Bergthal in South Russia also seeking land in America with the intention of immigrating to this country on account of the new military regulations coming into force in Russia at that time.

37 The Molotschna brethren lived in the valley of the Molotschna River in South Russia, not far from the Hutterian settlement.

Sunday, May 27. In the morning when I awoke all well, thanks to God, the spirit told me that this was Pentecost.[38] A longing immediately overtook me to be with my wife and children and celebrate Pentecost with them. I became very sad and began to think how I could possibly comfort myself in this wilderness. I took out my Martyr's Song Book and read a few songs. I then saw what people had been willing to suffer for the name of Christ. I took new courage and felt better. I reconsecrated myself wholly to God and to His Fatherly care. In the evening we attended a Lutheran church which was located in the neighborhood. Brother Funk preached a sermon in the English language of which we understood nothing. It was only a small congregation.

Monday, May 28. Awoke rested and much refreshed, praise to God. After breakfast we rode out for a distance of a few miles into the country on a wagon to see how the farmers were getting along in their work. There were as yet only a few pioneers settled in this region. Much of the land that had been plowed was yet under water. The wheat had only a poor stand and was very weedy due to late seeding. The grass was only thin and small. The land was very level and the soil was black, but somewhat sandy. It seemed to me that were we to settle here, we should never be threatened with famine, and, provided we were industrious and God-fearing, the Lord would not withhold His rich blessings. Since the region seemed somewhat cold and spring came rather late, we decided to go further south to investigate conditions there. All Monday we had our lodging place at the immigration house. In the afternoon we again journeyed out into the country in another direction. The land here seemed better than that which we had seen in the morning because it was richer in grass. We drove around the fields the entire afternoon and in the evening we met our brethren Jacob Buller, Bernhardt Suderman, Wilhelm Ewert of Prussia, Tobias Unruh of Poland, Andreas Schrag of Poland, Bernhardt Boer, Heinrich Wiebe and Jacob Peters of Bergthal. We drove on for another short distance and came to the little town of Fargo, where we remained for the night.

Tuesday, May 29. In the morning after we (sixteen of us) had rested, praise to God the Highest, we prepared at five in the morning to leave Fargo. The Red River is the boundary line between the state of Minnesota and the territory of Dakota. The land around Fargo, for a distance of 60 miles in length and 35 miles in width is extremely level and has few trees. Then it becomes more hilly and somewhat stony with numerous salt lakes, one of them being one-half mile across. This lake is spanned by a bridge. There are also streams here and there with trees along the banks. The lumber can be used only for fuel. The soil is black with a mixture of sand farther into the subsoil. At two o'clock we arrived at the James River. We were now one hundred miles from Fargo and we decided to go no farther. Funk said that he knew the land well in this region and there was no use in going any farther, since the land gets no better than that which we have already seen. The farther we go, the farther we get from Fargo and from the lumber regions, so that it would be quite difficult to settle for those reasons. The railroad continues for just another hundred miles and then ends. We took the same train back to Fargo at four o'clock in the afternoon because the land around that town looked better to us. At one o'clock, the same night we arrived at Fargo.

Wednesday, May 30. After breakfast six of us, in two wagons belonging to the railroad company, together with Funk and two agents drove out into the country to thoroughly investigate the land. We drove through many fields. The land is so extremely level, that it would be impossible for water to be drained in a rainy season. There is much tall grass around the wet spots but the ground is not marshy. The grass is only thin, the soil is black with a sandy subsoil and further down we find a gray loam, but less sandy. One man was seeding oats. We spent the entire day roaming through the fields. We had a lunch under the open sky which the agents provided for us and late in the afternoon we again returned to our quarters.

Thursday, May 31. I remained in my room the entire day and wrote letters home as well as some songs.[39] Late in the afternoon I walked down to the Red River to see the ship which was to take us to Manitoba, for we had decided to go there.

Friday, June 1. At eight o'clock in the morning we began our journey on the ship and at two o'clock in the afternoon we departed from Moorhead, down the Red River to Manitoba, twelve of us brethren from Russia. The steamship was five fathoms wide and twenty fathoms long. The Red River has a width of twenty fathoms. In the evening the ship stopped and soon the godless life of the people on deck began with music, card-playing and dancing.

---

38 The Roman calendar was reformed by Julius Caesar in 46 B.C. A small error of 11 minutes and 14 seconds yearly, however, still put the Julian calendar one year behind every 128 years. To remedy this, Pope Gregory XIII in 1582 introduced a slight change by omitting ten days from that year. The Gregorian calendar is now in use by all civilized countries except Russia and Greece. These two still follow the Julian calendar and are therefore 13 days behind the Gregorian. It is for this reason that Pentecost in Russia and Greece comes one week later, than in other countries.

39 During his travels in America, Rev. Tschetter composed words for several songs.

Saturday, June 2. Awoke well and refreshed, praise the Lord. I composed a song of thanksgiving to-day.

Sunday, June 3. We traveled by ship all day to-day. At one time the ship was unable to move, but after four hours of repair work, we again proceeded on our way.

Monday, June 4. At eight o'clock in the morning we arrived at Fort Pembina in North Dakota. Here I saw soldiers in uniform, also many cannons. They were the first soldiers that I had seen in America and I had traveled in this country for more than a month, in different cities, etc. We proceeded a little farther to the Canadian boundary line where we all marched out of the ship and then again back into the ship in single file. We were all inspected by the English Government officials. Everyone was asked where he was from, his age, name and occupation. All was put on record. This was at ten in the morning.

Tuesday, June 5. At five in the morning we stepped from the ship and walked to the city which was one-half mile from the river. The name of the city was Winnipeg. It is only a small town. Along the river there are numerous fortresses guarded by soldiers, belonging to the English Government. The soldiers wore red uniforms. From Fargo to Winnipeg is two hundred twenty-four miles by land and somewhat farther by water, but I am not certain how much. In the afternoon we were called before the governor. He was very kind and friendly and spoke much but all in the English language. Hespeler was our interpreter. The governor spoke of all the advantages that they could give us, but of course, one can not depend on that. In the afternoon twenty of us in three wagons drove out into the country to look at land and talk to the farmers. The people are lazy farmers of mixed Indian blood and are more cattlemen than agriculturalists. The land does not seem bad. The soil is a black loam with not much sand. The wheat stand was small but looked fresh and healthy. One could also see considerable unthreshed wheat left from the previous year.

Wednesday, June 6. At nine o'clock in the morning twenty-five of us again drove out into the country in five wagons with two extra wagons for tents and provisions going in advance. As we were about to leave with our wagons, we were all lined up and a man came carrying a tripod with a box and glass on top. I was wondering what he wanted and was informed that he would take a photograph of us, which was not to my taste, because I do not like to have my picture lying around in all parts of the world.[40] But what will you do with the world? World is world and will remain world until the Lord will come and end it all. We then took the ferry boat and crossed the Red River. After we had journeyed fifteen miles we halted, fed our horses, and had dinner while it rained quite hard. In the afternoon we continued our journey through many muddy and marshy places. At one place the horses slipped and fell and we had to draw the wagons out by hand. The roads were very bad.

After we had journeyed for sixty versts, the evening drew nigh and we came to a settlement inhabited by a people of mixed Indian blood. Our tent wagons had not arrived because they had taken the wrong route. Since we did not wish to sleep under the open sky, we asked these Indians to give us lodging in their homes but they would not. Finally they consented anyway and we remained there for the night.

Thursday, June 7. After breakfast we sang a song of thanksgiving and praise to the Lord, and Brother Suderman read the nineteenth Psalm, and led in prayer. At eleven o'clock the two tent wagons arrived and we had dinner and at three we continued our journey, one man on horseback accompanying us as guide to show us the land. He was a half-Indian. At five o'clock we arrived at the place where we were supposed to settle. We pitched our tents, ate supper, sang a few songs of thanksgiving and retired for the night.

Friday, June 8. At ten in the morning we continued our journey and soon we came to a house where only the wife was at home and she spoke a beautiful German. They had been living in Canada for two years and we talked many things to her and asked her many questions. She praised the country, very likely because she wanted neighbors. In America the people are all alike in that respect, i.e. everyone praises his own community because he wants it settled. "Every merchant praises his own ware." This region seemed more subject to drought. We crossed several streams and at noon had our dinner, but the mosquitoes were so bad that one could hardly defend himself. In the afternoon we drove on, crossing still other streams. On one occasion we led the horses across the stream. A little farther on we remained for the night, but the mosquitoes were terribly bad.

Saturday, June 9. After breakfast we again traveled on for fifteen versts, then had dinner and from thence proceeded on to the town of Winnipeg. The land through which we traveled that day was marshy and quite woody, but I reckoned that the lumber could be used only for fuel. At some places the land is good, but railroad facilities are poor. The town of Winnipeg is forty-five versts from this land and the roads are very bad. The lumber for building purposes must be shipped by way of the Red River from Minnesota. The half-breed Indians live on this land and it belongs to them. Grasshoppers are very plentiful. The price of stock and agricultural implements is more reasonable in the United States than in Manitoba and if

40 The writer and the Hutterians in general had religious scruples against photographs at that time.

the same is shipped across the boundary, a duty must be paid on it. To most of us, the Manitoba country was not to our liking, but seven of the brethren liked it and wished to journey another one hundred versts to the southwest, where there was some more land for sale. The five of us, Lorenz Tschetter, Ewert, Schrag, Tobias Unruh and myself and Brother Funk decided to return to Dakota and meet the other brethren at Moorhead, within two weeks. We took leave of the brethren and at midnight boarded our ship.

Sunday, June 10. I awoke somewhat sick. An English minister preached on board the ship. I understood nothing of the sermon. We sang German songs. This minister had with him his wife and two children who acted most vain and arrogant. It is really a pity that many of the ministers in this respect are worse than the other people. In the evening Brother Funk preached in English and we sang German songs. Brother Funk explained to the audience the purpose of our journey.

Monday, June 11. At eight o'clock in the morning we stepped from the ship at Fort Pembina after journeying on the river for one hundred versts. A large wagon with four mules and one wagon with one horse were given to us to go out and see the land. At noon we started out, going westward into Dakota. On one side of the road were thick woods of oak and lime trees with the Pembina River winding its way through the woods. A short distance (three to five versts) to the north is the Canadian boundary line. We drove on for twenty-seven versts and found very beautiful land with black soil and an excellent growth of grass. Some grasshoppers could be seen, but not as many as in Manitoba. We remained for the night at the home of a half-breed Indian. He himself was not at home. His wife and servants treated us very nicely. He had a beautiful house, the floors covered with rugs. He had about 40 head of horned cattle. The housewife gave us a good supper, for they are wealthy people. After supper we took a walk into the woods, where we found many beautiful trees such as oaks, poplars and limes, often so thick that two men could hardly reach around them. We came to a stream that flowed swiftly enough to drive a fair-sized mill. Then we again returned to our lodging place, where we sang a few songs, held a short prayer service and retired for the night.

Tuesday, June 12. We slept very well and had a good night's rest, praise to God. The lady gave us breakfast, for which he had to pay a little, but it was not much. We drove eight versts farther in the country. Here the land was quite sandy and the grass was thin. After going another twenty versts, we came to a German farmer who was very friendly to us. Here we fed our mules. The man seemed to be wealthy for he had several houses which he had purchased from the half-breed Indians. His name was Emerling. He lived near the Joseph mountains and advised us to go to the tops of these mountains for a good view of all the surrounding country. We went and found the mountains covered with a thick growth of trees. From here we got a most excellent view of all the surrounding country for miles around. We returned after a while and had dinner at his home. He told us many interesting things about the land. Barley is seeded about April 24 and cut about June 28. Wheat is seeded about April 20 and cut July 20. In the afternoon we again climbed two steep mountains. Here was a level plain forty-five versts long and five versts wide. After driving about nine versts around this plain we again returned and had supper at Emerling's place. We sang a few songs and Brother Schrag led in prayer. After that we retired for the night.

Wednesday, June 13. In the morning Brother Ewert led us in prayer and then we had breakfast. After breakfast, we decided to look at the land on the other side of the river, but since it had rained considerably during the night, Emerling said that it would be impossible to cross with our large wagon and four mules, but he thought it might be possible to cross with one horse and small wagon. Only one of us could go along with the guide, since the wagon was so small. I was selected to go along and see the land and report in the evening. We crossed the Pembina and two other small streams. After driving for nine versts, we came upon a level plain between the Pembina and Tongue Rivers, a stretch of land eighteen versts wide. The land is at first level and the soil black, but there is a great difference in soil at different places, here sandy and again heavier. The land seems a most excellent country for cattle raising with plenty of water and grass. The man with whom I drove could not speak German and I could not speak English but we managed to understand each other by means of signs. I spoke to him in the Low German (Platt Deutsch) and he could understand quite well for there is a great similarity between the "Platt Deutsch" and English. We then returned home crossing the Tongue River which flows into the Pembina three versts away from the Red River. At six in the evening we came to the town of Pembina. I was very hungry and went to a German man named Abels, who was a butcher in the town, and he gave me something to eat. A little later the other brethren also came and Abels also gave them something to eat. We remained in Pembina for the night.

Thursday, June 14. At four o'clock in the morning we boarded the ship for Fargo to look at some land in that neighborhood. The land from Pembina to Fargo is woody on the eastern or Minnesota side of the river, but the western or the Dakota side has no trees and the land would make an excellent cattle raising country. I composed a song today while sailing on the river, to the melody, "Barmherziger getreuer Gott."

Friday, June 15. At three o'clock this afternoon Brother Funk and I left the ship at a town called Grand Forks and traveled with the mailcoach instead, because we could get a better view of the land. At this point the great Red River branches off to the Minnesota side. Many logs are seen floating to Manitoba. From Pembina to Grand Forks is a distance of one hundred twenty versts and from Grand Forks to Moorhead is one hundred fifteen versts. At Grand Forks there is a saw mill and a large store where almost everything can be purchased. Since we could get no horses here, we remained in Grand Forks for the night. We were invited to supper by a man named Andreas. After supper I walked out into the country and found very fine level land, black soil, and a good growth of grass. Since it got to be quite late, I again returned to the town and remained at the post office for the night. I composed a song today, "The New Jerusalem."

Saturday, June 16. We continued our journey with a two-horse mailcoach, crossing a good farming country along the Red River. The soil is black and grass is plentiful. The land along the Minnesota side has many more trees than that on the Dakota side. After going for thirty-three versts we changed coaches, now taking a four-horse coach and a different driver. We drove on for eighteen versts. Here the land was lower and there was excellent hayland. The water in the streams was clear and the land was settled with here and there a home. We then changed to another four-horse coach and went on another twenty-one versts and changed again for the next twenty-one versts. Here we found many roses blooming. For the last twenty-two versts we again changed coaches and at ten in the evening we arrived at the town of Moorhead. I walked across the Red River bridge to Fargo, a distance of one verst to my old lodging place and found a letter waiting for me from my wife, and was very glad to hear from my loved ones at home. The other brethren, who had come by ship had not yet arrived and so I remained here for the night.

Sunday, June 17. I remained in my room all day Sunday, wrote a letter home and composed a song. At noon the other brethren came from the ship. Lorenz and Tobias had remained at Moorhead staying at the home of a German man.

Monday, June 18. At six o'clock in the morning we left Fargo for the west. After we had gone about twenty miles the train stopped. We stepped off and proceeded by wagon to our tents that had been pitched not far away. The land here is somewhat low. We took two teams and drove to the northwestward where we found numerous streams and fine level land with grass quite plentiful. At noon we returned and had dinner in our tents. After dinner the other brethren drove out to take a survey of the land. I remained at the tents, since I did not feel very well. After taking a nap I felt better. I walked six versts to the southward from the railroad and crossed numerous streams. The land seemed dry, although grass was quite plentiful. I returned home after dark and met the other brethren, who had just returned from their drive. We had supper in the tent. Tobias led us in a brief prayer service and then we retired for the night in our tents.

Tuesday, June 19. We sang a song of praise and I led the group in a short prayer service after which we had breakfast in our tents. We again drove toward the north and east to look at some lands. Here the land was woody at some places. There were numerous streams and grass was plentiful. The land is more rolling, but the low places are not marshy. Some sections are quite stony. In the evening we returned, had supper, Brother Ewert led in prayer and, after singing a song, we retired for the night in our tents.

Wednesday, June 20. After morning services and breakfast we drove ten versts to the northwest as far as Rush River. We found tall grass. We had dinner on a spot near two trees standing close together with another lone tree standing not far away. Then we crossed the Maple River and the railroad and drove to the southward. For four versts along the Maple River the land had plenty of moisture, but the last one hundred versts the soil was dry. When we arrived at our tents in the evening we found that a heavy rain had fallen. Brother Funk led us in prayer and we remained in our tents for the night.

Thursday, June 21. After breakfast and morning service, we packed our tents and drove seven versts south through a low and grassy valley, then seven versts west and again ten versts south, across the Maple River which here has steep banks. At places one could see trees. Then we drove ten more versts southwest. Here the land was higher and grassy, trees quite plentiful and many flowers especially along the river banks. Upon returning to our tents in the evening, we had supper and Brother Schrag led us in prayer. When we retired, a great rainstorm came with thunder and lightning, but we remained dry for our tents were well-made.

Friday, June 22. After morning services, conducted by Brother Ewert, and breakfast, we drove twelve versts westward. The land was somewhat higher and quite stony. Here we crossed the railroad and we saw a large machine operated by steam, with a long arm and shovel at one end. This arm raised, bringing up the shovel with a half-load of dirt and in this manner loaded a railroad car with dirt in a few minutes. We crossed the railroad track and proceeded northward for about ten versts. The land here was still higher and also stony. Then we again returned to the same spot where we had crossed at noon, drove west two versts, left our teams at that place and boarded a train for Fargo, which was thirty-seven versts east. Upon our arrival there, Lorenz, Tobias Unruh and myself walked across the bridge to Moorhead where our baggage was stored at the home of a German man. We remained there for the night. The man seemed rather frivolous and easygoing.

Saturday, June 23. Arose well and refreshed, thank God. I did not like my new lodging place. There was a saloon in the same building and all sorts of people came in. Furthermore there was no room to write and so I told the brethren that I would take my baggage and go to Fargo to the same place where I had formerly stayed. Here I wrote three songs with pencil upon scrap paper. In the evening brother Lorenz and Tobias also came to my room. We sang a few songs. Brother Unruh led in prayer service and we retired for the night.

Sunday, June 24. Shortly after our usual morning services and breakfast, several of our brethren, Jacob Buller, Bernhardt (Leonhard) Sudermann and Schrag came from Manitoba. The other brethren intended to remain in Manitoba a little longer in order to look at some other lands. I remained in my room all day and wrote some.

Monday, June 25. After prayer service and breakfast, the brethren Buller and Sudermann went out west to see the land along the railroad that we had gone over several days before. Lorenz and Tobias drove out to a farmer near Fargo. They found good land and an excellent stand of grain. The wheat that had been seeded April 19 and the barley that had been seeded May 8 were now heading on June 25. They brought samples of the grain along to town. This grain was the second crop on that land, it having been broken the year before.

Tuesday, June 26. I remained in my room in the forenoon. In the afternoon a man came over to our room with Dakota and Minnesota maps and showed us where we could have access to good pine-lumber. He was an official representing the forest department and advised us to buy woodland at $1.25 per acre eighty to one hundred miles from Fargo. The wood could be floated to Fargo on the Red River. The man was not able to speak German, so he went to get a German interpreter. He gave us Dakota and Minnesota maps. This German man invited us to his home and we accepted the offer. He lived with his father, mother, and two grown sisters. They were very friendly and told us many things. They had already lived at many different places, but liked it best here in Fargo. They gave us some good beer to drink. Their house had only very thin walls, and I asked the man if it was not too cold in winter. He said it was not. We again went to our rooms and in the evening the English man called on us again bringing a letter which I was to carry and deliver to the governor of Minnesota, at St. Paul. He also gave us a jar filled with sod. Later in the evening the other brethren who had gone out west to see the land returned and told us what they had seen. They liked the land very much.

Wednesday, June 27. We left Moorhead at ten in the morning with a four-horse mailcoach, seven of us brethren of the delegation and Funk. Since it was quite crowded, I sat with the driver which suited me very much for I could thereby get a much better view of the land. The land for the first eighteen versts was higher, with black soil and a fine stand of grass. We went another thirty-three versts and reached McCauleyville. Here the horses were again changed and after driving thirty-three versts farther horses were again changed. We continued fifteen versts more and arrived at Prickeritz at eight in the evening. We drove fifteen versts more and came to Breckenridge, where Seper of St. Paul and the railroad agent waited for us. We remained in Breckenridge for the night.

Thursday, June 28. We left Breckenridge at seven in the morning, by train with Seper and the railroad agent. At ten we arrived at Douglas which is sixty versts from Breckenridge. Here teams were already waiting for us to take us out to the land. For the first fifteen versts from Breckenridge the land was a low plain, then the next thirty versts somewhat higher and the last fifteen versts somewhat more hilly with small lakes on both sides of the railroad line. In the distance, one mile away, one could see some forests. At eleven in the morning, we went out in two wagons to look at the land. We drove for twelve versts and then returned. We found many small lakes, a number of them every mile so that about one-third of the country is under water. Near these lakes the grass is very tall and the land near the lakeshores is quite stony. The soil is black with a mixture of shiny sand slightly beneath the surface. Still further down there is a yellowish loam. The grass is not so thick, although the wheat along the roadside looked good and was just heading. The height of the wheat came up as far as my arms. The corn also looked nice and green. The region as a whole did not appeal to me, especially for village life as we have it in Russia, because there is too much water and bottomland. In the afternoon they took another drive to the other side of the railroad line, but I did not go along because it was too crowded. The brethren came back in the evening and reported that they liked this land much better than that which we had seen in the forenoon, but it was already settled considerably. We remained for the night at the railroad station.

Friday, June 29. At ten in the morning we took the train from Douglas to St. Paul and arrived at Willmar at two in the afternoon, the distance being one hundred eight versts, just half the distance to St. Paul. The land is hilly and has many small lakes. It is quite well settled. I saw many fields of wheat, oats and barley. The stand was good and the grain was just heading. From here we went to

Litchfield, a small town forty-eight versts from Willmar. At Darwin, one hundred eight versts from St. Paul, the land becomes wooded. Then we came to a small town called Delano. The land from Willmar to Delano is hilly and stony. From there we came to a large lake called Minnetonka, where two hotels are located, one of them being called the Weigalte. Then we came to Naples, a beautiful little town. We arrived there at eight o'clock in the evening and remained in the town for the night in order to look at different kinds of machinery and inquire as to the prices.

Saturday, June 30. In the morning after our usual services, we crossed the bridge over the Mississippi which is not supported as is usual by piers from beneath but is suspended from four high pillars, two on each side on the shores of the river. We saw the saw-mills of which there are seventeen in the city, some of them driven by steam and others by waterpower. A large saw-mill cuts about 22,000 feet of lumber per day. There are numerous waterfalls here, one of them having a fall of one hundred feet. We also saw factories making doors, window-sashes, and window-frames. Everything necessary for constructing a house, can be procured ready-made. In another factory we saw them make furniture such as chairs, bedsteads, etc. We also saw a paper-mill, but it was not in running order that day. Then we went to a cloth-factory, where many people were employed. After I had seen all these things, that worldly wisdom had accomplished, I thought of the words in the Scripture, that after all these things shall have reached perfection, God will destroy them, for in the eyes of the Lord it is all folly. When we arrived at our rooms, we found a man waiting for us who wished to show us the sights of the city. We went along with him and he showed us the whole town. After dinner, at two o'clock, we boarded the train for St. Paul, where we were to see the governor and get information from him in regard to the lands and the matter of exemption from military service. But he could speak only English and no German and so Brother Funk acted as our interpreter. He promised us the best of everything in his power, but in regard to the matter of exemption from military service, he did not say much because it was not within his power. Then we returned to our rooms for the night.

Sunday, July 1. After our morning services I wrote a letter and a song of consolation to my wife. I remained the entire day in my little room.

Monday, July 2. I felt somewhat sick this morning because I drank too much ice-water in the great heat yesterday. At eight o'clock in the morning we went to the railway station. A special car had been attached to the rear of the train. The car had sleeping accommodations, a very convenient thing, since I felt sick. The old man Seper was with us as well as a young man by the name of Rosen, who was a Mennonite. His father is a minister in Hamburg. A railroad agent was also with us. At two in the afternoon we arrived at St. James, where we had dinner. Then we came to the little town of Worthington which is two hundred fifty versts southwest of St. Paul. The land covering these two hundred versts is mostly rolling prairie-land with black soil. We arrived at the little town of Worthington shortly before evening. Here we stepped off in order to see the land. Sixteen of us went out in four wagons driving six versts and then returned to our rooms. The land was hilly with quite a good stand of grass. The grain along the roadsides was small.

Tuesday, July 3. In the morning we proceeded by special train thirty versts eastward to Heron Lake and from there we went out in four wagons, fifteen of us, to see the land. We drove until noon and then stopped for dinner at the home of a farmer who lived in a grove of trees. The growth of grass was quite plentiful, but the grain along the roadside was quite small, thin and of a yellowish color. In the afternoon we drove another thirty versts, following a different route. Then we returned to Heron Lake and took our train back to Worthington, where we remained for the night.

Wednesday, July 4. I did not feel well when I arose this morning. We again took the train to Worthington and went out by wagon twenty versts to see the land. Here the wheat was also small, thin and suffered from drought. The grass was quite plentiful. The soil is sandy and mixed with saltpetre. The water is likewise mixed with saltpetre. Later in the afternoon, a hot wind came up, the same as we sometimes have at home. The land is hilly and has deep valleys here and there. We drove as far as the town of Windom, which is forty-five miles from Worthington. Here we had dinner. Then we went to Sioux City, which is located in the state of Iowa, one hundred fifty versts from Worthington. The Minnesota line is twenty versts from Worthington. We had supper in the town of LeMars. At ten in the evening we arrived at Sioux City and were met by another railroad agent. The old agent who had been with us for the last few days then took leave of us. Rosen also took leave of us and we remained for the night in Sioux City.

Thursday, July 5. The town of Sioux City is located on the Missouri River near the boundary line between Iowa and Nebraska. We left Sioux City at seven in the morning and arrived at Council Bluffs, a small town. Here we changed trains, crossed the Missouri River over a large bridge, one verst in length and came to Omaha, Nebrasks. Omaha is one hundred fifty versts from Sioux City. Then we went as far west as Columbus, another small town, one hundred thirty-eight versts from Omaha. Here we stopped and became acquainted with some colonists, who had recently emigrated from Odessa, one of them by the name of Hildebrand. Most of these people had purchased farms, while one of them had entered the mercantile business. We talked many things with them. The women were especially anxious to tell of their trip from Odessa to America. They were all well pleased with their new location. We remained at the home of Hildebrand for the night.

Friday, July 6. After our usual morning services, we drove twelve versts to the north of Columbus in four wagons, fourteen of us. The country is excellently fitted for wheat, oats and corn. The grass was not particularly pentiful. The land is rolling and streams are scarce. Water is found one hundred thirteen feet in the ground. Wells are made by boring, so that a narrow pail can be used for drawing the same from the well. The soil is mixed with a grayish sand and loam. There are no forests here and the lumber for building purposes must be shipped from Minnesota. The cost of this lumber, delivered is $25.00 per M. feet. Planed and polished lumber costs $40.00 per M. feet. After we had viewed the land, we again returned to Columbus, where we boarded the train at four in the afternoon for Ayr Junction, one hundred four miles from Columbus. After we had left Columbus, I found that I had forgotten my little box which contained some valuable papers, at the place where we had stayed overnight. What I was most concerned about was the fact that among the papers was also my pass. I informed the agent about it and he wired back. When we arrived at Ayr Junction the reply was already there. The agent said that by Monday I would have my box. Two other agents joined us here while the two former ones who had accompanied us so far left us. We remained here for the night.

Saturday, July 7. We traveled by rail as far as Lamel, a small town fifteen versts from Ayr Junction. Here we had breakfast and then went out in four wagons, sixteen of us in number to view the land. We drove as far as a little stream known as the Little Blue River, thirty versts from Lamel. Here we ate dinner and went on another twenty versts as far as the Red Cloud River, where we remained for the night at the home of a man. During the entire stretch of fifty versts we struck only three farm homes. The land is quite sandy and grass does not seem plentiful, hardly enough for pasture. At places one finds ruins of old mounds and ditches. Water can be found only deep in the ground and in the entire distance we found only one small insignificant stream. The region is entirely treeless and far away from all "Handel und Wandel."

Sunday, July 8. We spent Sunday in the state of Nebraska, five miles from the Kansas boundary near the Red Cloud River. We spent the day in our rooms and attended services in a church in the evening. The sermon was preached in English by a minister who traveled with us, and we sang a song in the German language.

Monday, July 9. At three in the morning we traveled back fifty versts and at three in the afternoon we arrived at the little town of Hastings. Then we went to Sutton, Fairmont and Crete. In this last-named town I received my little box of papers which I had forgotten at Columbus, the week before. Here we had supper. At midnight we arrived in Lincoln, the capital of Nebraska. From Hastings to Lincoln, the distance is one hundred eighty-six miles and we remained in Lincoln for the night.

Tuesday, July 10. In the morning eleven of us took a car to get a view of the city. The car came to our door and took us all along. My, how tired I am of all this travel and sight-seeing by this time, but I could not refuse and so I went along. When the rest wished to go another one and one-half miles to bathe in a salt spring I refused and retired to my room. We left Lincoln at eleven in the morning and arrived at Plattsmouth at three, fifty-five miles from Lincoln. Here we boarded a steamboat and crossed the Missouri River, two miles wide to the Iowa side and traveled by train fourteen versts further on, where we took leave of the other brethren, Lorenz Tschetter, Tobias and myself going directly to Elkhart, while the other brethren went to Summerfield, Illinois. Bro. Funk went to the state of Missouri to visit one of his brothers. We were all to meet at Elkhart Sunday evening. We traveled throughout the night.

Wednesday, July 11. Early in the morning we came through Galesburg where we had breakfast and then to Aurora, a large city, and at three o'clock in the afternoon we arrived in Chicago. We were met there by a German man named Resla, who had orders to meet us from the railroad agents in Nebraska. He took us to a German hotel. From Plattsmouth to Chicago is a distance of four hundred fifty miles. At five in the afternoon we boarded the train and arrived at ten that evening in Elkhart, Indiana, one hundred one miles from Chicago. We went to brother Funk's home where I expected a letter from home, but was disappointed.

Thursday, July 12. At five in the afternoon Tobias Unruh and myself went with Isaac Kilmer out into the country to his farm. We had already been there before.

Friday, July 13. We remained the entire day at the home of Isaac, where we rested from our long journey. It rained all day long with much thunder and lightning.

Saturday, July 14. Felt somewhat sick when I arose in the morning. Could eat little and had constant stomach pains. At four in the afternoon Isaac took us to Holdemann, six miles away where we remained for the night.

Sunday, July 15. Felt somewhat sick when I arose in the morning. At ten we went to the church services where many people had assembled. I gave the opening sermon and Tobias Unruh gave the main sermon. After the services Isaac took us to Leatherman, one mile away, where we had dinner with some other brethren who were also ministers. In the afternoon we accompanied Isaac to another church six miles away where a service was to begin at four. There we also met Lorenz and Schrag. They informed us that Ewert, Buller and Warkentin's son had gone to Texas, and that Sudermann was in Elkhart. Tobias Unruh led in the opening sermon, and I gave the main sermon. My text was Col. II, 1, "I would that ye know what great conflict I have for you." The congregation was rather small, but when the sermon was over there were even less. Hardly any were left except the ministers. Very likely the sermon was not to their taste. After the service I went along with Rev. Heinrich Schaum, two miles from the church.[40] I had such a headache that I had to lie down as soon as we reached home and did not eat anything that evening.

Monday, July 16. My headache of yesterday had ceased, but somehow I could not eat breakfast for I had no appetite. The man at whose house I stayed took us to a place two miles away where Lorenz and Schrag stayed and from there took us to Elkhart, four miles away, where we met brother Sudermann. I went to a drugstore and purchased some medicine, and went to my room. I did not eat dinner. In the afternoon we had to talk over some matters in regard to conferring with the government. Some of the brethren first wished to go to Canada before conferring with the government officials, while others had gone to Texas. So we decided that Lorenz, Tobias Unruh and myself should make the journey alone, confer with the government officials and continue our journey homeward. We took leave of all the brethren and I led in a farewell prayer. They accompanied us as far as the railway station and we proceeded on our journey to Philadelphia.

Tuesday, July 17. This morning we were still traveling on with the train, passing through many cities and at eleven in the morning we were in Cleveland, Ohio, near Lake Erie, a large city with many hundreds of factories of various kinds. We were obliged to remain in Cleveland until four in the afternoon. At that time we departed from the city arriving at seven that evening in the city of Akron and at twelve in Pittsburgh where we changed. We stepped from the train and did not know where to find our train. Happily we found a German man who assisted us. We traveled throughout the entire night towards Philadelphia.

Wednesday, July 18. At ten we arrived at Harrisburg, at eleven at Lancaster, and at one o'clock in the city of Philadelphia, one of the most beautiful cities in America. The distance from Elkhart to Philadelphia is eight hundred miles. Here we had the address of a certain J. Cooke, who is one of the richest men in America. We went to the office of J. Cooke which was four miles from the station. We were asked whether we had seen Hiller a German man who was to meet us at the station.[41] We said, "No." We were given a lodging place which was paid for by the J. Cooke Co. man. Hiller then came in and informed us that Klassen and Cornelius with the three other Bergthal brethren had gone to New York City and expected to board the ship tomorrow. We asked Hiller to wire them and ask them to wait so that we might make the journey home together. We also inquired about the price of land and they informed us \$3.50 per acre. We said \$3.00 is enough, and they advised us to wait until tomorrow, when we could talk with the head official. We

---

40 * Henry Shaum was bishop of the Olive Mennonite Church.

41 Hiller early the following year was sent by the railroad company to South Russia to get the Hutterians and Mennonites interested in their lands. In Russia, Hiller called at the home of Rev. Tschetter.

42 The following is the Tschetter petition to President Grant.

TO THE PRESIDENT OF THE UNITED STATES.

We, the delegates, appeal in this petition that in case there should be a war, that we should be free for at least 50 years from everything that concerns war; after 50 years we are willing to pay as all others. The other governmental expenses we are willing to help bear as well as other citizens. We wish to be as obedient children to the government in all matters that are not against our conscience. But we cannot partake in anything that pertains to the military, and pray we may here enjoy in peace, what in Russia we are exiled for. We also desire to know whether we may be permitted to form our colony in one community; and have our own German schools; whether we may control our own schools; whether we may establish our own form of local government in our colonies as it fits us, and whether we may be freed from the holding of office and also jury-service and such like; and also whether we shall be free to vote or not.

We also desire to know under what conditions we may secure government land, and how many acres each person can have, and how old a person must be to obtain land; whether we may be freed from taking the oath, and whether our yea and nay will be regarded as sufficient, for swearing is just as much a matter of conscience with us as the matter of war, according to the word of our Lord and Saviour, Jesus Christ; and whether in case our consciences should be violated we might have the privilege of emigrating from America.

If we, the delegates, can secure the above-mentioned privileges, our brethren in Russia will be encouraged to emigrate to America. But if they cannot secure this, the emigration will be small; for most of them do not wish to risk the dangers connected with emigration with something uncertain.

Such is our humble prayer to his Excellency, the President of the United States, that he may give us a clear answer to this petition so that we poor and oppressed people may know what to do.

July 26, 1873.

Delegates
PAUL TSCHETTER
LORENZ TSCHETTER

decided to wait until the next day. We then went with Hiller to see the city waterworks which is one of the wonders of the world. The water from the river is forced one hundred feet into an elevated reservoir and then distributed through pipes all over the city.

Thursday, July 19. This morning I wrote a petition (Bittschrift) to the President of the United States.[42] At eight o'clock Hiller came to our rooms. I showed him the petition and he said that it was very satisfactory and that he would assist us in handing it to the President personally. At ten in the morning we went to the railway offices, where we were introduced to J. Cooke. He could not speak German and Hiller was our interpreter. Cooke said that he expected to leave the city for a time on business, but there was a man in New York City, who was the highest official over the land affairs and that he would be able to inform us regarding the price of the land. Mr. Cooke treated us with some very excellent wine which we had to drink with him. When he found that we wished to see the President he gave us a letter of introduction, which may be of great assistance to us. We were then called into another room where a group of Moravians wished to meet us and speak to us in regard to our belief and creed. We explained to them the chief principles of our confession of faith and they wrote them all down until we came to the point as to whether women could be teachers. I said, "No," and they inquired, "Why not?" I replied, "Because the apostle said, 'I suffer not a woman to teach, nor to usurp authority over the man, but to be in silence' " (I Tim. 11, 12). They said "We like all your principles, excepting this one. We are all in Christ, men and women." And I said, we are all equal, men and women in the eyes of the Lord, but the husband is the head of the wife and so we rather take the head then the feet." After I had said that, the discussion stopped and they took leave of us and went their way. We also retired to our rooms and at seven in the morning we boarded the train for New York City, one hundred miles from Philadelphia and arrived there at ten in the evening. We crossed a small body of water and then Hiller engaged a car to take us to his home, six miles out of the city where we remained at his home for the night.

Friday, July 20. At ten in the morning we boarded a steamship for New York City, six miles away. We were busy the entire day dealing with the land company. They did not wish to agree to points and asked us to come again the next morning at eleven o'clock when they would be ready with their decision. We returned to our rooms at the home of Hiller.

Saturday, July 21. Again went to New York City, and at eleven met the land agents. They agreed to all our points but wished us to come Monday. Since we expected to have an interview with the President that day, our meeting with the agents was postponed until Tuesday. We intended to wire home and inquire as to what was best to do in regard to this land business but upon being informed that the cablegram would cost twenty-five dollars we thought it was too much and so we again returned to our rooms.

Sunday, July 22. At ten we went to New York City and attended church services at a Mission where a sermon was preached in German. The minister spoke of the Cross and tribulations and faith and that we should leave all for His sake. But when I looked the congregation over, it did not seem as though they were learning very much. There was altogether too much of this worldliness. After the service we again returned to Hiller's home and had dinner there. We remained there in the afternoon. Many guests came to see us that afternoon, and we dined with them. They were anxious to see the Russian brethren and invited us to their homes, but we excused ourselves, saying that our time was very limited.

Monday, July 23. At ten we went to New York City to see the railway agent, but he was sick and so we could do very little. In the evening we intended to go to Washington. Since this traveling back and forth was expensive, we decided that Lorenz should stay at our room, while Tobias and myself would go to Washington with Hiller. Hiller telegraphed to the President at Washington, but received the reply that we should meet him at Long Beach. We then planned to return to our lodging place, but since there was no ship there at that hour I said that I would go to the mission and inquire whether we had received any mail. On my return I lost my way and wandered around a considerable time. When I finally found the place, neither Tobias nor Hiller were there. I waited for an entire hour and still no one appeared and so I returned to the mission and remained there for the night.

Tuesday, July 24. Received a telegram from Hiller that I should remain at the mission and that they would meet me there. At ten they arrived and we all went to the railway agent and he offered us the land for three dollars per acre. But we did not agree on a number of other points and so the deal remained open for further negotiation some time later. When we returned home we saw an oil steamer on fire in the ocean. The fire lasted throughout the day and night. That was not far from our rooms.

Wednesday, July 25. We spent the entire day in the city and returned to our quarters at Hiller's home in the evening.

Thursday, July 26. This was the day that we really intended to leave for home, for our ship was to sail today. But since we had some important work to do yet, we decided to remain longer. We had to take new courage and patience and wait until next Thursday, when another ship would leave for Hamburg. I wrote another petition to the President, for I did not particularly like the first one. At eleven in the morning we went to the city. Here I recopied my petition and had it translated into English. Then we again returned home. Oh, how I abhor life in the city. All the noise and music make me so disgusted, that I hardly stand it.

Friday, July 27. At eight we took the steamer for New York City, walked through a part of the city and boarded another ship to Long Beach where the President spends the summer and where we were to meet him. We sailed two hours by ship and traveled one more hour by rail when we arrived at Long Beach and remained at a hotel. Hiller went to investigate when we were to appear before the President. He soon returned and informed us that we were to meet him at eight in the evening. Shortly before eight we left our hotel to appear before the President, which was only one and one-half miles from our lodging place.

When we arrived at the President's home we were introduced to President Grant by Hiller. The President received us in the most friendly manner and we presented our petition to him personally. After reading it very carefully the President replied that we must have patience to wait for an answer to our petition. But since we are to leave New York for home on the Cimbria August 2, Hiller assured us that he would send us the President's reply.[43]

NOTE

The journey of Rev. Tschetter had important results. After his return to Russia, August 28, 1873, he reported on conditions in America and before another year was past several groups were on their way to America. Between 1874 and 1879 all the Hutterians with the exception of two families migrated to this country. They established three communistic colonies in the James River Valley of South Dakota, northwest of the city of Yankton, and a number of families settled on independent farms. Since that time, these three communistic colonies have increased to thirty-three, while the families on independent farms would count into the hundreds. Nearly all of the communistic colonies have since the World War moved to Canada and some of those still remaining in South Dakota are at this time in the process of doing the same. Most of the independent Hutterians still live in South Dakota. Rev. Tschetter, the author of the diary, died in 1919.

---

43 Several weeks after the Tschetters had reached their homes in Russia, they received the following reply to their petition to the President.

Washington, Sept. 5, 1873.

The President sent to me the petition of the Mennonite delegates, and the reason for the delay in the answer is this: At the time of the meeting of the Mennonites with the President he was told that they wished to depart in a few days. The only answer that could be given was that the President could not guarantee them the assurances they desired.

They wished guarantees of exemption from military service and also jury service. They desire also to be free from the payment of substitute money in case of draft; and the right to govern their own schools.

Since personal military service, citizenship obligations, jury service, and control over schools are all matters that fall under the jurisdiction of the various states in which they wish to settle, the President says that he cannot exempt them from the laws of the states and the laws to which other citizens are subject. As to the paying of substitute money for fifty years, that, too, is beyond his power of promising. It is true, however that for the next fifty years we will not be entangled in another war in which military service will be necessary. But should it be necessary there is little likelihood that Congress would find justification in freeing them from duties which are asked of other citizens.

It is impossible therefore to grant the answer which you (Hiller) and the delegates wished before their departure. I had to withhold the answer until I had opportunity to see the President.

With greatest obedience
Your Humble Servant
HAMILTON FISH.

CORRECTIONS (EDITOR'S NOTE)

Joseph W. Tschetter of Chicago calls our attention to the fact that the concluding sentence in his biography of his father, Paul Tschetter, which was published as an introduction to the Paul Tchetter diary in the April number of the *Review,* is erroneous. We are sorry for the error, which did not appear in the original manuscript and gladly print the correction. The last sentence should read: He was for over fifty years a minister of an independent Hutterite Mennonite Church which was organized like the churches of the General Conference of Mennonites, and was looked upon as a leader of the independent Hutterite Mennonite Churches.

Further corrections on the first installment of Paul Tschetter's Diary as printed in the April issue of the *Review,* are suggested by Timothy Brenneman of Goshen, Indiana, a son of Daniel Brenneman in whose home Paul Tschetter visited during his visit among the Elkhart County Mennonite churches, as reported in his diary. Mr. Brenneman is still much interested in Mennonite history though at an advanced age, and we are grateful to him for his valuable suggestions. Readers will please note the following points.

1. Note 16. Page 33. The identification of the church is wrong. What is said to be the Yellow Creek Church should be the Shaum or Olive Church, which was located one mile from the Isaac Kilmer home, whither Tschetter was taken for entertainment.
2. Page 34. Mr. Brenneman is certain that Tschetter was mistaken in his observation of Mennonite women chewing tobacco. He well remembers them smoking, but does not recollect a single case of chewing. The Isaac mentioned on this page was not Isaac Gelert, but Issac Kilmer, a prominent member of the Shaum or Olive Church, who lived one mile northwest of the church. Daniel Brenneman himself lived four miles northwest of the same church.
3. Page 34. The meeting mentioned under date of May 15, was a meeting at which an attempt was made to reunite the Wisler and Brenneman factions. It was held at the Yellow Creek Church.
4. Page 35. The church referred to is the Holdeman Church. The statement referring to the ministers smoking should be understood to mean that some of the ministers smoked, not all.
5. Page 36. The music box mentioned was an organ.

Copied from The Mennonite Quarterly Review Vol. 5- No. 2. April 1931 Pages 112-126 Vol. 5- No. 3. July 1931 Pages 198-220.

Chapter 3

The Migration of Hutterites from Russia to America

For three centuries the Hutterites had made a pilgrimage from land to land. From the Tyrolean Alps and Moravia where fierce persecution almost rooted out their faith, to Hungary where their sufferings and untold hardships continued, to Walachia where for a short time they enjoyed peace, only to have Turkish armies force them to seek yet another land of refuge. Then on to Russia, a group of about 40 families where at last the Hutterites and other German groups became a state within a state and were granted special privileges. In the year 1870, because of the growing democracy of the times and the spirit of militarism the Czar began a program of Russianization which not only meant the end of military exemptions, but complete government control of the school system and local governing policies as well. The days of special privileges were at an end and all Germans were to become full-fledged Russians.

The paths of the Mennonites and the Hutterites have often crossed throughout the years since both groups share a common Anabaptist ancestry and differ in their basic beliefs only in the communal way of life. Johann Cornies, a leader among the German Mennonite Colonists in Russia assisted the Hutterites to find good land on the Molotschna River and gave them valuable assistance when the Hutterites found themselves in dire need both spiritually and financially. The Hutterites divided into two groups, one remaining as a Bruderhof and the other locating in villages on private farms. In passing one should mention that the Bruderhof Hutterthal was founded in 1842, in 1853 Johannesruh was established, and Hutterdorf, and Scheromet and New Hutterthal after 1857.

In March of 1871 delegates from various Mennonite colonies and Hutterite settlements appeared at St. Petersburg in behalf of their common concern. This first attempt to get a favorable hearing was not very successful. The delegates returned home without definite assurance as to their future and with a growing conviction that their privileged days were numbered. Several more times delegations tried to obtain personal interviews with the Czar, but these too proved unsuccessful. The only result seemed to be that the Czar announced provisions in the forthcoming conscription act for exempting Mennonites and Hutterites from Combatant service. General von Todtsben, a man of German background was sent through the settlements in the spring of 1874 to explain the provisions of the act as it would effect them, and to try to have them reconsider the decision that had been made by this time, that again there would need to be a journey to a new land. The German culture and language was such an inseparable part of their life and religion that the loss of it was almost unthinkable.

In the meantime those who refused to accept any form of limited service under the military authorities, were casting about for a suitable refuge in case emigration should become unavoidable. Australia, South America, North America, and also other areas suggested themselves as possibilities. To each there were some objections. Each country had popular impressions that prevailed at the time. Of America it was said, "America was a country interesting for the adventurer, an asylum for convicts. How could one live in peace under his vine and fig tree amid such people, to say nothing of the native savage." Such a life might be possible "for those who had their pockets full of revolvers:" but for a non-resistant people it would be impossible to found homes amid such surroundings.

Then one had also to think of the long voyage across the Atlantic, loss of valuable property if a considerable number should decide to emigrate, the severing of ties of home and country—all these one must consider and these weighed heavily on the minds of those who loved their own beautiful homes and pleasant surroundings. Yet, considering all these facts they were willing to leave, because of their religious convictions, to a new frontier. America became the choice of almost all who decided to emigrate.

Cornelius Jansen who was a merchant and because of his official position and intimate knowledge of political affairs, from the very beginning preferred America to all other lands of freedom to those who might wish to emigrate. As early as 1871 Jansen and J. F. Funk, editor of the *Herald der Wahrheit* began a correspondence about the resources and industries of the different sections of the country, the customs of the people, and above all the laws regarding military service. He also inquired of the English Colonial Secretary of London whether Mennonite immigrants would be welcome in Canada and whether they would be free from military service.

In reply they were assured a welcome in Canada and yet the English government did not wish to encourage the emigration movement unless Russia would consent to their leaving. At about the same time the Ottawa authorities learned of the probable migration from another source, namely William Hespeler, a Canadian immigration agent. Hespeler who was of German birth had gained this information while on a visit to southern Russia and immediately forwarded the information to the Canadian Immigration Department. Hespeler was forced to leave Russia because the authorities suspected the purpose of his visit, which was of course to encourage the emigration. He had suggested that it would be wise to appoint a delegation of competent men to investigate the lands in Canada which might be suitable for the kind of settlement they desired.

Also in 1872 a group of four young men from the Molotschna Colony had set out on an adventure of their own, touring sections of the United States and visiting Mennonite groups already here. The favorable report brought back to Russia by these men no doubt also added considerable impetus to the emigration movement. It was decided at this time that a delegation would be sent made up of delegates from the various colonies to investigate the promised land more fully and to report it's findings to the respective villages.

In the early spring of 1873 delegates were chosen for this venture. The Molotschna Colony chose Jacob Buller and Leonhard Suderman, also chosen from other groups were Cornelius Buhr, Tobias Unruh, Andreas Schrag, Wilhelm Ewert, Heinrich Wiebe, Jacob Peters, Cornelius Toews, and David Klassen. Paul Tschetter, a young minister twenty-nine years old, and his uncle Lawrence Tschetter were chosen by the Hutterites. In this story we are primarily concerned with the emigration of the Hutterites and therefore we will follow the travels of the Tschetters.

In early May 1873 the Hutterites, Paul and Lohrentz Tschetter along with Cornelius Toews and David Klassen arrived in New York on the Silesia after an ocean trip of thirteen days. From the diary of Paul Tschetter one is able to travel the route that this delegation traveled, taking them to Elkhart, Indiana where they visited with among others John Funk who accompanied them because the group was not able to manage the English language very well. Old Mennonites and Amish groups were also visited. From Elkhart they traveled to Chicago, on to St. Paul, Minnesota to Duluth where they were joined by other members of the delegation.

The frontier of America in the early seventies, where cheap land or free lands were still available in quanities for large settlements ran from Winnipeg south through the Red River Valley, across the southeastern corner of the territory of Dakota, through central Nebraska and Kansas down into Texas. This was the region the delegates were interested in. The prospective colonists were a varied lot who desired to live together and consequently areas were sought where even the poorest would be able to purchase land. Since farming has always been the prominent vocation in the lives of these people so even now they were searching for land situations that were similar to those of Russia. Unsettled prairies, wilderness was by no means an objection because in Russia they lived in closed communities in large compact land areas which had originally been uninhabited crown lands at the time of purchase. To reproduce the same kind of settlements here would only be possible in such frontier regions where the government still owned large uninhabited stretches of land. The instructions to the delegates had included the following guarantees from the government where land would be purchased.

1. Religious freedom, and exemption from military service.
2. Land of good quality, in quantity sufficient to meet their needs, at moderate prices and easy terms.
3. The right to live in closed communities, have their own form of government, be able to use the German language as they had been permitted to use it in Russia.
4. To be desired was advance of sufficient money to cover transportation expenses from Russia to America.

Today these demands seem extravagant but at that time every western state as well as railroad companies still held vast areas of rich land anxiously awaiting industrious settlers. It was considered a worthy undertaking to employ every effort to get settlers, especially the Mennonites and Hutterites who were known as among the most successful farmers in Europe.

The delegates toured Winnepeg, which in 1873 was a village of nineteen houses and less than five hundred people. The nearest railroad was four hundred miles away. The only means of entrance was by the way of the Red River from the south or by a combined land and water route from Lake Superior on the east called the Dawson Route. After touring Manitoba for several days they were not favorably impressed because the land appeared to them as almost swamp land. Here it was the middle of June and the ground would not be ready even for seeding, where in Russia the grain was about ready for harvesting at this time of year. The Tschetters, Ewert, and Unruh felt that they had seen enough of Canada and started for Dakota. The region near Fargo was an original choice of the delegates as a possible site of a settlement. But because favorable congressional action could not be secured for land reservation in this region the hope of a settlement was abandoned. During the time of approximately three months that the delegates spent in the United States and Canada they stopped in various sections of Manitoba, Dakota Territory, Minnesota, Nebraska, and Kansas. Two of the delegation Buller and Ewert traveled as far south as Texas.

The Tschetters were concerned about securing something more definite in the way of a promise from the proper authorities for their people back in Russia, so they availed themselves of a few days of leisure to visit

President Grant. The visit, arranged by Hiller of the Northern Pacific railroad gave opportunity for a petition, mostly in the form of questions, to be presented in behalf of the Hutterite group. This petition concerned itself with the possibility of a fifty year exemption from military service or obligations, the privilege of living in colonies or villages, to conduct their schools in the German language, the right to be excluded from jury service, and the swearing of oaths with official papers. President Grant informed the Tschetters that he would need time to study the petition. It was after the Tschetters returned home to Russia that they were informed that to grant these privileges was beyond the power of the president as the states had jurisdiction over such matters.

The journey of this committee of twelve had important results. The lands of Canada and America had been investigated for settlements, and as they could preliminary arrangements for the emmigration of their people in the following year had been made leaving the completion of these plans in the hands of friends here in America.

While preparations for the great adventure were already under way in Russia during this time interest reached a new high when the delegation returned. Several small groups had already left Russia but now plans were made for a mass migration. The enthusiastic reports of the committee and the information that there was land to be had in any quantity and on easy terms with religious freedom in both America and in Canada aroused great interest in the winter of 1873 and '74. Where the emigration fever was the highest steps were immediately taken to dispose of their property so that an early departure the following spring to the new land would be made. Everybody wanted to sell and there was nobody to buy. The marketability of the land was restricted because some of the land was original Crown land with only limited ownership of the soil. So it was only the use of the land that could be sold. Although buildings and improvements belonged to them but without land they were not of great value. So often these farms were sold for a mere fraction of their actual worth.

Another task was to secure the necessary passports permitting emigration from Russia. Often this too was a tedious and long drawn out process demanding heavy fees and accelerated only by liberal gratuities to corrupt government officials. This often took several months before passports were obtained and every step was attended with heavy expense. It is reported that the average fee paid by each family for necessary emigration documents was about fifty dollars.

When the Russian government realized that a mass migration was underway and that there was a strong liklihood that Russia would lose forty thousand of its most industrious farmers in South Russia, efforts were underway to stem the tide. It is to be remembered that Hutterites and Mennonites were not the only ones involved in this migration. Even though the military issue was a most important consideration for Mennonites and Hutterites, other German groups such as German Lutherans, Reformed, and Catholics had also decided to leave Russia because of the program of Russianization the government had adopted. It meant that these groups too would lose their privileged status which they had enjoyed up to this time.

One needs also to recognize the fact that as in all groups, Mennonite, Hutterite, or others, there were those who decided to cast their lot with the religious absolutists for economic reasons. In every westward movement in history there has been a large contingent of the landless. So all these motives must be taken into consideration when seeking for the ultimate causes back of the emigration movement.

In America preparations for the emigration were also continuing. Not only American Mennonites, but western railroad companies and land departments were interested in this movement. Often serious rivalry between groups or state desireous of new settlers, led to crime and fraud as was the situation reported in the Daily Press and Dakotan of Yankton concerning a group of immigrants who with fraud and shrewdness inveigled an innocent, weary, and unsuspecting group into turning aside from their original destination. The Mennonites already settled in America offered their assistance both financially and in helping the new arrivals find suitable homes.

Rumors traveled quickly. Often derogatory reports were circulated to prevent settlements from being made in one state and thereby encouraging settlement of another area. One such rumor among others was a letter circulated in Russia in which the writer stated that Yankton has sunk, people in the region were starving, and that a war with the Indians was inevitable. The story supposedly was to have emanated from some confidence men employed by the great railroad companies having lands to sell. The frontier press too played a unique role in boosting their respective states and territories. Dakota was as well represented by these boosters as any region!

Jacob Brauch, a territorial immigration commissioner, was instrumental in bringing many Mennonites and Hutterites to Dakota who might not have come otherwise. The large groups of Hutterite Brethren who came in 1875 as well as others, came largely through his efforts. According to Brauch one of the best and cheapest mediums of advertising in countries abroad was the "American Letter." He believed that by writing relatives and friends in Russia about their experiences and opportunities more could be accomplished to further immigration to Dakota Territory than if an agent were sent to Russia.

Of the Hutterites, Elder Michael Waldner and his congregation at Scheromet and Elder Darius Walter with his congregation at Hutterdorf and others in private ownership in this village were of the first desiring to leave for America. Samuel Kleinsasser, Johannes Decker,

Christian Stahl, and Mathies Waldner journeyed to Alexandrowsk to make the necessary preparations for one hundred and nine individuals who were to arrive from Scheromet. The following day all the brethren and sisters arrived with their baggage. After a five day train trip they arrived at the German-Russian border. After the necessary pass and tariff inspections they crossed the border and camped for the night in the Eidtkunan Park near the railway station. The following day they left for Könegsburg and Berlin to reach Hamburg. After spending the night in the immigration home and being joined by Darius Walter with his congregation they embarked on the Harmonia which left the same day and was to be their home for the next sixteen days while sailing the Atlantic Ocean.

On Friday, July 17 full of hope and trust in God, they landed in New York. Shortly before sunset, after customs inspection and purchasing of railroad tickets, they began their journey to the Midwest. This journey took them through Detroit, Chicago, and to Lincoln, Nebraska where they had been influenced by railroad agents to establish their homes.

In Lincoln, finding the location unsatisfactory they sent three brethren from each group on a land inspection tour farther into Nebraska. The rest of the group remained in Lincoln. The six brethren returned several days later and since they had not found a suitable locality, they decided to travel to Dakota to investigate land there. The brethren remaining hired out for wages.

Because of inadequate provisions and the hot dry summer, soon after arriving in Lincoln an epidemic of dysentary broke out among the children causing thirty-six deaths. Here too an older man Darius Stahl died at the age of seventy-eight years. On August 17 they left Lincoln, arriving in Yankton the next day

The Michael Waldner congregation found a suitable tract of land in Bon Homme County, located on the Missouri River about eighteen miles from Yankton. It is probable that the rolling prairies of Dakota which reminded them of the Russian Steepes, the condition of the soil, and the climate made them decide for Dakota. Another reason was that they hoped to locate on a single large tract of land rather than individual homesteads and therefore did not consider taking advantage of the Homestead Act, where each individual of legal age could have a tract of 160 acres free simply by personally residing on the tract to qualify for ownership.

As the regulations of the Homestead Act were not advantageous to the establishment of a Hutterite Colony, they decided to buy a tract of privately owned land of 2,500 acres. The Dakota Herald, an English paper in Dakota reported in it's August 25, 1874 edition: "Honorable W. A. Burleigh yesterday sold 2500 acres of his large farm in the neighborhood of Bon Homme. The buyer is a group of Russian-Germans who have united after the fashion of Apostolic Communists. Of the purchase price 25,000 dollars, they pay 17,000 dollars cash, the balance they pay on time." This colony has been the mother colony from which several other colonies have been formed.

The other colony group led by Darius Walter and the minister Jörg Hofer located at Silver Lake in Turner County on government land. This was a temporary location. The winter which was a severe one with terrible storms was spent in earthen huts. In the spring of 1875 the group moved to the James River near Wolf Creek from which the colony derived it's name. This tract of land consisted of 5,400 acres.

The other Hutterites who had lived in private ownership in Hutterdorf who accompanied this group to Dakota Territory settled near Freeman on government land, which consisted of 160 acres per settler. In the fall of 1874 Paul Tschetter from Neu Hutterthal with several families and single men followed the earlier settlers. The group spent the winter in Elkhart, Indiana, where John Funk and other helpful Mennonites helped them through the winter. The following spring of 1875 they too came to settle in Dakota on private tracts about nine miles from the Darius Walter Colony along the Wolf Creek.

The two colonies just mentioned as well as all the other congregations of the Hutterites emmigrated to America in the years 1874-1879. Several groups came at various times, some groups were as large as 350 and others as small as five families. The usual estimate is that 800 Hutterites came to America but 1,200 or more would probably be a more accurate number. It is to be said that those Hutterites who had practiced community of goods in Russia, continued to do the same in Dakota. About one third of the Hutterite immigrants lived in colonies, while the other two-thirds lived on private farms.

Although practically the entire group left Russia, several families did remain. Among these were a Stahl family, Tschetter family, Knels family, and a Wollman family. Wollman owned in partnership with Lepp a large factory and it is very probable that his economic status kept him from emmigrating. The descendants of these families suffered along with others who remained in Russia as they lived through the hardships of the revolution that came later.

We are informed that this Mr. Wollman who had become extremely wealthy encouraged a nephew of his to come back to Russia from America for funds that Wollman made available for the Hutterites here. The nephew never returned to his home in Dakota although a trunk containing a Russian fur coat and about $300 arrived here. After investigation it was discovered that the nephew had arrived in New York but disappeared and no further evidence of his where abouts has ever been found. It has been suggested that the character and the personality of the nephew was inclined toward a boastful and rather arrogant nature and that this may have been in part responsible for his disappearance as this was in the with sorrow and woe, a man educated to the work of carrying the gospel of peace to the heathen, rises up and declares that to do this even *voluntarily* is not wrong. Surely, If the blind lead the blind shall they not both fall into the ditch? We rejoice however, that this is not the sentiment of most of our Russian Brethren, as they are sacrificing much of their earthly possessions to come to America, to enjoy their full liberty of conscience.

We trust, however, our friend Dirks will harmonize his faith a little nearer with that of the gospel, and learn to give an answer to his friends, in similar questions, which will correspond nearer with the gospel. We trust that none of our friends in Russia nor yet in America will feel inclined to accept such teachings. Let us all hold to the true gospel principles and be faithful even unto death.

Russian Aid Fund.

CASH RECEIVED.

From Amish Mennonite Church in Mc Lean co., Ill. by Chr. Nafziger	$150.00
From Amish Mennonite Church in Woodford co., Ill by Chr. Rjessor	80.00
Chr. Honderick	5.00
From Church in Tuscarawas co., O. by Peter Bitschy	74.75
From Church in Juniata co., Pa., by S. K. Beiler & J Riehl	67.00
Jacob Buzzard, Yellow Creek	2.50
From Deer Creek Church, Johnson co., Iowa, by J. J. Swartzentruber	64.00
D. Z. Yoder sends as a loan, loaned by Peter Kauffman	100.00
From Church in Stark co., O., by David Mourer	190.00
From Amish Mennonite Church in Holmes co., O., by Sam. Miller	3.00
Christianity Requires Peace 2.50 & 10 00	12.50
From Church in Whiteside co., Ill., by L. Hendricks	46.03
From Church at Danvers Mc Lean co., Ill., by Jos. Stuckey	148.00
Anna Sangree	2.00
From Church near Davidsville Pa., by S. Foust	28.00
G. Brown	5.00
From Amish Mennonites at Croghan Lewis Co., N. Y., by Joseph Stiri	112.50
D. K. M	.25
Holdeman's Church, by J K Beutler	86.00
From the Community at Lena Stephenson co., Ill., by Allen Boyer	32.75
John Rupp	6.00
Daniel B. Smith Ottowa O.	81.50

Herald of Truth.

Elkhart, Ind., Aug. 1874.

TO OUR SUBSCRIBERS. — If any of our subscribers do not get their papers regularly, or if any persons who send for books, &c., do not obtain them in due time, they will confer a favor by informing us, and we will do our best to have everything properly forwarded to its destination.

HOW TO SEND MONEY.—If in sums of more than a dollar, it is best to obtain either a draft, or a Post Office Money Order, or where these cannot be obtained, get the letter registered.

THOSE of our subscribers who do not wish to take the Herald of Truth any longer, will please to inform us of the fact by letter and pay up all arrearages, and the matter shall have our prompt attention, otherwise it will be considered that they wish to continue their subscriptions

FROM A PRIVATE LETTER we learn that the grasshoppers have again infested the southern region of Minnesota, and have destroyed much of the growing crops. This is unfortunate as our Russian brethren settled in Mountain Lake, in that state, unless they should have been so favored as to have escaped the ravages of these destroyers.

A Misconception.—It seems that some of the brethren in Russia have conceived the idea that the Aid offered to those who are without means, is offered only to those who will settle in the United States, while those who settle in the Provinces of British America, should be excluded from the benefits of this assistance. This information was given us by a letter from Bro. Henry Wiebe, of the Bergthaler Church, to Henry Schutt, of Hamburg. But the idea is entirely incorrect. The committee makes no difference where the brethren settle in America, whether in the United States, the Canadian Provinces, or Manitoba, they shall fare alike so far as the aid of the committee can be applied to their assistance. But in order to secure the Aid of the Mennonite Board of Guardians they must have the proper certificates of identification and must come by the Inman Line; and to obtain the Aid of the Executive Aid Committe of Pennsylvania, they must come over the Red Star Line, from Antwerp to Philadelphia. These are conditions that must be complied with. But when the brethren are once here they can go and settle where they please. May God's blessing be with them.

The Russian Emigration.—On the 8th of July, seven families from Russia arrived at Summerfield, Illinois, where they remained over Sunday, and proceeded on to Kansas, where they propose to settle.

On Sunday morning, July the 19th, some thirty families, under the direction of Bishop Jacob Wiebe, arrived at Elkhart, from the Crimea, six of whom went directly on to Kansas, while the remainder stopped here, where they expect to remain until they have determined upon a place of settlement. Of these a number came at the expense of the Mennonite Board of Guardians, amounting to 28½ tickets. They had a pleasant trip, were well cared for, and with the exception of sea sickness, enjoyed good health.

The brethren David Klaasen and Cornelius Toows, are also on the way, going by the English line of Steamers to Quebec, and thence through Canada to Manitoba, where Bro. Schantz has already provided for their reception, and before this reaches our readers, they may have reached their destination.

Thirteen other families also from the Crimea, who started with Bro. Wiebe's party, came in another Steamer and went to Yankton to join the settlement commenced there last Fall by the brethren Unruh and others.

Twenty-five families from Jakaterinoslaw arrived on the 18th, and are now stopping at Buffalo till they have made their selection of land.

Some eighty families from the Hudderthal Church arrived in New York about the same time as the above, and proceeded to Burlington, Iowa, intending, if we are rightly informed, to settle in Nebraska.

We exceedingly regret that the latter party did not come over the Inman Line, as they were compelled to pay a much higher rate of fare than by this Line. We trust that those who represent themselves as the friends of the Mennonites, will manifest their friendship in a different way, than by heaping unnecessary expense upon them, and compelling them to pay hundreds of dollars to enrich designing agents. We hope our brethren will guard against being misled, and hereafter come by those Lines of Steamers with which arrangements have been made by the brethren, at reduced rates. Those coming through Hamburg will be provided for at Hamburg by Henry Schuett, and come over the Inman Line to New York, where they will be met by Bro. Warkentin.

Those coming by way of Antwerp and Philadelphia will be received at Antwerp by Mr. Von der Becke, and come on the Red Star Line, to Philadelphia, where they will also be received by the brethren.

The whole number of Mennonites that arrived at New York during the week ending July 18th, was almost six hundred, and we have reports that some six hundred more

From Manitoba.

Bro. Jacob Y. Schantz writes from Winnepeg, Province of Manitoba, in the British Possessions, under date of June 20th, that he arrived safely there with a span of horses, and went out on the land reserved for the settlement of the Russian Mennonites and proposes there to build four temporary houses, as stated in the last Herald, secure water and make other necessary provisions for the comfort of the expected emigrants.

He says: Two young friends came with me to see the country, and work a while. They will help me build. Two brethren were also with me, who had intended to help me, but because the lumber did not come in time, they returned home on the 18th of June. I bought the lumber for the reception houses in Minnesota, and received the promise that it should be here in two weeks from date of purchase. We then went on the reserved land, and after finding a proper days before checks, bank drafts, and other security measures available today.

So a pilgrimage of some one hundred twenty years traveled thousands of miles; on foot, on horseback, on wagon, by boat, steamship, and finally by train ended in Dakota Territory.

Today as we reminiscence of one hundred years since our forefathers came to this land we are reminded of the words in Deuteronomy 6:20-25. That in days to come when our children ask what these stories mean we shall be able to tell them. We need to ponder and appreciate the heritage that is ours, remembering we have a torch to hold high that we did not light, but it was given to us by other hands. The torch is ours to keep burning bright, ours to pass on to other generations.

Deloris Stahl

Mrs. Franz (Sarah) Wollman and children Frank, Jacob, and Katherina. She joined the Jamesville Colony and migrated to Canada.

Prairieleut Settlement in Langham, Saskatchewan

Source: "Rooted and Grounded in Love—History and Family Records of the Langham Prairie People" by Edna Wurtz and Catherine Masuk—Published in 2000.

As the population of the Prairieleut increased in the Freeman and Bridgewater, SD, area, need for suitable land for farming led to families moving to Canada to establish homesteads. This began in the 1890's with families moving to southern Manitoba and later moving to Langham. Langham is about 15 miles northwest of Saskatoon, which in 1900 was a very small village in what was then called North West Territories as Saskatchewan did not become a province of Canada until September 1, 1905.

The largest numbers immigrating directly from Freeman to Langham was in early spring 1901 when five families and in 1902 when another six families immigrated. Over the next several years, according to JJ Mendel, about 45 Prairieleut families (page iii) moved to Langham and surrounding communities, some directly from the Freeman area and some via Chaseley, North Dakota. Also, Low German families such as from Mountain Lake, Minnesota, also moved to the Langham area during this time.

These families had strong ties to their very close relatives in the "States." In several cases the oldest children who were already married remained in South Dakota and the parents and youngest children moved. Thus, there were parents, siblings, grandparents, cousins (some who never met), and in laws separated by the 1,000 plus mile distance from Freeman and the Saskatoon area. Transportation by train was the most practical method. By the mid 1920's there were recorded instances of travel by car to see the "Canadian family". In the early years traveling such a distance back and forth from Freeman and Langham typically occurred only to attend marriages, anniversaries and funerals or to visit a very ill relative. Long distance courtships led to a few brides following their grooms to Canada. By the time of the 2001 Langham Prairie People centennial celebration, most close connections back to Freeman were elderly cousins, and second and third cousins.

The Bethesda Mennonite church was built in 1907 and the Emmanuel Krimmer Mennonite Brethren church south of Langham was built in 1917. Attendance at church conferences provided some opportunities to visit relatives and keep in touch.

During World War One (1917 and 1918) military draft aged men and several families with draft aged children moved to Canada, as there was no alternative to military service for United States draftees. The typical destination was Langham where they had cousins and other close relatives. The reason for the move to Canada was the US military's harsh treatment of four imprisoned South Dakota Hutterite colony men who as conscientious objectors refused to bear arms After the war most if not all returned to the States . (Note: Anti German feelings and the imprisonment at Alcatraz of four draftees of whom two Hofer brothers from Rockport Colony died in a Ft. Leavenworth military prison in 1918, led to the then 17 of 18 South Dakota Hutterite colonies immigrating to Canada. By 1932, all but Bon Homme colony moved.)

INMAN STEAMSHIP COMPANY

GENERAL WESTERN AGENCY

32 South Clark Street, Chicago, June 21, 1875.

RATES OF STEERAGE PASSAGE.

To take effect AT ONCE.

New York, To or From Liverpool, Queenstown, Londonderry, Belfast or Glasgow,	$28 00
" " " Dublin,	29 00
" " " London, Bristol or Cardiff,	31 00
" " " Hamburg, Havre, Antwerp, Rotterdam, / " " " Amsterdam and Harlingen,	32 00
" " " Christiania, Bergen, Stavanger, Christiansand, Gothenburg, Malmo, Copenhagen, Mannheim, Drontheim, Paris, Berlin or Bremen	35 00
Children under 12 years, Half Price. Infants to New York,	3 00

Commissions:

On British Passengers, for each adult,	$2 00
" Continental " " "	3 00
Children, Half Rates. Infants, when paid for,	50

The **COMMISSION** shall cover all charges for bill-posting, exchange, and all other expenses except newspaper advertising.

Prepaid (*Westward*) tickets may be issued for passage from any of the points mentioned above, through to destination, the *through rate* being the sum of the Ocean and Railroad fares. *No separate Railroad order, or ticket, is required.*

For "***Inland Fares,***" New York to Western Points, *See "Castle Garden Emigrant R. R. Tariff."*

Note. — *All persons over twelve years of age pay full fare on both Ocean and Railroad; those between five and twelve years, half fare on both Ocean and Railroad; and those between one and five years, half fare on Ocean and free on Railroad, and infants under one year $3.00 on Ocean (to New York) and free on Railroad.*

Outward (*Eastward*) tickets are to be issued only for passage from New York to Europe (passengers from the interior to provide their own railroad transportation to New York); and as the tickets are printed to read to Queenstown and Liverpool, please remember, when you book passengers to points beyond these places, to write across the face of the ticket the name of the port to which they are booked.

FRANCIS C. BROWN,

General Western Agent.

Ein Auswanderungs Lied

Jetzt ist die Zeit und Stunda da,
Dass wir ziehn nach Amerika,
Viel tausend Seelen geht's dort gut,
Dass tröstet uns und gibt uns Müt.

Jetz ist die Zeit und Stunda da,
Dass wir ziehn nach Amerika.
Die Wagen stehn schon vor der Tür
Mit Weib und Kinder ziehen wir.

Jetz ist die Zeit und Stunda da,
Dass wir ziehn nach Amerika.
Die Pferde stehn schon angespannt,
Wir ziehen in ein fremdes Land.

Ihr alle die mit uns verwandt,
Reicht uns zum letzen mal die Hand.
Ihr Freunde weinet nicht zu sehr,
Wir sehn uns nun, und nimmer mehr.

Seid alle Männlich, und seid stark,
Macht uns den Abschied nicht zu hart.
Wir ziehen ja nicht aus der Welt,
Auch da ist Gott, der uns erhält.

Wenn unser Schiff zur See einschwimmt,
Dann werden Lieder angestimmt.
Wir Fürchten keinen Wasserfall,
Der Liebe Gott ist überall.

Und kommen wir gen Baltimor,
Dann heben wir das Land empor,
Und rufen laut "Victoria!"
Jetzt sind wir in Amerika.

Willkommen fremdes Vaterland,
Wo sich mein Herz hat hin gewandt.
Du Land wo ich geboren bin,
Muss meiden und muss weit dahin.

Leb wohl du altes Vaterland,
Lebt alle wohl die uns gekannt.
Wir werden uns einst wiedersehn,
Dort wo die Friedens Palmen wehn.

The time and hour is now at hand,
We're moving to a foreign land;
Where souls by thousands prosper well,
Dauntless with tears, we say farewell.

The time and hour is now at hand,
We're moving to a foreign land;
Our wagons loaded stand in row
With wives and children we shall go.

The time and hour is now at hand,
We're moving to a foreign land;
Our horses hitched, to wagons stand,
We're leaving for an unknown land.

To our beloved ones and our kin,
We say farewell and sigh within;
Weep not so hard that we must part,
It grieves our weary saddened heart.

Be manly and renew your strength,
As time goes on we'll meet at length;
We still remain upon this sphere,
Where God's protection will be near.

When we embark the ship at sea
We'll join in songs of jubilee;
We fear no water and no waves,
For God is there and His love saves.

When we'll arrive on yonder shore,
God's holy name we will adore;
We'll shout when we step on the strand,
America, thou blessed land!

Welcome, thou fatherland, afar
Where favored gates stand wide ajar;
We now our land of birth disown,
We've chose a home in lands unknown.

Farewell, farewell, my fatherland,
Farewell, again, my kindred band;
Some day we'll meet on heaven's shore,
'Neath peaceful Palms forever more.

Translation is by Mr. Abe J. Unruh, Montezuma, Kansas.

This song was sung by Mennonites and Hutterites before leaving Russia. It was written by Jakob Stuku, Elder of Mennonite Congregation at Kotosufka, Shitomir district in Volhynia, Western Russia. At this writing some Hutterite descendents near Freeman can still quote parts of this song by memory.

Remembrance in Rhyme

THE MIGRATION STORY IN GERMAN

by M. J. Hofer, Bowden, N. D.

.Ich will euch was erzählen
Von etwas wert und hold,
Von Herzen soll's euch freuen,
Daß ihr euch wundern sollt.

Es sind die vielen Lieben
Einstens im fernen Land.
Sie wuchsen wie die Eichen
Am fetten Meeresstrand.

Sie lebten dort viel Jahre;
Dann kam ein Aufruf drein:
Ihr müsset aus dem Lande,
Wenn ihr wollt wehrlos sein.

Der Älteste, Paul Tschetter,
Der wurde dann gesandt
In einer fremden Gegend
Zu suchen Heimatsland.

Nachdem er seine Botschaft
Nach Rückkehr dargebracht,
Da fing es an zu tagen,
Weichen mußte die Nacht.

Dann sind sie ausgewandert,
So wie es ward bestellt,
Mit ihren lieben Kindern,
Hin in die weite Welt.

Viel Tränen sind geflossen,
Viel' Seufzer flogen weit
In jenen bangen Tagen
Zum Thron der Ewigkeit.

Die Neuwelt voll Erbarmen
Die Arme reichte zu:
"Kommt her, ihr Heilsbedürft'gen,
Hier habt ihr Glaubensruh!"

Dann sind wir noch gewandert
Weit weg vom Meeresstrand,
Und ließen uns dann nieder
Auf einem ebnen Land.

Sie bauten kleine Häuser
Von Rasen und von Holz,
Man nannt sie "Similankis,"
Worauf sie waren stolz.

Der Mann, der grub den Brunnen,
Die Frau die Erde zog
Mit einem großen Eimer,
Dann auf den Haufen trug.

Pflügen tat man mit Ochsen,
Vor einem kleinen Pflug,
Und hinten auf dem Rücken
Man eine Geißel trug.

Wo sind die vielen Jahre,
Wo ist die Jugendzeit?
Wo sind die zarten Kräfte?
Zurück, sehr weit--weit—weit.

Die meisten lieben Alten,
Die sind schon alle fort;
Dort in der ew'gen Heimat,
An jenem Ruheort.

Der alte Bruder Tschetter,
Der wirkt im Segen noch;
Er trägt auf seinen Schultern
Getreu noch Christi Joch.

Die Zeit, die fährt geschwinde
Wie'n Pfeil zur Ewigkeit;
Drum laßt uns alle streiten
Für Jesus, weil's noch Zeit.

Es will schon Abend werden,
Die Dämmrung bricht herein;
Drum, Heiland, hör' das Flehen
Und kehre bei uns ein.

Und wenn der Kampf vollendet,
Nimm uns hin, wo du bist.
Zu dir, du lieber Vater,
O Heiland Jesus Christ.

Autobiography — D. J. Mendel

Translated From German by Mrs. Joe G. Hofer

Published here is that part of the autobiography which pertains to living in Russia, the migration to America, and getting established here.

David J. Mendel
Born November 4, 1868
Died April 28, 1951

In the beginning of the 1780's, three companions—Willman, Tittel and Paul Mändel—left Szobotch in Ungerland (today's Czechoslavakia) and came to the Colony (Bruderhof) in Wischenka, Russia. Paul Mandel was a Bohemian and was my great-grandfather. He died in Hutterthal in 1846. He had two children, a son named Paul (my grandfather) and a daughter named Lea. Paul, my grandfather, had one son also named Paul with his first wife, and he died at the Elmspring Colony in South Dakota at the age of 99 years. From his second wife he had three sons and four daughters: Jacob (my father), Michael, Peter, Maria, Elizabeth, Anna and Kathryn.

My father, Jacob, married Elder David Hofer's daughter, Anna, on December 4, 1849. They established their home in Hutterthal.

In 1868, 20 families (I can name them all) agreed to relocate and start a new dorf or village. They were fortunate to secure several thousand desjatin (2½ acre equals 1 desjatin) 200 Werst (2 / 3 mile equals 1 Werst) northwest of Hutterthal. Here I was born as the seventh child of the family on November 4, 1868. I was very welcome since I had five older sisters.

Now I shall begin about my childhood. My father operated a large farm, a windmill, and a brick burning factory. He had the plans and materials bought for a large barn or grainery and a new home at the time of his death. When he made a business trip to Ekoternoslof, 100 Werst away from home, he did not know that cholera was on a rampage there. While there he came in contact with this disease and a few hours after his return home he passed away on June 2, 1872. I was three and one-half years old at the time, and I distinctly remember his death. Mother with her eight children (oldest at 21 and youngest three weeks) mourned his passing. Later mother told me how I had waited daily for two weeks at the gate for his return, but I gradually forgot him.

The great migration was during the following years because of Russian conscription laws. All Mennonite and German citizens were granted a ten year reprieve. They had the choice of leaving Russia or accepting the military training service. Neu Hutterthal dorf had an unanimous decision to go to America. The village consisted of 20 families or farms. Ten were located on each side of the street which was almost two-thirds of a mile (1 Werst long). Between the farm yards were beautiful orchards and gardens. It was difficult to leave these beautiful yards and farms behind. However, everything was sold and preparations were made to leave for America. Five families left in 1874 and the remaining in August of 1875. The last group included my mother and her children. I was six and one-half years old and remember many of the happenings such as traveling though large cities and driving through Germany and the streets of Berlin. The many statutes were very interesting to me. When we came to the harbor, Bremen, we waited four days until our ship, "Main," was ready for sailing. After 16 days on the great Atlantic Ocean, we arrived in the millionaire city of New York on September 5, 1875. The next three days final arrangements were completed so that we could continue our trip. I took advantage of these three days and visited the New York zoo where I saw animals from the large elephant to the small birds. This was my greatest thrill of the whole adventurous trip.

The train was our next mode of travel, and we headed toward the west. On September 11 we arrived in the small city of Yankton. The railroad ended here so we waited another four days while necessary arrangements and preparations were made to continue our journey. Some bought wagons and horses while others hired traveling necessities. Turning northward, we arrived at the Wolf Creek Colony which had been settled that spring. From there we traveled ten miles northeast where the five families who had left the previous year lives. As they saw us coming, they came out to meet us and their greeting was most heart warming. We stayed at the home of my brother-in-law, Jacob Tschetter, now known as Christ Hofman's place. Within a few days Uncle Joseph Hofer, (Yos), Mother's brother, advised Mother to buy the 640 acre ranch two miles south of the Wolf Creek Colony. She paid $4000 for the 640 acres including cattle, horses, sheep and everything that was there. The buildings were made of logs. It was on this farm that I spent my youth.

Since there were no organized school districts, sessions were held in private homes two to three months a year. When the districts were organized, a four month term was ordered by the government.

I attended school at seven different places. I sat 26 months on a school bench, from ABC's to my 16th year. The rest of my youth was spent on the farm.

At the age of 18, I accepted a teaching position. I felt very inadequate with my limited education to do such a noble task, but with the Lord's blessings I enjoyed teaching for ten years, although my main occupation was and remained farming.

Hutterite Names

Shown is a list of common Hutterite names and how they came into our history. Through the generations, the spelling of many of the names have changed.

DECKER (DEKKER)—In 1783, a group of 15 Mennonites from a Low German village, joined the Hutterites at Wischink, Russia. Among them were Elsie Dekker, a widow with her five children, Hein, Jacob, Heinrich, Benjamin, and Eva. The name Decker, is carried on from the descendants of Benjamin, to America and Canada, and is found among the Lehrerleut, Schmiedleut and the Prairieleut.

ENTZ—This name comes from West Prussia. Four Entz families came to America; among them, John Entz who was chosen preacher of the Elm Spring Colony in 1892.

FAST—Through inter-marriage this Mennonite name from a Low German village came into the Hutterites.

GLANZER—A family name from Carinthia. They were expelled because of their refusal to accept the Catholic faith. Christian Glanzer and family joined the colony in 1755. There are many Glanzers among the Schmiedleut and the Prairieleut today.

GROSS—A German name possibly from Austria Tirol. The name was recorded in 1528 during the early Antibaptist movement, first appearing among the Hutterites in 1782 when Andreas Gross, his wife Christina, and son Jerg came to the group. Christina and Jerg accepted the faith and were baptised. Jerg is the ancestor of all the Grosses in the Brotherhood and the Prairieleut in America and Canada.

HOFER—A name that originated in Carinthia, Austria where they were staunch Lutherans. Around 1750 the country demanded the Catholic religion; therefore many people were driven from their homes and fled to Transylvania where they met with the Hutterites. Among these were Michael and Mathias Hofer from Amlach and their brother Johannes Hofer of St. Petersburg with his wife, Anna, and their seven children, Johannes, Michael, Christian, Paul, Jacob, Anna, and Barbara. All the Hofer's in the Brotherhood and Prairieleut derive from these Hofers.

JANSEN—A Mennonite name that came into the Hutterites through inter-marriage with the Low Germans in Russia.

KLEINSASSER—A name also originated from Carinthia, Austria. Johann Kleinsasser was leader of the group of Lutherans expelled from Carinthia and who fled to Transylvania, under the leadership of Maria Theresa. In 1755, this group went to Alwinz where they joined the Hutterites. With Johann Kleinsasser were his wife Barbara, a daughter Christina, and his brothers Stephanus, and Mathias and Joseph. In 1763 Johann was ordained the leader of the Hutterites. This name is very common among the Brotherhood and the Prairieleut of today.

KNELS— A name first seen in the Hutterites in 1783 when a widow Lisel Knels and her two sons Abraham and Johannes joined at Wischink, coming from Low German Mennonites of Prussia. This name is almost extinct today.

MENDEL (MAENDELIG, MENDL)—Among the group from Sabatisch to Wischink in Russia was Paul Maendelig of Czeck origin. He became the ancestor of the Mendels of today in the Lehrerleut, the Schmiedleut and the Prairieleut.

MILLER (MULLER)—A common Mennonite name. A Peter Muller and Joseph Muller with his wife Elizabeth and two children, Joseph and Barbara were among the Lutherans who fled to Transylvania from Carinthis, Austria. Miller descendants are found among the Prairieleut in America.

POLLMAN-PULLMAN (POLMAN-BOLMAN)—In 1784, with a group coming from Sabatisch and Lebar to join the Hutterites at Wischink, Russia were, Tobias Bolman and wife Susanna (son-in-law of Jacob Walther) and Andreas Bolman with his wife Roesel and six children: Johannes, Adam, Maria, Barbel, Katherina and Eva. Joseph Bolman and his wife

Judith and children, Lisel, Mariela, Annele also joined this group. This name is common anong the Prairieleut of America, but not found in the Brotherhood.

STAHL—A Hutterite name that first appeared in 1663 when a Johannes Stahl was taken prisoner at Zobelhof, Hungary. In 1757, another Johann Stahl is mentioned, at Alwinz. After this the name is common among the Hutterites and is found among the Dariusleut, the Schmiedleut, and the Prairieleut of America.

TSCHETTER (CZETERLE)—This name is recorded in Hutterite history as far back as 1760 when Abraham Tschetter, at Sabotiste, Hungary was arrested for opposing the government church. He gave up the faith and became a Catholic. Lorenz Tschetter was arrested in 1766, and imprisoned for one year because of his faith. He rejoined the Bruderhof at Walachia upon his release. The Tschetter name carries on from these and is found in the Dariusleut, Schmiedleut and the Prairieleut of America.

WALDNER (WALTNER)—A Hutterite family name coming from Amlach, Carinthia, Austria. Jerg Waldner, his wife Anna and their three children, Christian, Johannes and Maria fled to Translyvania in 1755. There they joined the Hutterites where John was chosen preacher, and is the chronicler of the Klein Geschichtsbuch. Johann's son Andreas married Kathrina Schrag from a nearby Swiss Mennonite village in 1797. Upon Andreas death his wife Katherina took her six children back to join the Swiss group. They took the name Waltner, which is common among the Swiss Mennonites in Kansas, and South Dakota. Waldner is common among the Brotherhoods and the Prairieleut of today.

WALTER (WALTHER)—The oldest Hutterite family name in exsitence today. The earliest Antibaptist member of the family was Franz Walther, a barber-surgeon from near Maulbronn, Wurttemberg who joined the Hutterites in 1580. In 1746 Zacharias Walther was chosen elder of the Hutterites, but was imprisoned for his faith. Later he joined the Catholic State church. His only son Jacob emigrated to the Ukraine with his wife Katherina and two sons Jacob and Darius in 1784. All the Walters in the Dariusleut and Prairieleut are descendants.

WIPF—The name is believed to have been one of the few surviving "old Hutterites" in Transylvania prior to the coming of the group from Carinthia in 1756. The Klein Geschichtsbuch mentions a widow Annela Wipf and her five children, Johann, Gretel, Elias, Samuel and Joseph. This name is also common among the Brotherhood and the Prairieleut of America.

WOLLMAN (WALEMANN WOLEMAN)—The name of Hans Waleman is mentioned in the Klein Geschechtsbuch during the 30 years war. Later Jacob Waleman with his wife Asseneth and five children, Andreas, Mechael, Barbel, Judith, Asseneth and a Katherina Waleman and her two children Joseph and Gretel are listed as joining the colony, at Wischink, Russia in 1784. The descendants are found among the Schmiedleut, the Dariusleut, and the Prairieleut.

WURZ (WURTZ)—An old Hutterite name. Joseph Wurtz was chosen as preacher in 1611 at Neumuhl, Moravia. In 1650 Moses Wurtz was chosen preacher at Sabatisch in Hungary. In 1755 Andreas Wurz from St. Peter with his wife Margreta and five children, Christian, Elizabeth, Magdalena, Christina and Anna joined the Hutterites at Alwinz and Kreuz, Transylvania. The descendants in the Brotherhood and the Prairieleut in America and Canada all come from Andreas Wurz.

Michael D. Hofer
(Oberschulz)
Born May 8, 1841
Died October 26, 1902

Michael R. Hofer
(Rutschield)
Born August 4, 1829
Died October 25, 1932

Mrs. Maria J. (Wipf) Kleinsasser was born in Russia on October 31, 1878. She is believed to be the only Hutterite alive today that was born in Russia at the time of the migration. She lives in Freeman with her daughter, Viola Kleinsasser.

(4—405.)

THE UNITED STATES OF AMERICA,

To all to whom these presents shall come, Greeting:

Homestead Certificate No. 3936 }
APPLICATION 3557 }

Whereas There has been deposited in the GENERAL LAND OFFICE of the United States a Certificate of the Register of the Land Office at Yankton Dakota Territory, whereby it appears that, pursuant to the Act of Congress approved 20th May, 1862, "To secure Homesteads to Actual Settlers on the Public Domain," and the acts supplemental thereto, the claim of David Wipf has been established and duly consummated, in conformity to law, for the south east quarter of section twelve in township ninety nine north of range fifty seven west, of the Fifth Principal Meridian in Dakota Territory containing one hundred and sixty acres

according to the Official Plat of the Survey of the said Land, returned to the GENERAL LAND OFFICE by the Surveyor General:

Now know ye, That there is, therefore, granted by the United States unto the said David Wipf the tract of Land above described: To have and to hold the said tract of Land, with the appurtenances thereof, unto the said David Wipf and to his heirs and assigns forever; subject to any vested and accrued water rights for mining, agricultural, manufacturing, or other purposes, and rights to ditches and reservoirs used in connection with such water rights, as may be recognized and acknowledged by the local customs, laws, and decisions of courts, and also subject to the right of the proprietor of a vein or lode to extract and remove his ore therefrom, should the same be found to penetrate or intersect the premises hereby granted, as provided by law.

In testimony whereof I, Grover Cleveland, President of the United States of America, have caused these letters to be made Patent, and the seal of the General Land Office to be hereunto affixed.

Given under my hand, at the City of Washington, the twenty sixth day of January, in the year of our Lord one thousand eight hundred and eighty seven, and of the Independence of the United States the one hundred and Eleventh.

By the President: Grover Cleveland

By M. McKean, Secretary.

Robt W. Ross, Recorder of the General Land Office.

RECORDED, Vol. 8, Page 360

When our forefathers came to America they were able to secure land from the Government through the Homestead Act of 1862. Shown is a homestead paper for 160 acres. They were also able to secure a second quarter (160 acres) through a tree claim, where they had to plant a given amount of trees on the property.

Letter From Paul Tschetter Found

Rev. Paul Tschetter was one of twelve delegates who in 1873 came from Russia to America to view the land with the intention of relocating here. Just recently Lawrence Klippenstein of Altona, Manitoba, discovered a letter that Rev. Tschetter wrote to Mr. John F. Funk of Elkhart, Indiana who had accompanied the delegates on their inspection tour. In this letter he reports the status of the emigration as of the date written.

With the permission of Mr. Klippenstein, the Steering Committee of the Hutterite Mennonite Centennial is herewith printing this letter. We are using his translation as it was printed in the Mennonite Historical Bulletin, page 2, October 1974 issue. (Footnote: To conform to American calendar add 12 days.)

Neuhutterthal
Nov. 29, 1873

. . . You will wonder perhaps why I had not written much earlier. I will mention the reason why I did not answer immediately. I was to report something definite, but even now cannot report with certainty about our migration, as to how many are involved. I returned on August 6, according to our calendar, protected by the hand of our Lord, and found my family well. Our joy was so great that I cannot describe it to you: they had thought that we no longer among the living . . .

Our emigration is still in a sorry state since we have not received word from Hiller as to the petition we submitted to the President. Everyone is waiting for this message since there is much evil spoken about America, especially among those who do not wish to emigrate. So I beg you to encourage Hiller that he send word. I have also written him that he should do so, but if you will urge him he will make greater efforts since there is nothing we can do without word from him.

The members of the Hutterian community, among us have already sold their land, but do not know how they may leave. If we receive the letter from America they will most likely travel with us to America if they can be together, can serve God there, and can hold their land in common. The Russian law remains as it was, and there is still no change, because it has only now been presented to the Emperor. And three delegates have again gone to meet him to find out something definite. I believe the emigration will not be large because faith is weak. However, I trust that I may be able to come along with several families, if it is God's will and my health holds up. Those who reside on crown lands are the worst off of all since they cannot sell until three years have elapsed, and without selling they have no means for travel, and without such means it is impossible to come to America. But I trust that the Lord will lead everything according to His purposes and for the best, as he has brief letter . . . Give greeting to Isaac and Golldemann and Sommerfeld.

I remain, your brother,
Paul Tschetter

It is recorded in J. J. Mendel's, "History of the People of East Freeman, Silver Lake, and West Freeman," and in the "Mennonite Encyclopedia" that Andreas Wallman left the Hutterite group of Russia and joined the Mennonites of Chortitza—a Low German group. Here he married Katharina Lepp. He worked for Peter Lepp (possibly her father), a well known industrialist, and later became a shareholder in the factories in Cortitza and Alexandrovsk. Andreas's son became a manager of the Cortitza factory, which became known as Lepp and Wollman factories. Andreas was a brother to Franz Wallman No. 431 on the Hammonia which came to America in 1874. An ad is shown advertising their machinery.

Josua Wollman

He was born in South Russia on January 12, 1840 to Mathias and Rebecca (Pollman) Wollman. His brother Michael Wollman "Motzela" came to America on the ship Mosel (No. 365).

Josua, as learned from descendents, owned a flour mill in Russia and was very wealthy at the time of the migration; therefore he chose not to come to this country. He also never married. Little else is known of his later years.

Chapter 4

Ship List—Colony Census (1880)

A Listing of Hutterites Who Came to America

Compiled From Ship Records Obtained From:

National Archives and Records

8th and Pennsylvania Ave. N.W.

Washington, D.C.

Compiled by
Arnold M. Hofer, Dolton, S.D. 57023

The desire to compile a list of all Hutterites who came to America was first dreamed when I was told that there is still available a census that Michael Hofer (uberschultz) had made in 1872 in Russia. Since this didn't cover all Hutterite dorfs this was inadequate.

The first real hope for such a task came when I learned that a certain Mr. Jacob A. Duerksen of Washington, D.C., was compiling a list of ships that carried Mennonite and/or Hutterite immigrants to America. Available from the Archives were micro-film copies of the passengers that these ships carried, listed by families, giving the ages, occupation, country of origin and class of travel.

The next step was to find all the ships that carried these people. Mr. Duerksen had already found a number of such ships and was very helpful in a future search as well as helping me get photo-copies of the passenger lists from the micro-films. It was through a search of old obituaries, visits with old people, etc., and the untiring efforts of Mr. Duerksen who spent many hours in this behalf, that I am now fairly certain that I have located all the ships and have compiled a list that is as complete as possible from the records available.

All Hutterite men are listed as farmers except a few unmarried listed as laborers. All gave their country of origin as Russia with the exception of the Lawrence Tschetter who had been a delegate in 1873. He gave his country of origin as U.S.A. This certainly is an error and stems from his previous visit.

All passengers traveled as "Between Deck" (second class) or "Steerage" (third class). In all cases they traveled the most economical class offered by that particular ship. Among Low-German Mennonites one notices that occasionally some traveled more luxuriously. In this centennial publication, a photo copy of an advertisement of a steamship line gives one a good idea of the cost of ocean travel.

These lists are a very good source of general information, but one must accept details with some reservation. Some allowance must be made for the usual errors, oversight, carelessness, and difficulties because of language differences between the recorder and the passenger. Also, there must have been an effort on the part of some to cut the costs of fare. The number of children below age one versus two and three year olds bears this out. Below age one travel was at greatly reduced rates.

Orphans that came along with another family were listed on the ships as part of the family they came with, even using the same surname. I discovered a few cases where children have the wrong name. Ages given also are not always correct. Sometimes an older child accompanied relatives ahead of his family. Some of these instances I discovered but probably not all. Stories, still existing, relate that those with infected eyes couldn't pass medical inspection and had to accompany later groups when this cleared up. I can't point out any instance of this. The story of the individual who is supposed to have come as a stow away, this list proves false because he is listed as a passenger.

An indentification of individuals is given in many cases. Sometimes only one or two members of a family are pointed out even though others are known, because this was thought sufficient to "place" the family. As often as possible, ministers and doctors were used for these purposes as they are usually well known. "Rut schield" who is used a lot, was Michael Hofer, who attained the age of 103 years, the oldest man among Hutterite people. "Uberschultz" was another Michael Hofer who is so called because he was over the "Schultz's" or mayors of the dorfs. He was the father of Rev. D. M. Hofer who in 1923 visited our dorfs in Russia. You will find an account of his visit in this publication. John Hofer No. 34 is also used for identifying purposes. Because he was not a prominent man, I need to explain that he was my paternal grandfather. His three brothers joined Wolf Creek Colony, so for most prairie Hutterites there were no well known people to whom I could attach certain people in this relationship. Numbers after the name stem from the house number they had in Russia.

Some people among Hutterites are best identified by some name that is a dirivitive of their real name. The many Josephs are differentiated by names such as Yussepel, Yos, Chew or Sep. The Jacobs may be known as one of the following: Yocobel, Yoppela, Yop, Chek or Checkela. The list for John is the longest, namely, Yahone, Yahonella, Hons, Honsel, Hannas, Hansella, Chandel and Chavan. These many dirivitives make possible many combinations for identifying purposes. Three different Jacobs, each with a father named John, are commonly referred to as Hons Yȯkob, Hannas Chek and Yahonella Chek. Some system like this becomes necessary when an ethnic group limits itself to a few names.

In identifying individuals, all nicknames that I felt were offensive were omitted. The ones used are in very common use by the people, and I trust that no one will be offended. My apologies if my judgement is wrong.

Of this list of 1254 persons, approximately 40 never made it to South Dakota. This is mostly due to the 36 children who died in Lincoln, Nebraska. About 800 settled in private ownership and more than 400 in communal ownership in Bruderhofs. As of this writing, June 1, 1974, only one of these 1254 persons is still alive. She is Mrs. John (Maria) J. Kleinsasser, Freeman, daughter of passenger No. 393 on the Mosel.

I am certain that there is no other ship that brought any sizeable group of Hutterites. It may be that a few individuals came with Mennonites on some other ship. Mrs. Helena Wipf, age about 75, is definitely not located even though she came to South Dakota. According to 1880 government census, there may be a few more, but the total would be less than a dozen.

Recognition must be given to Elenora Wipf of Huron, S.D., for the help she has been in identifying many of these passengers. Also John A. Mendel of Marion, S.D., was of great help as long as his health permitted. Andrew Wurz of the Hutterville Colony, Magrath, Alberta, also worked on the 1877 passenger list, identifying those that founded the Elm Spring Colony. I appreciate this help very much as well as many others who gave me snatches of information. Then without the services of Jacob A. Duerksen this project would not have been possible. His acquaintance with the archives, his interest in records as complete as possible, his willingness to spend countless hours searching for more ships and names, and for the much correspondence he was willing to carry on with me—all this gratis—makes it impossible for me to properly recognize such a contribution.

May this effort, which I enjoyed, in some ways serve a useful purpose. For those with interest in family trees, this may serve to some advantage. It may be of interest to many to know that there still exists a record of the births, deaths, baptisms and marriages of Hutterites from 1757 to the time of the migration.

One of the earliest groups of Russian Mennonite immigrants sailed on the *Hammonia* (above), arriving in New York on August 15, 1873. After a stay in Elkhart, Indiana, some of them arrived in Yankton on October 18, 1873, as the first Mennonite settlers in Dakota Territory. This was the Daniel Unruh group. This is the same ship that brought the first group of Hutterites in 1874.

German French

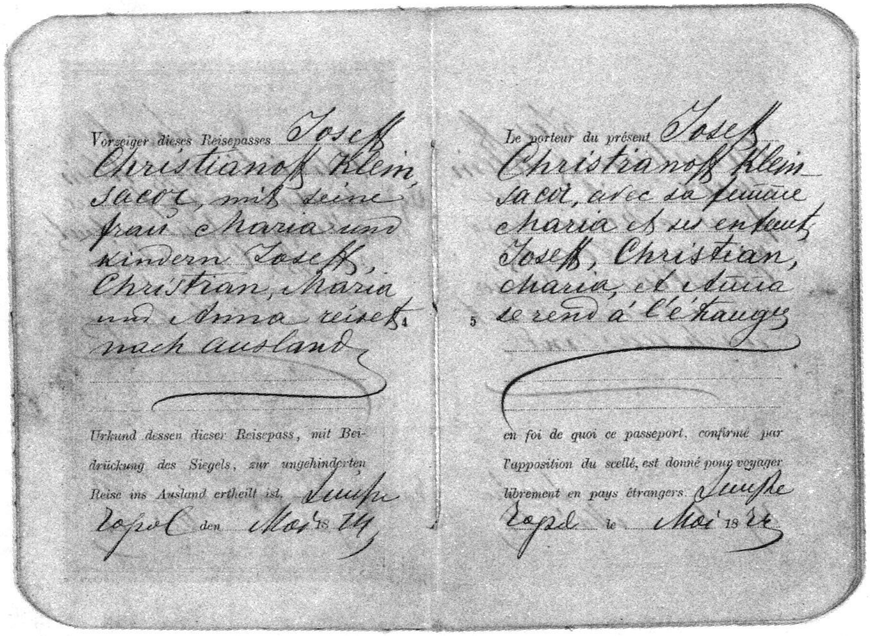

The Passport was written in three languages, German, French and Russian. This Passport was for Joseph C. Kleinsasser and his family Passage Number 294 on the ship Hammonia.

Russian

PASSENGERS ON THE HAMMONIA
Left Hamburg, Havre
Arrived in New York June 17, 1874

The Hammonia brought the first as well as the largest group of Hutterites to America—382 souls. The passenger list shows 767 passengers. About 150 were Low German Mennonites. The ocean voyage began at Hamburg, Germany. Next was a stop at LeHavre, France, before sailing for New York.

This group, commonly known as ''Kutschaber'' because their dorf in Russia was also known as Kutchewa, came from the dorfs known as Hutterdorf and Scheromet. Among this group were Michael Waldner and his followers, the founders of Bon Homme Colony and Darius Walter and his followers, the founders of Wolf Creek Colony as well as 35 to 40 families who settled in private ownership on the present site of Freeman and the area south and west of Freeman. This group led by Rev. William Tschetter and Rev. David Waldner formed the Hutterdorf church southwest of Freeman.

From New York this group traveled to Lincoln, Nebraska, with intentions to settle there. Not finding the area to their liking and after dysentary claimed the lives of 36 of their children as well as the aged Darius Stahl, delegates were sent to South Dakota to look for a more suitable location.

While the intentions of the followers of Darius Walter and of Michael Waldner were to reconcile their differences and form one ''Bruderhof'' they again proceeded to part ways with the Michael Waldner group founding Bon Homme Colony about 20 miles west of Yankton and the Darius Walter group founding Wolf Creek Colony about nine miles west of Freeman. In Bon Homme, some original buildings are still in use today while at Wolf Creek only the shell of some can still be seen.

For a better description of the migration of this group read pages 127-130 in *Banished for Faith* by Emil J. Waltner.

* Means writing is not clear on the original ship list.

20	Jacob Waldner	23	Passenger Nos. 20-25 ,93-94 and 141-145 are listed among the Low German passengers on this ship. They may or may not be Hutters. They cannot be identified
	Catherine	30	
	Agnetha Friesen	14	
	Gerhard Friesen	9	
	Claas Friesen	17	
	Anna Waldner	6 months	
93	Michael Wurz	21	
	Barba (wife)	20	

No.	Name	Age	Remarks
141	Jacob Walter	39	
	Cath (wife)	29	(Stahl)
	Elise	9	From first wife
	Cath	8	From first wife
	Sara	4	From second wife
287	Christ Kleinsasser	52	Father of Joseph Kleinsasser, (No. 294)
	Elizabeth (child)	27	
	Sara (child)	22	
290	Peter Kleinsasser	26	Parents of Mrs. Printer J. J.Mendel, first marriage
	Marie	23	
	Anna	11 mo.	
	Peter	1 mo.	
294	Joseph Kleinsasser	32	Parents of bachelor Peter J Kleinsasser of Freeman
	Marie	32	
	Jos	9	
	Chr.	6	
	Marie	8	Mrs. Rev. Paul F. Gross
299	David Walter	23	Father of Mrs. Sam J. Hofer, Huron known as Dabela
	Anna	20	
301	Wilh. Tschetter	44	Minister, Hutterdorf Church
	Elizabeth	41	(Waldner)
303	George	21	Father of George G. Tschetter
304	Catherine	20	(Kleinsasser) Daughter of # 287
	Anna	18	Mrs. George "Greysold" Gross
	Paul	15	Father of Rev. P.P. Tschetter
	Rebecca	9	
	Susanna	8	Mrs. Joseph Kleinsasser, Freeman, SD
	Catherine	7	Mrs. Peter H. Unruh
	John	5	Father of Banker Tschetter
	Jacob	11 months	Father of Ernest Tschetter
	Elizabeth	11 months	
313	Frid. Waldner	38	In Colony, Tripp, SD. (1880 Census)
	Cathrine	37	(Kleinsasser) Sister to #573
	Jos.	15	
	Anna	9	
	Frid.	8	
	Joh	7	
	Jacob	4	
	Cath.	10 months	
	Susanna	10 months	
322	Jos. Walter	29	Wolf Creek. Twp. (1880 Census). Parents of Paul Jos. Walter, Carpenter, SD.
	Sarah	28	(Stahl)
	Joseph	9	Father of Mrs. J. J. Miller, Bancroft, S.D.
	Anna	6	
	Jacob	3	
327	Elias Kleinsasser	48	Lived in Wolf Creek Twp. (1880 Census)
	Susanna	50	(Hofer)
	Hich *	20	Heinrich & Rachel are married m-10-22-1872
	Rachel	19	(Kleinsasser) Daughter in law
	Jacob	18	Bon Homme Colony
	Paul	9	Father of Mrs. John A. Mendel, Marion, SD
	Math	7	Rev. Math. Kleinsasser, Ebenezer Church
334	David Hofer (boy)	14	"Bofa David"
335	Michael Wurz	52	Lived west of Freeman, SD
	Esther	53	(Wollman)
	Chr.	21	Father of Mike C. Wurtz, Langham,. Sask
	Esther	16	
	Barba	13	
340	Andr. Wurz	29	Bon Homme, Later at Milltown
	Susanne	26	
	Susanne	4	
	Barba	10 mo.	
343	Jacob Wurz	22	Bon Homme, died young Son of #335
	Anna	21	(Decker) "Langsanna Anna"
346	George Waldner	52	"Kammer Jerg"
	Cath	50	(Miller)
	Andr.	19	Father of "Slim" Waldner, Freeman, SD
	David	17	
	Christ *	14	
	Cath	9	
352	Joseph Waldner	32	
	Susanne	24	
	Jacob	10 mo.	
355	George Waldner	22	Langham, Saskatchewan area
	Cathe	19	(Wurtz) Daughter of # 335
	Mich	4 mo.	

No.	Name	Age	Notes
358	Paul Wollman	62	Bon Homme
	Justine	50	
	Paul	18	
361	Zacharias Walmann	26	Bon Homme, miller
	Susanne	28	
	Zacharias	7	
	Jacob	4	
	Cathe	7 mo.	
366	Johann Stahl	55	
	Cath	47	
	Susanne	20	
	Joh	9	
	Cath	21	
	Marie	8 mo.	
372	Michael Tschetter	44	
373	Paul Tschetter	42	
374	Jacob Tschetter	21	
375	Marie Tschetter	23	Single
376	Moses Stahl	61	Lived near Freeman
	Marie	51	(Walter)
	Paul	24	Grandfather of Cal Stahl, Seattle, WA
	Cath	20	(Wipf) Grandmother of Cal Stahl
	Marie	9	Mrs. Jaocb Hofer, Standoff, Alberta
381	Joh Hofer	30	Minister at Hutterdorf Church
	Susanne	29	(Stahl), daughter of Moses, #376
	Joh	8	Deaf and dumb
384	David Waldner	31	Moved to Canada. Was a brother to Mrs. Rev. Wm. Tschetter
	Cath	32	
	David	9	
	Cath	4	Died Lincoln, Nebr.
	Susanne	11 mo.	Died Lincoln, Nebr.
389	Joh Hofer	65	"Dratzel Johannes" Wolf Creek colony
	Susanne	62	(Walter) made spinning wheels
391	Joh Hofer	27	Son of #389 above
	Susanne	26	(Stahl) daughter of Christian Stahl & Justina Wollman
	Cath	6	
	Marie	8 mo.	
	Susanne	8 mo.	Mrs. Lawrence Tschetter, Olivet, SD
396	Samuel Wipf	30	
	Marie	28	
398	Elias Wipf	22	Minister at Hutterdorf, Parents of Jacob E. Wipf west of Freeman, SD
	Marie	18	
400	John Stahl	57	
	Esther	52	(Walter)
402	Joh Wipf (boy)	6	
403	Joh Stahl	36	Colony, Tripp, SD. Son of Darius #637
	Cath	36	(Hofer) daughter of # 389 Hammonia.
	Joh	11 mo.	
	Cath	1 mo.	
407	George Wipf(boy)	9	
408	David Hofer	36	Brother to Rev. John Hofer, Hutterdorf Church
	Anna	36	(Waldner)
	Anna	18	Mrs. Andreas Kleinsasser
	Georg	9	Father of Mrs. Rev. Joe E. Wipf, Huron
	Joh	8	Father of Mrs. Joe M. Walter, Freeman
	Joseph	7	"Goskala"Father of "Elevator Joe", Freeman
	Peter	4	Died Lincoln, Nebr.
	Marie	8 mo.	
416	George Wipf	18	Bro to Rev. Elias Wipf, Hutterdorf
417	Jacob Walther	27	"Gritt Jacob"
	Cath	28	
419	Hich * Walther	23	"Gritt Henrich"
	Marg	20	(Knels)
	Joh	4 mo.	
	Jacob	4 mo.	
423	Zacharias Wipf	38	Lived near Freeman
	Marie	40	(Miller)
	Zacharias	13	Father of Zack Z. Wipf, Freeman
	Joh	6	
	Elias	3	
	Anna	8	Mother of Math. Kleinsasser, Freeman
	Susanne	9	
	Cath	9	

No.	Name	Age	Notes
431	Franz Wollman	49	Settled north of Wolf Creek, moved to Huron area
	Sarah	47	
	Andreas	23	
	Cath	22	
	Joseph	20	
	Franz	14	Visited uncle in Russia, Disappeared in New York in 1884
	Paul	9	
438	Jacob Hofer	41	Minister, Bon Homme Colony
	Rebecca	38	(Pullman)
	Jacob	14	
	Joh	9	
	Jos	8	
	Michael	7	
	Zacharias	6	
	Samuel	4	
	Peter	4	
447	Marie Hofer (single)	17	In 1880 Census the above minister Jacob Hofer has a daughter, age 23, This is she most likely
448	Jacob Waldner	35	Teacher, Bon Homme Colony
	Susanne	33	
	Michael	14	
451	George Wipf	31	"Zonder Yerg" Both Mr. and Mrs. Wipf
	Anna	32	died of Carbon Monoside gas, Freeman
	Anna	8	Mrs. David L. Tschetter, Bridgewater
	Sarah	11 mo.	
	Geo	1 mo.	
456	Samuel Wipf	15	
457	Sam Kleinsasser	60	Bon Homme, Died in Pennsylvania Basket maker
	Sara	48	
	Cath	18	
	Eliz	9	
	Marie	8	
	Joseph	4	
463	Lorenz Stahl	56	Bon Homme Colony
	Susanne	47	
	Johann	20	
	Marie	15	
	Susanne	9	
	Rebecca	8	
	Jos.	8	
470	Joseph Waldner	28	Bon Homme Colony, Tinsmith
	Annie	28	
	Joseph	7	
	Joh	5	
	Marie	3	
	Fried.	11 mo.	
	David	1 mo.	
477	Joseph Wipf	23	Brother to Rev. John L. Wipf, Colony Tripp, SD. 1880 Census
	Cath	20	
	Cath	3	
	Joseph	11 mo.	
	Marie	1 mo.	
482	Michael Waldner	25	
	Helene	23	(Does not say "wife.")
	Jacob	2 mo.	
485	Michael Wurz	29	Bon Homme Colony
	Reichel	29	Lived to be 97 years old.
	Rachel	9	
	Susanne	7	
	Sara	11 mo.	
	Cath	1 mo.	
491	David Hofer	31	Bon Homme Colony
	Susanne	27	
	David	8	
	Samuel	4	
	Sara	5	
496	Michel Waldner	38	Colony, Tripp, SD (1880 Census)
	Sara	24	
	Michael	15	
	Sara	17	
	Joh	9	
	Zacharias	8	
	Jacob	6	
	Sarah	4	
	Eliz	10 mo.	
	Rachel	10 mo.	
506	Paul Gross (boy)	9	Rev. Paul F. Gross. N. Dakota.
507	Tobias Walter	58	Colony, Tripp, SD. 1880 Census
	Sara	56	(Stahl)

No.	Name	Age	Notes
	Tobias	9	
	Cath	8	
511	Math Waldner	26	Colony, Tripp, S.D. 1880 Census
	Sara	30	
	Joseph	5	
	Elizabeth	3	
515	Christ Stahl	52	Bon Homme Colony
517	Justina	59	(Passenger #516 is void)
	Rebecca	19	
	Marg.	15	
520	Justine Stahl	28	Bon Homme (in 1875 records)
	Anna	8	
	Justine	4	
	Christ	11 mo.	
	Daniel	1 mo.	
525	Peter Janzen	19	Tripp, SD Colony (1880 census)
526	Sara Janzen(single)	20	
527	Johann Decker	41	Bon Homme
	Susanne	38	
	Cath	20	
	Marie	15	
	Johann	17	
	Jacob	9	
	Barba	8	
	Susanna	4	
	Anne	4	
	David	9 mo.	
537	Jacob Knels	28	Bon Homme
	Sarah	27	
	Jacob	3	
	David	8 mo.	
541	Susanne Knels	58	Bon Homme. Both listed as widows; daughter, disabled
	Susanne	35	
543	Jacob Hofer	31	Bon Homme
	Anna	30	(Stahl)
	Jacob	9	
	Susanne	8	
	David	3	"Miller David" Had furniture store in

No.	Name	Age	Notes
	Joseph	8 mo.	Bridgewater
549	Andr Gross	22	Molan Twp. In 1880, wife Rebecca
	Wilh Gross	18	Wolf Creek Colony, wife Anna (1880)
	Fried* Gross	16	Wolf Creek Colony, wife Maria (1880)
	Marie Gross(single)	13	These are siblings of Rev. Paul F. Gross
553	Joseph Waldner	57	Bon Homme Colony
	Marg	53	
	Eliz.	20	
	Joseph	18	
	Jacob	13	
	Marg	9	
559	Sam Kleinsasser	36	Bon Homme
	Susanne	33	
	Susanne	14	
	Marie	9	
	Samuel	8	
	Joseph	7	
	Andr	6	
	Joh	4	
	Sara	4 mo.	
568	Darius Walter	63	Wolf Creek Colony
	Cath	57	
	Barba	17	
	Marie	14	
572	Darius Walter	39	Minister, Wolf Creek Colony
	Susanne	39	1880 Census list wife as Anna
574	Jacob Walter	34	Brother to minister Darius Walter
	Cath	32	In 1880, wife listed as "Maria, second wife," Wolf Creek Colony
	Elias	9	
	Darius	6	
	Jacob	11 mo.	
	Mich or Hich*	1 mo.	
580	Elias Walter	25	Wolf Creek Colony
	Susanne	23	
	Elias	3 mo.	
	Susanne	3 mo.	
584	Georg Hofer	58	Minister, Wolf Creek Colony, father of Rev. John Hofer of Hutterdorf
	Barb	32	(Wurz, second wife)
	George	9	

	Peter	11 mo.	
	Cath	6	
	Marie	1 mo.	
591	Jacob Hofer	32	Wolf Creek Colony,son of George above
	Elizabeth	30*	
	Jacob	9	
	Elizabeth	5	
	Susanne	10 mo.	
	Sara	10 mo.	Died in Lincoln, Nebraska
596	Josef Hofer	21	
	Anna	21	
	Sara	11 mo.	
599	Josua Hofer	19	Wolf Creek Colony
600	Anna Hofer(single)	19	
601	Hich* Stahl	60	
	Barb	55	(Kleinsasser)
	Barb	9	
			Son of #601 above
604	Hich* Stahl	25	Wolf Creek Colony listed as school teacher in 1880- census
	Marie	25	
	Hich*	4 mo.	
607	Daniel Wallman	39	Wolf Creek Colony, both died at Spring Creek Colony, Montana
	Susanna	44	
	Daniel	14	
	Jacob	11 mo.	
611	Paul Hofer	40	Wolf Creek "Tonkey Paul"
	Sara	32	(Walter) daughter of #572 above
	Sara	9	
	Cath	6	
	Paul	3	
616	Jacob Hofer	50	Bon Homme
	Anna	59	(Kleinsasser) Her 1st marriage to ______ Walter
	Barba	19	
619	David Hofer	21	Bon Homme, shoemaker
	Sara	20	
621	Josef Hofer	35	Lived near Olivet, "Yos"
	Anna	36	(Walter)
	David	15	Grandfather of Jake Hofer, Sioux Falls

	Josef	9	"Yos Yusep" father of Joe H. Hofer
	Jacob	8	Rev. Jacob J. Hofer, Salem & Ebenezer churches
	Peter	7	Killed by lightning in 1887
	Paul	3	"Yos Paul" Olivet
	Anna	10 mo.	
	Darius	10 mo.	Died as a young child
630	Zacharias Walter	57	Wolf Creek Colony
	Marg	53	
	Joh	29	
	Marg.	19	
	Marie	9	Died Wolf Creek, Raymond, Alberta
	Anna	8	
636	Cath Walter	39	Wolf Creek Colony, sister in law to Daniel Wollman #607
637	J. Darius (Stahl	80	Stahl, Died in Lincoln, Nebraska before migrating to South Dakota
638	Jacob Stahl	27	Wolf Creek Colony, son of Moses #376
	Susanna	26	Hofer, daughter of Rev. George #584
	Jacob	4	
	Paul	11 mo.	
	Joh	1 mo.	
643	Martin Stahl	40	Colony, Tripp, SD
	Esther	49	Stahl, her second marriage
	Sarah	19	Mrs. Rev. Paul Walter
	Anna	16	Mrs. Wilhelm Gross
	Joh	17	He married widow of Johann Tschetter
	Cath	15	Mrs. Rev. Mike Waldner, Bon Homme
	Marie	9	
	Susanne	8	
	Marg.	6	Mrs. Joseph Stahl
	Rebecca	4	
653	Hech* Walter	74	Wolf Creek Colony, brother to #572
654	Paul Walter	19	Rev Walter
655	Esther Stahl	84	Mother of Benjamin & Moses Stahl
656	Sara Stahl	55	Mrs. Mathias Kleinsasser

PASSENGERS ON THE SUEVIA
Left Hamburg, Havre
Arrived in New York November 6, 1874

This group originated from Neu Hutterthal village also known as Dabritscha. They arrived at Elkhart, Indiana, and spent the winter there. In the spring of 1875, they proceeded to South Dakota. In this group was Rev. Paul Tschetter who had been one of the delegates looking for a suitable location in 1873. According to his diary, he had decided on the Red River Valley in North Dakota. Now in 1875, he followed those who had come earlier to South Dakota. These five families settled along the Wolf Creek, 12 miles southwest of Bridgewater, all within the span of about one mile. The Neu Hutterthal Church was later built in the middle of this group on the land of Rev. Paul Tschetter. Thirty-two passengers identified as Hutterites are listed.

No.	Name	Age	Remarks
26	Hoffer, Josua	37	Brother of Michael R., Rutschield
	Susanne	34	(Tschetter) daughter of delegate Lawrence
	Josua	9	Father of John Joshua, Emery
	Johann	6	
	Jos	5	Yale, S.D., known as "Shapkela"
	Paul	7 mo.	
	Hanna	9	
33	Tschetter, Paul	32	Rev., delegate, founder of Neu Hutterthal Church
	Marie	31	(Walter)
	Susanne	9	
	Paul	8	Known as "Big Paul"
	Marie	4	
	Barba	2	
	Jacob	11 mo.	Father of Emil Tschetter, Emery
40	Tschetter, Lorenz	14	These are sons of Lawrence Tschetter, the delegate. Homesteaded east of Olivet.
41	Tschetter, Paul	16	
42	Tschetter, Joseph	37	Brother of delegate Rev. Paul
	Marie	37	(Wipf)
	Jacob	17	"Dika Chek" land agent, Bridgewater
	Paul	14	"Sep Paula," grain buyer, Bridgewater
46	Hoffer, Josef	30	Brother to Michael R., Rutschield
	Susanne	28	(Tschetter), sister to delegate Paul
	Joseph	8	Father of Rev. Eil L., St. Paul
	Susanne	6	
	Anna	4	
	Jacob	11 mo.	"Yokka," lived near Onida
	Anna	11 mo.	
53	Gross, Georg	20	Father of Mrs. E. M. Wipf
54	Gross, Wilh	15	Foster father of Mrs. Maria Schultz, Freeman
55	Tschetter, Jacob	32	Brother to delegate Paul
	Marie	21	
	Jacob	4 mo.	Rev., missionary to N. Caroline, known as M.

It may be of interest to add here that passenger number 51, Jacob Hofer, was kidnapped by gypsies in New York. However, it was discovered in time, they were pursued and he was rescued.

PASSENGERS ON THE STATE OF NEVADA

Left Antwerp, Belgium

Arrived in New York on August 5, 1875

This is another error on ship lists. This family has been identified as the Elias Wipf family. Mrs. Wipf was a Cornelson. They went directly to Kansas and lived in the Inman, Kansas, area. The name Wipf was commonly written as Wipp before coming to America. However, Elias being listed as Eliz and as a female is the error. They are being listed among this list of Hutterites because of his heritage even though they identified with Low-German Mennonites. He has three brothers who came to South Dakota—George No. 451 in 1874, Alex No. 330 in 1877 and David No. 79 in 1879. The mother Helena also came to America and to South Dakota, but has not as yet been located or identified. In the 1880 census she was living with son David. Her age was listed as 79.

Name	Age
Wipp, Eliz. (female)	45
Agatha (female)	43
Anna (female)	16
Maria (female)	14
Cath (female)	1

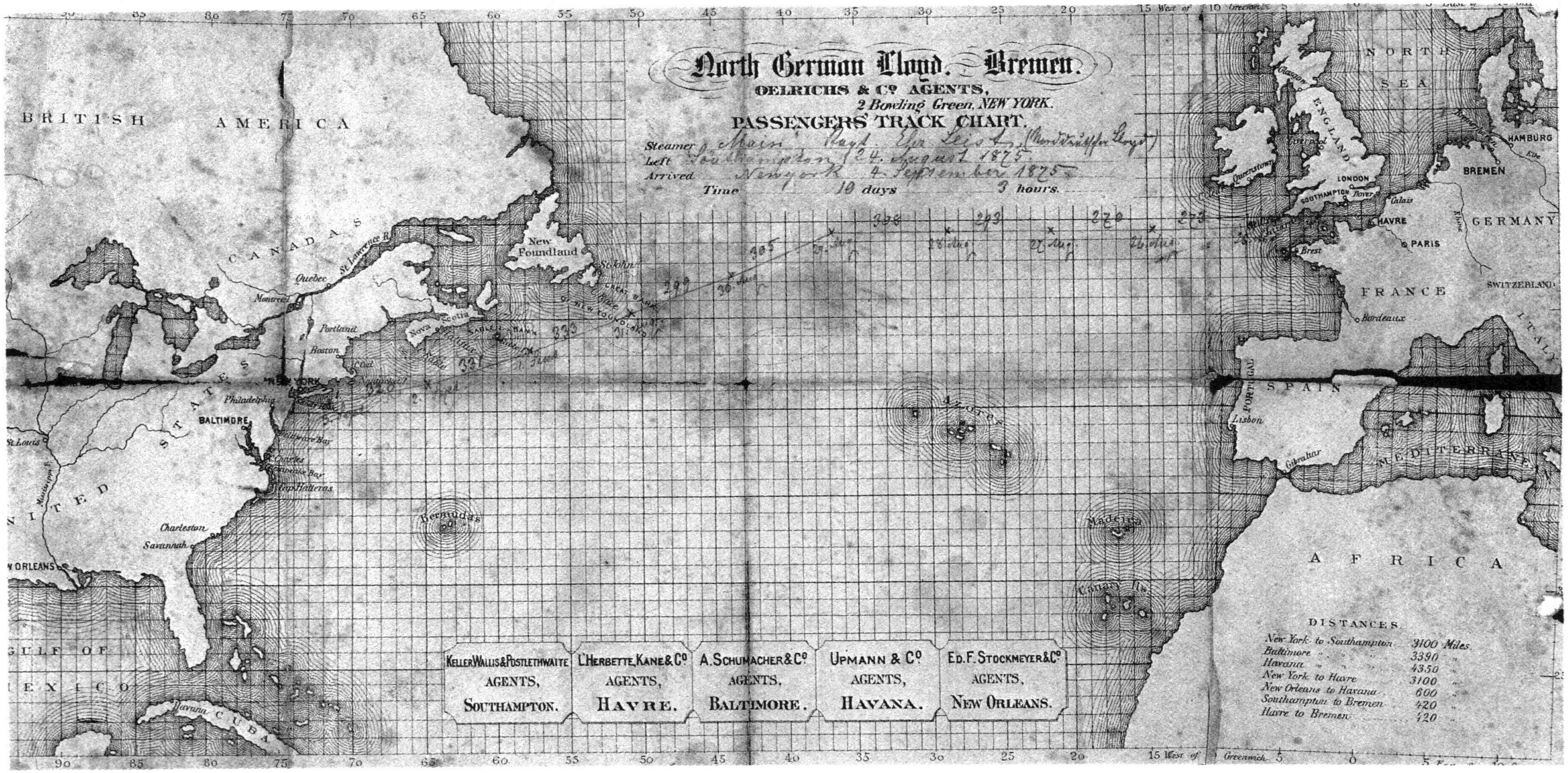
North German Lloyd. Bremen.
OELRICHS & Co. AGENTS,
2 Bowling Green, NEW YORK.
PASSENGERS' TRACK CHART.
Steamer
Left
Arrived
Time 10 days 3 hours.
BRITISH AMERICA
CANADAS
UNITED STATES
New Foundland
St. John
Nova Scotia
Quebec
Montreal
St. Lawrence R.
Portland
Boston
NEW YORK
Philadelphia
BALTIMORE
St. Louis
Charleston
Savannah
N. ORLEANS
GULF OF MEXICO
CUBA
Havana
Bermudas
Azores
Madeira
Canary Is.
NORTH SEA
ENGLAND
LONDON
SOUTHAMPTON
Queenstown
BREMEN
HAMBURG
GERMANY
HAVRE
PARIS
Brest
FRANCE
Bordeaux
SWITZERLAND
PORTUGAL
Lisbon
SPAIN
Gibraltar
MEDITERRANEAN
AFRICA
KELLER WALLIS & POSTLETHWAITE AGENTS, SOUTHAMPTON.
L'HERBETTE, KANE & Co. AGENTS, HAVRE.
A. SCHUMACHER & Co. AGENTS, BALTIMORE.
UPMANN & Co. AGENTS, HAVANA.
ED. F. STOCKMEYER & Co. AGENTS, NEW ORLEANS.
DISTANCES.
New York to Southampton 3100 Miles.
Baltimore 3390
Havana 4350
New York to Havre 3100
New Orleans to Havana 600
Southampton to Bremen 420
Havre to Bremen 420

PASSENGERS ON THE MAIN
Left Bremen, Southampton
Arrived in New York on September 4, 1875

These were the remaining families of Neu Hutterthal also known as Dabritscha. Consequently, these people were often referred to as the "Dabrishers."

Aside from a few who joined the colony, these settled mostly near the Wolf Creek next to the Rev. Paul Tschetter group and along the Jim River north of Olivet. It is of interest that there is still in the late D. J. Mendel family a log of this trip. On a map the route is penciled showing the miles traveled daily as well as the position each day. It is a track chart of the North German Lloyd Line giving the travel time from South Hampton to New York as ten days, three hours and the distance as 3100 miles. Capt. Ehr. Leist.

Listed here are 122 Hutterites including those born on the voyage.

No.	Name	Age	Remarks
176	Wipf, Joseph	40	Minister at Neu Hutterthal Church
	Maria	36	(Glanzer)
	Susanne	16	
	David	9	Minister Neu Hutterthal
	Joseph	7	
	Elias	6	Minister, Hutterthal Church, Carpenter
182	Hofer, Andreas	26	Bro. to Michael R., Rutschield
	Anna	26	(Hofer)
	Susanne	6	Mother of Banker J. J. Tschetter
	Joseph	4	Joe A. Lived near Wolf Creek (ditscha fritz)
	Anna	11 mo.	
187	Walter, Franz	28	
	Rebecca	25	(Hofer)
	Anna	5	Married Jacob A. Wollman
	Joseph	11 mo.	Joe F. Walter, Bridgewater
191	Walter, Isaac	25	Father of Rev. Jacob I. Walter, Bridgewater
	Anna	22	(Gross)
	Joseph	11 mo.	Father of undertaker Mike Walter, Freeman.
194	Tschetter, Anna	30	Her husband John died in Bremen, Germany on way to America. He was a son of delegate Lawrence.
	Johann	8	
	Paul	6	
	Lorenz	4	This family joined Wolf Creek Colony
	Jacob	11 mo.	
	Born, Aug. 24, a boy		Born on ship
199	Walter, Paul	30	Known as "Stunna Paul"
	Justina	26	(Wollman.) They had no children.
201	Walter, Rebecca	20	Should be Wollman, blind
202	Walter, Elias	13	Father of Joe M. Walter, Freeman
203	Hofer, Christian	73	Wolf Creek Colony. Grandfather of John Hofer No. 34
204	Tschetter, David	35	Brother to delegate Paul. "Schneidela"
	Marie	33	(Hofer), sister to Michael Hofer No. 28
	David	9	Lived in Huron area
	Barbara	8	
	Anna	6	
	Maria	4	
	Jacob	2	Father of Joe H. Tschetter, Emery
	Sara	11 mo.	Mother of Joe D. S. Glanzer
212	Tschetter, Jacob	59	Father of delegate Paul
	Barbara	56	(Kleinsasser)
	Barbara	16	Rev. Johann Vetter, minister at Salem, Bethel
	Johann	14	
	Paul	8	A nephew Paul Hofer, brother to John Hofer No. 34
217	Tschetter, Jacob	32	Son of delegate Lawrence, "Pfoff"
	Catherine	30	(Decker)
	Anna	8	
	Susanna	6	
	Sara	4	
	Jacob	11 mo.	Accidently shot about 1897
223	Mendel, Jacob	25	Son of Anna Mendel, below
	Sara	22	(Tschetter) daughter of delegate Lawrence
	Jacob	11 mo.	J. J. Mendel, printer
226	Mendel, Anna	47	(Hofer) grandmother of printer Mendel
	Anna	19	Mrs. Jacob Tschetter, Businessman, Bridgewater
	Margr	17	Grandmother of David P. Gross, Freeman
	Elizabeth	15	Mrs. David M. Wollman
	Susanna	9	Mrs. Rev. Johann Tschetter
	Catherine	4	Mrs. Mike M. Hofer, Bridgewater
	David	6	D. J. Mendel, Freeman

No.	Name	Age	Notes
233	Tschetter, Johann	45	Tschetter Hannas
	Rebecca	43	(Hofer)
	Anna	15	
	Johann	9	Colony, Darius leit
	Catherine	8	
	Paul	7	Minister, Neu Hutterthal "Hannas Paul"
	Peter	4	"Hannas Peter" Bridgewater
	Maria	11 mo.	
241	Tschetter, Johann	18	John Hofer No. 34, my grandfather a nephew of No. 233 above
242	Hofer, David	36	Bro. to Michael R. Hofer, Rutschield
	Catherine	32	(Waldner)
	David	8	"Bingo"
	Catherine	4	
	Joseph	11 mo.	Father of Dr. Ernest Hofer
247	Decker, Johann	31	Settled along Jim River near Milltown
	Catharine	26	(Wollman)
	Paul	9	Bro. to above Johann, school teacher, moved to Canada
	Johann	6	Beadle County
	Samuel	4	Farmer, trucker, near Milltown
	Born Aug. 25, a girl		Mrs. Rev. J. M. Tschetter, N. Carolina missionary. Born on ship
252	Tschetter, Lorenz	56	Delegate, uncle to delegate Paul
	Anna	50	(Hofer)
	Jacob	9	Nephew of No. 233 and 252, a brother to John Hofer No. 34, passenger No. 241
	David	7	Lived southwest of Bridgewater
	Sara	3	(Not their daughter)
257	Waldner, Johann	30	Bro. to Peter Waldner M.S.
	Susanne	28	(Wipf)
	Jacob (farmer)	18	Probably his brother, father to John S., Huron.
	Susanna	9	
	Anna	7	
	Johann	5	
	Jacob	3	
	Marie	11 mo.	
	Born, Aug. 29, a boy		Born on ship
265	Walter, Michael	28	Tripp Colony, 1880
	Maria	27	
	Anna	7	
	Marie	4	
	Michael	11 mo.	
270	Gross, Georg	46	Bro. to Wilhelm Gross. (Two of their boys came in '74)
	Marie	37	(Wollman)
	Catharina	18	
	Joseph	9	
	Anna	6	Wolf Creek Colony
	Jacob	4	Canada
	Andreas	11 mo.	
277	Wallman, Joseph	38	Grandfather of Paul P. Wollman
	Catherina	36	(Stahl)
	Elizabeth	20	A niece
	Catharine	9	
	Susanne	7	
	Paul	3	
	Jacob (farmer)	17	
284	Wallmann, Jacob	38	Father of Mrs. Sam P. Hofer, Bridgewater
	Marie	35	(Stahl)
	Marie	18	
	Jacob	16	
	Anna	9	
	Andreas	8	
	Josine (?)	7	
	Rebecca	6	
	Susanne	4	
	Joseph	2 mo.	
	Johann	11 mo.	Father of Edwin Wollman, Spink Co.

PASSENGERS ON THE CIMBRIA
Left Hamburg
Arrived in New York on July 12, 1876

Why there were two groups coming to America in 1876 spaced only about two weeks apart instead of coming in one group is a mystery. This group of five families came from Hutterthal dorf. The Stahl families (brothers) and Christian Waldner joined Wolf Creek Colony. Twenty-one Hutterite passengers are on this ship.

No.	Name	Age	Remarks
61	Stahl, Michael	29	Should be 39. Minister, Wolf Creek Colony
	Susanna	41	(Hofer)
	Peter	17	
	Rebecca	15	
65	Stahl, Johann	32	Wolf Creek Colony
	Justine	25	(Wurz)
	Johann	5	
68	Walter, Jacob	38	''Dermitz ke Jacob''
	Barbara	28	(Decker)
	Jacob	8	"Bismarck" near Clayton
	Samuel	7	Lived at Freeman, County Treasurer
	Johann	5	Freeman businessman
73	Waldner, Sara	69	(Hofer) Mother of Martin Waldner
74	Waldner, Christian	21	Minister, Wolf Creek Colony, (son of Martin, first marriage)
	Anna	20	(Hofer), died at 99 years
76	Waldner, Martin	40	Son of Sara Waldner above
	Anna	28	(Mendel) sister to first wife
	Martin	15	Father of Martin who lived at Carpenter
	Anna	12	
	Sarah	9	
	Marie	7	

PASSENGERS ON THE GILLERT
Left Hamburg, Havre
Arrived in New York on July 29, 1876

In the fall of 1875 Rev. Michael Waldner and Joseph Waldner of Bon Homme Colony were sent to Russia to visit the remaining Hutterites in Johannesruh and Hutterthal, with the purpose of encouraging them to establish communal ownership after coming to America. In these two dorfs such an effort had been made a few years previously but had failed.

The group on this ship was made up of those who were persuaded to accompany the Waldners back. The effort to interest them in communal ownership was considered mostly a failure. See Kleine Geschichtbuch, page 460.

Of the passengers of this ship, 69 are identified as Hutterites, not counting the two Waldners.

No.	Name	Age	Remarks
25	Kleinsasser, Jacob	25	Father of Joe K. Kleinsasser, Freeman
	Catherine	25	
	Johann	5	
	Wilhelm	3	
	Jacob	10 mo.	
30	Waldner, Friedrich	56	Unidentified
	Barsolomeuse	59	
	Paul	5	
33	Wurz, Johann	23	Miller, Wolf Creek Colony, parents of Bishop John Wurtz, Sr., Wilson Siding
	Rachel	20	(Hofer)
35	Fast, Jacob	42	
	Catherine	40	(Waldner)
	Catherine	15	
	Jacob	17	
	Marie	9	
	David	4	
	Elizabeth	11 mo.	
	Kleinsasser, David	33	Homesteaded where Freeman stands, died 1879
	Catherine	32	Remarried to Geo. Gross, later to Rev. John L. Wipf
	Catherine	9	
	Anne	7	
	Marie	3	
	Susanne	11 mo.	

No.	Name	Age	Notes
48	Gross, Andreas	78	Bon Homme, father of Wilhelm Gross
	Catherine	50	(Wollman)
	Christian	13	Died at New Elm (S.D.) 1951
	Paul	9	Shot by neighbor on Bon Homme Island, 1892
52	Wurz, Josef	30	
	Marie	30	
	Marie	5	
	Rebecca	11 mo.	
	Anna	1 mo.	
57	Hoffer, Jacob	50	Wolf Creek Colony, "Tatala"
	Rebecca	49	(Gross) third marriage (mother of Andreas Wipf below)
	Jacob	16	(Tatala Yakob)
60	Wipf, Andreas	30	Wolf Creek Colony, 1876-1879, southwest of Bridgewater afterwards
	Sussane	33	(Glanzer) lightning 5-23-1885
	Sara	9	
	Andreas	8	Dr. A. A. Wipf
	Jesef	6	
	Susanne	4	Mrs. A. R. M. Hofer
	Samuel	11 mo.	Died at 5 years
	Rebecca	1 mo.	
68	Kleinsasser, Andreas	25	
	Anna	20	
	Catherine	10 mo.	
71	Waldner, Michael	43	Delegates sent by Bon Homme Colony to Russia to persuade others who will come to America to join Bon Homme Colony
	Josef (wife)	30	Joseph, listed as wife, is another ship list mistake
73	Glanzer, Paul (workman)	21	Bro. to father of Sam W. Glanzer, Bridgewater
74	Wipf, Johann	30	Bon Homme. Bro. to Rev. Elias Wipf of Hutterdorf Church
	Susanne	30	(Wurz)
	Johann	7	
	Daniel	5	
	Samuel	11 mo.	
	Susanne	1 mo.	
80	Mandel, Jacob	25	Probably Bon Homme
	Susanne	30	
	Susanne	9	
	Paul	7	
	Marie	4	
	Anne	4 mo.	
86	Janzen, Jacob	54	See Mendels book, page 13
	Marie	45	Sister to Rev. Mike Waldner of Bon Homme
	Susanne	16	
	Wilhelm	13	
	Anne	9	
	Elizabeth	8	
	Johann	6	
	Cornelius	5	Lived in Parkston
	David	11 mo.	
	Marie	1 mo.	

PASSENGERS ON THE POMMERANIA

Left Hamburg, Havre

Arrived in New York on July 3, 1877

The Hutterites on this ship originated from Johannesruh and Hutterthal. Among this group are also those who founded the Elm Spring Colony which is the mother colony of the Lehrer leut colonies. Others settled between Bridgewater and Freeman.

182 Hutterite passengers.

No.	Name	Age	Remarks
225	Wipf, Jacob	40	Minister, founder of Elm Spring Colony
	Rebecca	36	(Mendel) known as "lehrer"
	Jacob	15	
	Joh	13	
	Paul	9	
	Anna	8	
	Maria	7	
	Elizabeth	5	
	Rebecca	11 mo.	
234	Decker, Jacob	24	Probably a brother to Mrs. Rev. John P. Hofer
	Marie	25	(Kleinsasser), daughter of "Kuller Zacharias"
	Zacharias	10 mo.	
237	Wipf, Elias	46	Elm Spring Colony, Bro. to lehrer
	Magdale	46	(Kleinsasser)
	Elias	19	
	Joh	8	
	Andr	7	
	Jacob	4	
	Josef	3	
	Paul	9	
	Sara	4 mo.	Died on voyage
246	Wipf, Josef	36	Second marriage
	Susanna	33	(Kleinsasser)
	Maria	9	
	Anna	7	Married into Colony
	Cathe	5	Mrs. D. D. Wipf, Parkston
	Susanna	3	Mrs. John M. S. Hofer
	Sarah	11 mo.	Frankfort, S.D.
	Joh	11 mo.	
254	Hofer, Saml *	32	Wolf Creek Colony. Bro. to "Oil Michael"
	Rachel	32	(Hofer)
	Samuel	9	
	Jacob	6	
	Susanne	3	
	Rachel	11 mo.	
260	Hofer, Samuel	24	Bro. to Paul S. Hofer, joined Rockport when old
	Susanne	28	(Kleinsasser)
262	Glanzer, Samuel	63	Great grandfather of Jacob H. Glanzer, Bridgewater
263	Waldner, Georg	63	Elm Spring Colony
264	Waldner, Cather	36	Elm Spring Colony, not married
265	Mendel, Michel	44	Second marriage, Elm Spring Colony
	Marie	26	
	Marie	17	Mother of Mrs. Banker Tschetter, Freeman
	Anna	14	
	Michel	9	
	Joh	8	
	Josef	7	
	Lorenz	11 mo.	
273	Kleinsasser, Andr	29	Second marriage
	Marie	26	(Wipf)
	Jacob	7	Father of Lewis Kleinsasser, Freeman
	Joh	14	Brother to above Andrew. Matt Kleinsasser's father, Freeman
	Susanne	19	Sister to above Andrew. Mother of John S. Waldner
278	Hofer, Peter	42	Minister, Elm Spring Colony, uncle of "Peter Paul"
	Susanne	50	(Hofer), second marriage, mother of "Peter Paul"
	Josef	5	
	Susanne	19	
	Anna	15	
	Marie	13	
	Rachel	9	
	Sara	7	
	Rebecca	10 mo.	
287	Hofer, Peter	24	Elm Spring Colony. Parents of Dave Hofer Sr., Calif.
	Marie	24	(Wollman)
	Marie	11 mo.	
	Susanne	1 mo.	
291	Waldner, Georg	26	Elm Spring Colony
	Marie	27	(Kleinsasser)
	George	2 mo.	Was minister at Miami Colony

No.	Name	Age	Remarks
294	Waldner, Jacob	20	Elm Spring Colony, Brother of Geo. No. 291
	Barbara	20	(Hofer)
	Anna	2 mo.	
297	Stahl, Paul	18	Father of Mrs. Rev. Peter G. Hofer
298	Hofer, Michael	21	Son of Michael R. Hofer, Rutschield
	Elizabeth	21	(Gross) Parents of Dr. M. M. Hofer, Freeman
	Marie	1 mo.	Married Jacob J. Kleinsasser
301	Waldner, Joh	38	Elm Spring Colony
	Susanne	36	(Walter)
	Joh	14	
	Georg	8	Married "Hofer Katherina"
	Josef	6	
	Anna	4	
	Susanne	11 mo.	
	Jacob	1 mo.	
309	Kleinsasser Josef	63	Father of Enoch Kleinsasser
	Justine	58	(Tschetter)
	Josef	16	
	Rebecca	20	Mrs. John Waldner, Beadle
313	Kleinsasser, Enoch	25	
	Elizabeth	24	(Wipf)
	David	3	"Enoch David" near Freeman
	Anne	2 mo.	
317	Gross, Andr	22	Andrew C. Gross, father of Mrs. Zack Walter, Bridgewater
318	Kleinsasser, Josef	44	Elm Spring Colony, "Hansela Joseph"
	Anna	45	(Hofer) sister to "Paulela Paul"
	Anna	16	
	Josef	13	
	Samuel	9	
	Sara	8	
	Susanne	6	
	Joh	4	
	Peter	2 mo.	
327	Kleinsasser, Marie	20	
	Joh (her baby)	3 mo.	
329	Kleinsasser, Joh	20	
330	Wipf, Alexander	29	"Zonder" father of Elias A. Wipf, "Miala"
	Rachel	27 *	(Stahl)
	Yoh	11 mo.	
	Jacob	1 mo.	Died on voyage
334	Hofer, Yoh	63	Second marriage, Bon Homme Colony
	Susanne	40	
	Michl	18	
	Marie	13	
	Rebecca	9	
	Sara	9	
	Yoh	7	
341	Kleinsasser, Zacharias	51	
	Marie	56	(Hofer) sister to "uber Schultz"
	Joh	12	Rev. John Z., Calif., father of Rev. J. J. Colony
	Cathe	17	
	Anna	8	Mother of Mrs. Rev. Peter G. Hofer
346	Kleinsasser, Andr	20	Son to above Zacharias
	Anna	20	(Waldner)
	Joh	2 mo.	John A., Beadle Co.
349	Kleinsasser, Joh	56	
	Susanna	49	(Tschetter)
	Zacharias	18	Stepfather to John S. Waldner
	Paul	14	
	Marie	16	
	Anna	9	Mrs. Enoch Hofer
	Sara	5	
356	Kleinsasser, Sara	82	(Wipf), Mrs. Hansela Kleinsasser, Elm Sp. Colony
357	Hofer, Joh	49	Elm Sp. Colony. Father of John L. , Calif.
	Rachel	47	(Kleinsasser) daughter of above Sara
	Jacob	18	
	Michael	12	
	Susanna	14	
	Cath	7	Mrs. Geo. Waldner, died in Hutterville in Alberta at about 95
363	Hofer, Joh	37 (27)	John L. of Calif., son of above John, first marriage
	Cath	33 (23)	(Hofer) daughter of Michael R., Rutschield
	Jacob	3 *	Jacob L. Sr., near Silver Lake
	Cath	10 mo.	Mrs. Druggist Hofer, Bridgewater

No.	Name	Age	Remarks
367	Wipf, Jacob	30	Lived south of Freeman (1880)
	Cath	29	(Stahl)
	Sara	8	
	Maria	7	Mother to Mrs. Rev. Joe E. Wipf, Huron
	Anna	4	Mrs. Sam Wipf
	Cath	11 mo.	
	Anna	1 mo.	
374	Gross, Georg	28	Elm Sp. Colony, Bro. to Paul C. Gross, Clayton
	Sara	25	
	Georg	5	
	Andr	11 mo.	
	Josef	1 mo.	
	Sara	3	
380	Entz, Peter	52	Elm Spring Colony
	Marie	52	(Wipf)
	Josef	9	
	Marie	19	
	Susanne	13	
	Cath	8	
386	Entz, Peter	28	Elm Sp. Colony. Son of Peter above
	Sara	29	(Decker)
	Peter	9	
	Josef	5	Married Anna, daughter of Rev. Paul Hofer. (turned blind) Hutterthal Church
	Joh	3	
	Jacob	11 mo.	
392	Entz, Joh	25	Son of Peter No. 380
	Susanne	26	(Hofer)
	Jacob	3	
	Peter	7 mo.	
396	Entz, Jacob	23	Son of Peter No. 380. Grandfather of Jacob Entz near Huron
	Rebecca	18	(Glanzer)
398	Wurz, Joh	27	Elm Sp. Colony. Bro. to Mrs. John Hofer No. 34.
	Cath	25	(Knels)
	Cath	4	A son John, age about 5, is missing
	Anne	3	
402	Wurz, Josef	52	This probably is a mistake. Should be Kathrina Wurz and daughter Anna, ages would be correct. Katherina is mother of John, Josef, and Andr., also Anna married John Hofer No. 34.
	Andr (son)	18	
404-410	not Hutterites		
411	Wurz, Josef	13	Elm Sp. Colony. They are half brothers of No. 398. Sons of Kathrina No. 402.
	Andr	9	

Passenger numbers 413 thru 440 are not Hutterites.

No.	Name	Remarks
441	Mendel, Susanne	Infant born at sea to No. 265

PASSENGERS ON THE LESSING

Left Bremen, Havre

Arrived in New York on July 17, 1878

This group settled on the prairie, some along the Wolf Creek about eight miles southwest of Bridgewater and others near Freeman. Several families chose the colonies. These originated from Johannesruh and Hutterthal.

106 Hutterites on this ship.

No.	Name	Age	Remarks
268	Waldner, Johann	43	''Fritz Hannas'' Rev.
	Anna Barbera	46	Daughter of No. 278
	Susanna	19	
	Catherina	16	Mother of Mrs. Joe M. Walter, Freeman
	Sara	8	
	Rebecka	4	
	Barbera	11 mo.	
275	Dekker, Samuel	25	Elm Spr. Colony. Bro. to John near Milltown
	Marie	22	(Waldner) daughter of No. 268
	Rebecka	6 mo.	
278	Kleinsasser, Enoch	66	See Mendel's book, page 11
	Anna	57	
280	Hofer, Paul	27	''Peter Paul''
	Anna	26	(Wurz)
	Elizabeth	4	Adopted (Eliz Fast)
	Susanne	11 mo.	Deaf, died in 1966, Beadle Co.
284	Pollman, Paul	41	Parents of Joe and Sam near Bridgewater
	Rachel	40	(Glanzer)
	Johannus	9	
	Andrias	8	
	Rachel	19	
	Catherine	16	
290	Mandel, Peter	33	
	Susanne	31	(Stahl)
	Peter	9	Father of Joe and Peter near Freeman
	Jacob	5	Father of Sam Mendel, Freeman
	Paul	6 mo.	Spink County
	Susanne	7	
296	Walter, Joseph	21	''Sepel'' near Bridgewater
	Rachel	19	(Wipf) daughter of No. 299
	Marie	6 mo.	Mrs. Peter M. Tschetter, Bridgewater
299	Wipf, Zacharias	44	
	Sara	40	(Glanzer)
	John	14	Probably should be Joseph, Emery
	Samuel	9	Father of Rev. D. S. Wipf, Emery
	Marie	4	
304	Hufer, Susanne	69	(Kleinsasser) widow
305	Wipf, Elias	66	Killed by tornado, 1884, brother to No. 299
	Rachel	67	(Miller)
307	Wipf, Elias	26	Southwest Bridgewater, father of Rev. Joe E., Huron
	Justine	24	(Hofer), sister to ''uber schultz'' died in tornado
	Marie	6	Mrs. Joe Hofer, mother of Rev. Eli L. Hofer
	Elizabeth	6 mo.	Mrs. Paul W. Glanzer near Bridgewater
311	Miller, Andreas	43	Second marriage
	Susanne	35	(Tschetter)
	Joseph	15	Father of Mrs. Banker Tschetter
	Peter	12	Father of Peter Miller, Marion
	John	7	Probably adopted John Fast, see Mendel's book, page 13
	Paul	4	
	Andreas	3 mo.	
318	Hofer, Jacob	39	Wolf Creek Colony, (1880)
	Catherina	36	(Wipf) sister to No. 307
	David	15	
	Sara	12	
	Rachel	9	
	Jacob	7	
	Marie	4	
	Joseph	3	
	Catherina	6 mo.	
327	Wurz, Michael	25	Probably lived in Canada, Gurnsey, Sask.
	Sara	27	(Tschetter)
	Jacob	10 mo.	
330	Wurz, Jacob	19	

331 and 332 are not Hutterites

No.	Name	Age	Notes
333	Hofer, Michael	26	Ruta-Michaela
	Sara	26	(Stahl)
	Rachel	5	Mrs. Jacob M. Hofer, Spink County
	David	3	
	Sara	11 mo.	Mrs. Sam S. Hofer
	Jacob	1 mo.	
	Marie	13	Child not theirs, no doubt
340	Tschetter, Peter	33	Founder of Tschetter Colony, was a brother to "Tschetter Hannas"
	Sara	31	(Hofer)
	Sara	9	
	Jacob	8	
	Michael	6	
	Johann	4	
	Peter	11 mo.	
	Paul	1 mo.	
348	Tschetter, Anna	80	Mother to above Peter, also mother to Prediger Paul's father
349	Stahl, Benjamin	64	Father of John and Michael of Wolf Creek Colony
	Paul	12	
	Martha	17	
352	Stahl, Andreas	26 *	(Maybe 21) Son of No. 349, Father of Rev. Paul Stahl of Langham, Sask.
	Cath	20	(Wollman)
	Susanne	6 mo.	
355	Wollman, Joseph	15	Probably bro. to above Cath No. 353
356	Glanzer, Samuel	30	
	Barbera	28	(Walter) sister to "Sepel"
	Marie	9	Mrs. Joseph Pollman
	Samuel	6	Sam W. near Bridgewater
	Paul	11 mo.	Paul W. near Bridgewater
361	Glanzer, Joseph	25	Bro. to above Samuel
	Barbera	24	(Tschetter)
	Sara	5	Mrs. Jacob S. G. Hofer, Onida
	Josef	11 mo.	Father of missionary Rebecca Glanzer
	Samuel	1 mo.	

366, 367, and 368 are not Hutterites

No.	Name	Age	Notes
369	Tschetter, Lorenz	65	Probably parents to No. 362
	Marie	64	
371	Tschetter, Lorenz	22	Son of above No. 369, no doubt
	Sara	21	(Pollman)
	Marcus	10 mo.	
374	Hofer, Jacob	48	Father of No. 375. Also John Hofer No. 34. Lived west of Neu Hutterthal Church
375	Hofer, Christian	25	Wolf Creek Colony, later Standoff, Alberta. Bro. to John Hofer No. 34
	Justine	25	(Stahl)
	Rebecca	4	
	Susanne	6 mo.	

PASSENGERS ON THE MOSEL

Left Bremen, Southampton

Arrived in New York on July 21, 1879

This was the final group to leave Russia. It was also the second largest, totaling 334 individuals. These originated in Johannesruh and Hutterthal. Some of these settled along the James River near Olivet. Others filled in the land that was still available between Freeman and Bridgewater. Except for marriage into a colony, these settled on the prairie in a private ownership.

With the coming of this group the movement from Russia was complete. Less than a dozen remained there, and these were ones that had married with Low-German Mennonites into their villages. For an account of these see page 13 of Mendel's book.

No.	Name	Age	Remarks
71	Wipf, Joseph	31	Father of Dentist J. H. Wipf, Freeman
	Susanna	32	(Wurz) daughter of Andrew (pass No. 329)
	Joseph	6	Lived in N.D.
	Andrew	9	Lived in Colony
	David	3	Manager in W. C. Colony
	Rebecca	8	Married Darius Walter, W. C. Colony, died young
	Susanna	5	Lived in Colony
	Johann	1	Lived in Colony
79	Wipf, David	34	"Zonder David" lived where Johnny I. Walter lives
	Catherine	26	(Stahl)
	David	6	D. D. was Sec. of State of S.D.
	Anna	5	Mrs. Paul Wollman, N.D.
	Catherine	3	Mrs. Jacob B. Hofer, N.D.
84	Knels, Jacob	41	Grandfather of Mrs. John A. Mendel, Marion
	Wilhelmine	44	
	Jacob	17	Died in State Hospital, Yankton
	Maria	19	
	Rebecca	14	
	Barbara	11	
	Anna	9	
	Magreta	7	
92	Glanzer, Paul	60	
	Barbara	60	
94	Glanzer, Matthias	37	Settled southwest of Dolton
	Anna	34	(Wurz)
	Paul	13	Father of Rev. J. P. Glanzer, Calif.
	Michael	10	Married Rebecca Hofer, "Motz Mike"
	Samuel	5	Married Anna Walter
	Matthias	3	Married Kathrina Waldner
	Susanna	14	Mrs. Jacob M. Wipf, Carpenter
	Barbara	7	Mrs. Jacob J. Walter, Carpenter
102	Glanzer, Paul	34	Bro. to Samuel No. 109
	Katherine	33	(Janzen) first wife was Anna Gross. All children listed are from Anna
	David	8	D. P. Glanzer married Maria Hofer
	Barbara	13	Mrs. Joe J. Wipf, Calif.
	Susanna	10	Mrs. Jacob M. Wollman
	Anna	6	Mrs. Sam J. Walter
	Maria	3	Colony, Mrs. Andrew Kleinsasser
109	Glanzer, Samuel	27	Brother to above No. 102. Lived southeast of Bridgewater
	Susanna	29	(Gross) daughter of No. 200
	Susanna	6	
	Samuel	1	Father of Dr. A. S. Glanzer, Menno
113	Wurtz, Daniel	54	Homesteaded the Sam K. Hofer farm
	Susanna	53	(Tschetter)
	Maria	19	Mrs. Jacob Hofer No. 28. Mother of Rev. Mike J. Hofer
	Rebecca	15	Mrs. Cornelius Wedel, Yale
	Barbara	11	Mrs. Michael Tschetter, first marriage; Mrs. Paul S. Hofer, Carpenter, second marriage
118	Verheis, Jacob	23	A mistake, should be Jacob Wurz. Son of above Daniel, "Daniel Yop." Moved to Canada later
	Sarah	21	
	Susanna	6 mo.	
121	Wollman, Jeramias *	49	
	Anna	27	(Hofer) second wife
	Jacob	19	
	Michael	11	
	Joseph	4	
	Andrew	2	Father of Mike Wollman, Bridgewater
	Rebecca	9	Mrs. Joe Hofer, mother of "Elevator Joe," Freeman
	Maria	6	

No.	Name	Age	Remarks
129	Hofer, Michael	37	"Uber schultz"
	Maria	35	(Gross) daughter of No. 200
	David	9	Rev. D. M. Hofer, co-founder of Gospel Mission in Chicago. Relief worker in Russia
	Michael	8	Lived south of Bridgewater
	Paul	6	Lived south of Bridgewater, Michael Paul
	Johann	4	Died at age 20
	Peter	2	Father of Rev. Peter G. Hofer Jr.
	Maria	15	Mrs. Elias Wipf
	Elizabeth	11	Mrs. D. J. Mendel, 1st marriage
	Susanna	6 mo.	Mrs. D. J. Mendel, 2nd marriage
139	Hofer, Johann	31	Rev. at Neu Hutterthal Church. Bro. to "uberschultz"
	Anna	37	(Gross, Wolman), her second marriage
	Andrew	13	Wollman, Anna's son, died in N.D., half brother to blind Katherina Wollman
	Johann	5	Furniture store, undertaker at Emery
	Anna	11	Mother of Mrs. John Joshua Hofer near Emery
	Maria	7	Mrs. Paul J. Hofer near Olivet
	Elizabeth	3	Mrs. Joe J. Walter
146	Hofer, Katherine	22	Should be Wollman. "Blind aunt Katherine." Step-daughter of above Anna No. 140
147	Hofer, Jacob	28	Bro. to "uberschultz." Father of Sam J. Hofer of Huron
	Susanna	24	(Dekker)
	Susanna	2	Mrs. Sam Wipf, Bon Homme Colony
150	Hofer, David	22	"Davidetl" lived in Bridgewater. Bro. to "uberschultz"
	Anna	23	(Polmann). Had no family
152	Hofer, Paul	37	Rev. at Hutterthal Church, "Paulela Paul"
	Anna	38	(Wipf)
	Paul	14	Father of Rev. Jacob D. Hofer, Calif.
	Johann	11	Rev. at Hutterthal. Father of Rev. Jacob B. Hofer, Dolton
	Samuel	5	Sam P., Bridgewater
	Joseph	3	Druggist in Bridgewater. Father of Mrs. Rev. J. J. Kleinsasser, Calif.
	Sara	19	Mrs. Geo. Gross. Mother of Mrs. Sam K. Hofer
	Maria	12	Mrs. D. P. Glanzer near Bridgewater
	Anna	1 or 8	Married Entz, Elm Sp. Colony, known as "blind aunt Anna."
161	Hofer, Michael	50	"Rutschield" reached age of 103 years
	Anna	37	(Tschetter) second wife
	Joseph	20	Should be Joshua, known as "old man"
	Enoch	17	Married Anna Hofer
	Paul	12	Was nursery salesman in Freeman, known as "Paul Tschetter"
	David	11	Father of "Diamond Dick" known as "Gossen"
	Andrew	6	Father of Ed A., near Freeman "Andree"
	Maria	18	Mrs. Paul Tschetter, "Sep Paula"
	Anna	7	Mrs. Jacob J. Gross
	Elizabeth	3	Mrs. John J. Decker, Huron area
	Susanna	1½	Mrs. John M. Wollman, near Bridgewater
172	Tschetter, Isaac	44	Brother to Jacob No. 397
	Elizabeth	46	(Hofer) sister to "Rutschield"
	Josua	21	Father of Isaac, Joshua, Mary Tschetter near Freeman
	Lorenz	10	
	Jacob	4*	
	Maria	15	Mrs. Wm. Gross, mother of "Schultz Maria"
	Susanna	7	
179	Hofer, Samuel	50	Brother to "Paulela Paul" No. 152, second marriage
	Maria	51	(Hofer, Dekker) second marriage
	Paul	14	Paul S. Hofer, Carpenter
	Anna	17	Mrs. Paul W. Gross, mother of Sam P. Gross, Bridgewater
	Maria	20	Dekker, Mrs. Zacharius Kleinsasser, "Honnes Zacharius"
	Margarethe	15	Dekker, Mrs. Paul Hofer, mother of Rev. J. D. Hofer, Calif.
	Barbara	13	Dekker, Mrs. Rev. John P. Hofer, mother of Rev. Jacob B. Hofer
186	Hofer, Johann	24	Son of above Samuel No. 179, father of Rev. Sam J.R. Hofer, Carpenter
	Rebecca	21	(Dekker) This family was in Elm Spring Colony in 1880, but left
	Samuel	1	Died young
189	Kleinsasser, Paul	25	Father of John P. Kleinsasser, (Morgan)
	Anna	22	(Tschetter) daughter of No. 172
	Paul	2	Rev. P. P. Kleinsasser, Freeman
	Elizabeth	3	Mrs. Jacob L. Hofer, Sr.
193	Dekker, Barbara	70	Grandmother of Mrs. Paul E. Kleinsasser
194	Mendel, Paul	61	Second marriage, died in Colony at age 99. Grandfather of John A. Mendel, Marion.
	Catherine	56	(Polmann, Gross) second marriage
	Anna	21	Mother of John Joshua Hofer, Emery
	Elizabeth	17	Mrs. Joe Z. Wipf
	Sahra	19	
	Susanna	11	

No.	Name	Age	Remarks
200	Gross, Paul	58	''Schultz'' lived 1 mile south of Olivet
	Susanna	54	(Hofer)
	George	20	''Schultz yerg,'' father of Mrs. Sam K. Hofer
	Rebecca	13	Mrs. Paul S. Hofer, Carpenter
204	Gross, David	28	Son of Paul No. 200, ''Schultz David''
	Sara	26	(Hofer)
	David	6	D. D. lived north of Freeman
	Paul	2	''Gretel Paul'' father of David P. Gross
	Rachel	5	Mrs. Andrew M. Wollman, Olivet
209	Gross, Wilhelm	53	Second marriage
	Catherine	32	(Mendel)
	George	21	''William Yerg'' Spink County
	Paul	18	''William Paul'' Bridgewater, father of Sam P
	Wilhelm	1	Father of mail carrier, Andrew W. Gross, Freeman
214	Waldner, Matthias	60	
	David	18	
	Paul	14	Lived at Seneca, S.D.
	Peter	10	M. S. ''Motzel Peter,'' lived north of Freeman.
	Anna	19	Mrs. John Stahl, Wolf Creek Colony
219	Tschetter , Joseph	29	
	Maria	30	
	Joseph	7	
	Anna	6	
223	Mendel, Paul	32	Father of John A. Mendel, Marion
	Anna	29	(Kleinsasser) sister to Paul Kleinsasser No. 189.
	Paul	6 mo.	Killed by lightning about 1896
226	Mendel, Sara	19	Should be Kleinsasser, sister to Anna No. 224
227	Mendel, Catherine	16	Should be Kleinsasser, sister to Anna No. 224
228	Mendel, Rebecca	10	Should be Kleinsasser, sister to Anna No. 224
229	Mendel, Maria	11	Should Fast, married Jacob Decker
230	Walter, Joseph	36	Known as ''Groupeta''
	Maria	30	(Gross) daughter of Wilhelm No. 209
	Maria	9	Mrs. Peter Mendel
	Susanna	7	Mrs. A. A. Wollman
	Joseph	4	''Groupeta Joe'' lived south of Bridgewater
	Catherine	1½	Mrs. John J. Hofer, Emery (undertaker)
236	Dekker, Andrew	36	
	Maria	36	(Stahl)
	Jacob	10	
	Joseph	4	
	Joachim	1½	Should be John, lived in Huron
	Catherine	7	
	Maria	5	
243	Tschetter, Paul	34	Probably father of Joe P. Tschetter near Huron
	Sara	33	(Wipf)
	Jacob	3	
246	Tschetter, Isaac	25	Known as ''Klana Isaacel,'' lived north of Huron
	Sara	24	(Wurz) daughter of Cathrina No. 402 '77 ship
	Catherine	4	Mrs. Jacob A. Dekker
	Elizabeth	1	
250	Wipf, Johann	44	Second marriage
	Catherine	50	(Hofer, Stahl) second marriage, sister to ''Rutschield''
	Johann	17	Stahl, Wolf Creek Colony
	Josua	14	Stahl, father of Joshua B. Stahl, Yale
	Jacob	9	''Knox,'' Beadle Co.
	Sara	15	Stahl, married Franz Wollman, who disappeared in New York.
	Maria	4	Married Joseph Knels, Montana
257	Dekker, Samuel	56	(Bammal Sömmel)
	Susanna	50	(Gross) sister to Paul No. 200
	Jacob	10	Father of Paul J. Decker, Freeman
	Rebecca	19	Mrs. Christian Wurz, Canada
261	Stahl, George	28	Known as ''Tarretz,'' father of Mrs. D. R.M. Hofer, Dolton
	Sahrah *	28	(Dekker) daughter of Sam No. 257
	George	5	
264	Hofer, Michael	61	Second marriage. Brother to ''uber Schultz's'' father David
	Anna	54	Second marriage
	Susanna	15	
	Barbara	13	Mrs. Joseph C. Gross, Freeman
	Rebecca	10	Mrs. Mike Glanzer, Spink Co.

No.	Name	Age	Remarks
269	Hofer, Michael	22	Known as No. 28, son of Michael No. 264. Father of Mike K. Hofer who had elevator in Freeman
	Catherine	27	(Wurz) daughter of Catherine No. 402, '77 ship
	Jacob	6	"Chekela," father of Albert Hofer, Spink Co.
	Johann	3	John K., who lived in Yale
	Catherine	5	Mrs. Jos. Hofer, Yale, mother of Mrs. John M. Tschetter, Huron
	Anna	1	Lived with Martin Waldner's, Carpenter
275	Hofer, Jacob	25	Known as No. 28, son of Michael No. 264, father of Rev. Mike J. Hofer, Bridgewater
	Anna	24	(Stahl) died young
	Catherine	2	Half sister of Mrs. Joe D. Hofer, Bridgewater, stayed with them
278	Hofer, Peter	61	Father of Baer Yop, joined Elm Spring Colony, also grandfather of Dave Hofer Sr., Calif.
	Rebecca	20	
	Catherine	18	Mrs. Paul W. Tschetter, mother of Rev. P. P. Tschetter
281	Hofer, Andrew	37	Son of Peter No. 278, brother to "Baer Yop."
	Susanna	37	(Wurz)
	Michael	8	
	Andrew	6	
	Jacob	4	
	Peter	2	
	Susanna	10	
	Anna	1 (or 7)	
289	Hofer, Jacob	35	Son of Peter No. 278 known as "Baer Yop."
	Rebecca	31	(Stahl) daughter of Benjamin Stahl
	Jacob	10	N.D.
	Peter	7	Had hardware store in Tripp
	Michael	4	N.D., father of Mrs. Sam M. Tschetter, Carpenter.
	Susanna	8	
295	Walter, Jacob	64	Second, grandfather of Joe M. Walter, Freeman
	Susanna	51	(Wollman) second
	Heinrich	18	Had a wooden leg, never married
	Susanna	8	
299	Glanzer, David	35	Brother to father of Sam W. Glanzer near Bridgewater
	Anna	35	(Wipf) sister to Dr. A. A. Wipf's father. This family joined Wolf Creek Colony
301	Hofer, Michael	55	Known as "Ruta-Michael"
	Maria	50	(Waldner)
	Joseph	18	Rev. Joseph Hofer, Hutterthal Church, Beadle County
	Anna	11	
	Peter	22	
	Barbara	20	
	Susanna	1½	
308	Hofer, Mathias	37	Brother to "Rutschield"
	Maria	37	(Wurz)
	Andreas	12	Killed by wagon accident
	Josua	10	"Motz Joshua" Beadle County
	Joseph	6 mo.	
	Maria	16	Mrs. Elias Walter, mother of Joe M. Walter, Freeman
	Anna	6	Mrs. Andrew Pollman
	Elizabeth	4	Mrs. Isaac Tschetter
	Catherine	2	Mrs. Jacob Decker, mother of Paul J. Decker
317	Gross, Jacob	33	Son of Andreas No. 48 Gillert ('76)
	Sara	28	(Hofer) sister of "Oil Michael"
	Jacob	10	Father of Paul Gross, Lake Byron
	Andreas	6	Father of Geo A. Gross, trucker, Freeman
	Sara	4	Never married
	Susanna	2	Mrs. Peter W. Tschetter (first wife)
323	Gross, Daniel	17	Half brother to above Jacob No. 317, never married
324	Wurz, Joseph	30	Settled southwest of Hutterthal Church, known as "Koller Sep"
	Barbara	31	(Glanzer)
	Joseph	9	Lived near Doland
	Andreas	3	
	Sara	4	
329	Wurz, Andreas	71	Father of above Joseph No. 324
330	Polmann, Joseph	52	
	Justina	46	(Hofer) sister to "Rutschield"
	Paul	13	Lived near Emery, father of Mrs. John Joshua Hofer
	Andreas	5	Lived 10 miles southeast of Emery, father of Jake Pollman, Menno
	Justina	16	
	Catherina	11	
	Rebecca	7	
	Sara	4	Mrs. John P. Gross, north of Huron
	Elizabeth	2	Mrs. Paul M. Hofer, south of Bridgewater

No.	Name	Age	Notes
339	Polmann, Joseph	24	Son of above Joseph No. 330
	Sara	23	(Wipf)
	Sara	4	Mrs. Geo. G. Wipf, Beadle County
	Anna	6 mo.	Married David Hofer, furniture business, Bridgewater, known as "Miller David"
343	Polmann, Joseph	36	
	Maria	34	(Mendel)
	Joseph	16	Father of Martin Polmann, Yale
	Jeremias	9	Sully Co., father of Mrs. Mike Walter, undertaker, Freeman (first wife)
	Paul	2	Lived east of Bridgewater, father of Mrs. John A. Hofer
	Maria	12	Mrs. Jacob J. Walter, Clayton, "Bismarck"
	Sara	11	
	Rebecca	7	
351	Gross, Joseph	32	Father of Sam J.C. Gross, Freeman
	Maria	30	(Walter)
	Joseph	10	Father of Jake T. Gross, Freeman
	Paul	8 *	Beadle County
	David	2	Father of Joe D.M. Gross, N.D., now of Freeman
	Christian	6 mo.	Huron area
	Catherine	4	
358	Gross, Paul	26	Lived near Clayton, brother to above Joseph No. 351, father of George and Joe, Freeman
	Catherine	25	(Stahl), sister to Mrs. Rev. Peter G. Hofer's father
	Johann	5	Beadle County
	Catherine	1	
362	Hofer, David	24	In Elm Spring Colony in 1880
	Rebecca	21	
	Maria	1	
365	Wollmann, Michael	53	Lived near Olivet
	Catherine	49	(Hofer)
	David	24	Father of Jake D. and D. D. of Freeman
	Jacob	14	Father of Banker Jake Wollman, Freeman
	Andrew	8	Near Olivet, father of Andrew R. of Menno
	Johann	5	Near Bridgewater, father of Clifford
	Anna	19	Mrs. Rev. Jacob J. Hofer, "Yos Jacob"
	Elizabeth	11	Mrs. D. D. Gross, mother of John D. Gross
373	Wollmann, Michael	25	Son of above Michael, was Freeman businessman, "store Michael."
	Anna	24	(Waldner)
375	Wollmann, Johann	25	Grandfather of Elgin and Harris Wollman, lived south of Bridgewater
	Susanna	32	(Hofer, Wollman) second marriage
	Susanna	14	Mrs. W. W. Gross, Freeman, mother of mail carrier A. W. Gross
	Andrew	9	Businessman A. A. Wollman, Freeman
	Jacob	7	Lived west of Freeman, father of Mrs. Paul Matt Hofer
	Justina	3 mo.	Married John M. Wollman No. 370, died shortly after marriage
381	Wallner, Jeremais	42	
382	Wallner, Ester	72	
383	Gross, Peter	24	Son of Andreas No. 48 on Gillert '76. See Mendel's book, page 12
384	Kleinsasser, Mathias	72	
385	Hofer, Michael	36	"Oil Michael" father of John M.S. Hofer
	Sara	36	(Kleinsasser)
	Michael	6	Drowned in 1906
	Susanna	12	Mrs. Peter Waldner, M.S., Freeman
	Sara	10	Mrs. Andrew G. Gross
	Rachel	4	Mrs. Joe A. Wipf, mother of Elenora R. Wipf, Huron
	Anna	2	Mrs. Peter W. Tschetter
	Catherine	6 mo.	Died young
393	Wipf, Johann	31	Rev. John L. Wipf, Hutterthal Church, Freeman
	Catherine	30	(Kleinsasser)
	Johanna (female)	7	Should be Johann, businessman in Freeman, father to John A. Wipf
	Catherine	5	Mrs. John J. Kleinsasser, Freeman

Missing is Maria, age 5 months, married John J. Kleinsasser (his second marriage). She is the only Russian born Hutterite still alive on 6-1-1974.

No.	Name	Age	Notes
397	Tschetter, Jacob	36	Brother to Isaac No. 172
	Catherine	35	(Gross)
	Jacob	9	Known as "Billy Jacob"
	Mathias	9	Known as "Billy Motz"
	Isaac	7	Known as "Billy Isaac"
	Paul	4	Known as "Billy Paul"
	Joseph	3 mo.	Known as "Billy Joseph"
	Susanna	14	

Next is listed a census of the four colonies in existence in South Dakota in the 1880 census report available from the South Dakota State Historical Society in Pierre.

1880 Census
Hutterian Brethren Society
Bon Homme County

Name	Age	Occupation
Hofer, Jacob	47	Clergyman
Maria	23	
Joseph	17	Miller
Michael	15	
Zacharias	13	
Samuel	10	
Peter	10	
Jeremias	2	
Waldner, Jacob	42	Teacher
Susana	39	
Wipf, John	30	Overseer
Susana	29	
John	10	
Daniel	8	
Samuel	5	
Susana	3	
Anna	1	
Wurz, Michael	35	Farmer
Rachel	35	
Rachel	14	
Susana	12	
Sahra	8	
Catharine	6	
Michael	2	
Stahl, Lorenz	62	Farmer
Rebecca	18	
Joseph	16	
Hofer, David	37	Works in mill
Susana	33	
David	14	
Samuel	10	
Sahra	11	
Catharine	5	
John	2	
Susana	4 mo.	

Name	Age	Occupation
Waldner, Joseph	34	Tinsmith
Anna	34	
Joseph	13	
John	11	
Maria	9	
Fred.	8	
David	7	
Anna	5	
Jacob	3	
Susana	1	
Wurz, Jacob	29	Farmer
Anna	28	
Hofer, David	27	Shoemaker
Sahra	26	
Sahra	6	
David	3	
Rebecca	1	
Kleinsasser, Samuel	67	Basket maker
Sahra	54	
Elizabeth	17	
Maria	15	
Joseph	10	
Hofer, Jacob	61	Farmer
Anna	65	
Hofer, John	66	Carpenter
Susana	48	
Maria	18	
Rebecca	14	
Sahra	14	
John	9	
Stahl, Christ	58	Farmer
Justina	65	
Dekker, John	47	Farmer
Susana	44	
John	23	
Susana	15	
Jacob	15(?)	
Anna	10	
David	5	

Name	Age	Occupation
Kleinsasser, Samuel	45	Farmer
Susana	39	
Susana	20	
Maria	18	
Samuel	15	
Joseph	14	
Andrew	12	
Jacob	10	
Rebecca	1	
Hofer, Jacob	37	Farmer
Anna	36	
Jacob	16	
Susana	14	
David	9	
Anna	5	
Rebecca	6 mo.	
Wurz, Andrew	32	Blacksmith
Susana	32	
Susana	9	
Barbara	5	
Anna	2	
Wallman, Zacharias	32	Miller
Susana	34	
Zacharias	12	
Jacob	10	
Paul	5	
David	1	
Wipf, John	26	Farmer
Barbara	33	
Sahra	5	
Wallman, Paul	24	Farmer
Catharine	24	
Paul	2	
Samuel	1	
Glanzer, Paul	24	Farmer
Margret	21	
Sahra	2	
Maria	1	
Waldner, Joseph	24	Miller
Catharine	21	
Michael	2	
Joseph	1	

Name	Age	Occupation
Kleinsasser, Jacob	23	Works in mill
Barbara	24	
Jacob	2	
Susana	4 mo.	
Hofer, John	20	Farmer
Maria	23	
Jacob	1	
Hofer, John	19	Farmer
Rebecca	21	
Jacob	2	
Knels, Susana	64	Farmer, widowed
Susana	41	Widowed, handicapped
Grosz, Catharine	56	Farmer, widowed
Christian	16	
Paul	12	
Hofer, Anna	26	Farmer, widowed
Anna	6	
Susana	4	
Sahra	1	
Knels, Jacob	34	Farmer
Sahra	33	
Jacob	9	
Catharine	2	
Wallman, Justina	56	Farmer, widowed

1880 Census
Wolf Creek Russian Hutterite Colony, Dorias Walter, Pres.

Name	Age	Remarks
Walter, Dorias	45	Brother of Pres., colony herder
Anna	44	
Walter, Jacob	43	Pres. of Colony, priest, preacher
Maria (second wife)	31	
Elias	17	Son of first wife
Catherine	16	From first wife
Sarah	12	From first wife
Maria	9	From second wife
Rebecca	7	From second wife
Anna	5	From second wife
Barbara	5	From second wife
Susan	3	From second wife
Stahl, Jacob	33	Works on farm
Susan	33	
Jacob	10	
Paul	9	
John	5	
Susan	4	
Maria	1 mo.	
George	1 mo.	
Stahl, Michael	43	Preacher
Susan	44	
Hofer, Paul	46	Works on farm
Sarah	37	
Sarah	16	
Catherine	13	
Anna	4	
Paul	1	
Stahl, Peter	21	Works on a farm
Maria	18	
Susan	2 mo.	
Waldner, Christian	25	Works on farm
Anna	24	
Elizabeth	3	
Anna	1 mo.	
Hofer, Samuel	35	Works on farm
Rachel	35	
Sam	13	
Jacob	10	
Susan	7	
Hofer, Jacob	58	Has charge of hennery fowls, part deaf from sickness 40 yrs. since.
Rebecca	57	
Hofer, Jacob Jr.	20	Works on farm
Barbara	20	
Hofer, George	19	Second miller in mill
Rebecca	19	
Stahl, Henry	31	Teaches Church school
Maria	31	
Maria	3	
Catherine	2 mo.	
Walter, Elias	30	Works on colony farm. Grandfather of John Wurtz Wilson Sid.
Susan	31	
Susan	5	
Maria	2	
Wertz, John	25	First miller in mill. Koller Wurtz, grandfather of John Wurtz Wilson Sid.
Rachel	22	
Susan	3	
John	1	
Hofer, Christian	26	Works on colony farm
Ustina	27	
Rebecca	7	
Susan	3	
Hofer, Joshua	25	Works in mill
Anna	25	
Catherine	5	
Anna	2	
Hofer, Jacob	39	Works on farm
Elizabeth	36	
Jacob	14	
Elizabeth	12	
Susan	4	

Name	Age	Remarks
Walter, Paul	40	Attends to colony swine
Sarah	39	
Paul	16	
Dorias	11	
Henry	7	
Sarah	3	
Jacob	7 mo.	
Hofer, ——	72	Makes spinning wheels, $120 year
Susan	69	
Walter, Paul	25	Works on colony farm
Sarah	25	
Paul	2	
Jacob	2 mo.	
Wollman, Daniel ? (David)	20	Works on colony farm
Marg.	19	
Gross, William	25	Works on colony farm
Anna	22	
Anna	3	
William	1	
Stahl, John	24	Shoemaker
Anna	35	
John	12	Step son
Paul	10	Step son
Lawrence	9	Step son
Jacob	8	Step son
Peter	3	Son
Anna	2 mo.	
Hofer, Jacob	40	Colony blacksmith
Catherine	38	
David	17	
Sarah	15	
Rachel	12	
Jacob	11	
Maria	7	
Joseph	5	
Catherine	3	
John	1 mo.	
Walter, Zacherias	63	Works on farm
Marg.	55	
Marg. (daughter)	26	Sick for 2 yrs., from taking a severe cold
Maria	20	

Name	Age	Remarks
Stahl, John	38	Works on colony farm
Christina	30	Ailing for 4 yrs., otherwise sound
John	10	
Susanna	3	
Wollman, Daniel	46	Works on colony farm
Susan	51	
Catherina Walter	45	Sister-in-law
Gross, Frederic	23	Works on colony farm
Maria	22	
Frederic	3	
Maria	1	
Stahl, Henry	65	Works on colony farm
Barbara	65	
Barbara	20	
Walter, Darius	69	
Catherine	63	
Hofer, Jeremiah	64	Works on farm
Barbara	41	Second wife
Catherine	13	
Maria	9	
Barbara	1	
Stahl, William	76	Works around garden
Paul	15	Son
Walter, Henry	80	Laborer

1880 Census
Elm Spring Russian Colony, Jacob Wipf, Pres.

Name	Age	Notes
Whipf, Jacob	43	President, preacher
Rebecca	40	
Jacob	18	
John	16	
Paul	14	
Anna	12	
Elizabeth	10	
Maria	8	
Rebecca	6	
Joeph	1	
Hofer, Peter	44	Preacher
Susanna	53	
Anna	19	
Maria	17	
Rohanna	14	
Sara	12	
Joseph	8	
Waldner, John	41	House? (horse) overseer
Susanna	39	
John	17	
George	12	
Joseph	10	
Anna	6	
Susanna	4	
Jacob	3 mo.	
Entz, Peter	32	Colony blacksmith
Sara	32	
Peter	11	
Joseph	9	
John	7	
Maria	9 mo.	Step daughter
Entz, Peter	56	Works on colony farm
Maria	55	
Susanna	16	
Joseph	13	
Katherine	11	
Entz, John	28	Colony herder
Susanna	29	
Jacob	7	
John	2	
Hofer, John	52	Colony gardener
Rohanna	52	
Susanna	17	
Michael	15	
Katherine	11	
Mendel, Michael	47	Works on colony farm
Maria (second wife)	28	
Maria	20	
Anna	17	
Michael	15	
John	13	
Joseph	11	
Paul	9	
Lawrence	5	
Wertz, John	30	Works on farm
Catherine	28	
John	8	
Catherine	6	
Joseph	2 mo.	
Sam	2 mo.	
Catherine	55	Mother
Joseph	16	Brother
Andreas	14	Brother
Whipf, Elias	47	Works on farm
Magdaline	39	
Elias	19	
John	14	
Andrew	12	
Jacob	10	
Joseph	8	
Paul	6	
Michael	5 mo.	
Waldner, George Jr.	28	Works on farm
Maria	30	
George	5	
Joseph	1	
Waldner, George Sr.,	66	Works on farm
Catherine	38	Daughter

Name	Age	Remarks
Waldner, Jacob	24	Works on farm
Barbara	23	
Anna	3	
Jacob	10 mo.	
Hofer, Peter	63	Works on farm
Maria	28	Daughter
Rebecca	23	
Gross, George	31	Carpenter
Sarah	28	
George	8	
Sara	6	
Paul	1	
Kleinsasser, Zacherias	54	Works on farm
John	15	
Anna	13	
Kleinsasser, Joseph	48	Works on farm
Anna	49	
Anna	19	
Joseph	17	
Samuel	16	
Sarah	12	
Susanna	10	
John	8	
Peter	4	
Hofer, David,	25	Works on farm
Rebecca	23	
Maria	2	
Hofer, Jacob	21	Works on farm, son of John Hofer, gardener.
Susanna	21	
Jacob	10 mo.	
Hofer, John	25 (or 23)	
Rebecca	22	
Sam	2	
Anna	6 mo.	

1880 Census
Hutterite Colony, Tripp, S.D.

Name	Age
Wipf, Joseph	29
Katherine	26
Katherine	9
Joseph	7
John	3
Sara	1
Waldner, Michael	46
Sara	31
John	18
Zacherias	17
Jacob	12
George	10
Elizabeth	9
Rachel	7
Susanna	4
Sarah	1
Waldner, Frederic	44
Katherine	34
Anna	20
Frederic	18
Jacob	11
Baldasser	10
Susanna	8
Maria	3
Walter, Tobias	64
Sara	61
Katherine	18
Stahl, Martin	46
Hester	55
Maria	17
Susanna	14
Rebecca	10
Stahl, John	43
Katherine	43
John	9
Madeline	2

Waldner, Mathias 32
Elizabeth 35
    Joseph 11
    Elizabeth 9

Waldner, Michael 30
Justina 35
    Justina 14
    Christian 11
    Anna 8

Johnson, Peter (Janzen) .. 26
Sarah 26
    Katherine 4
    Sara 1

Waldner, Joseph 23
Maria 22

Waldner, Michael .... 23 Son of Michael and Sara
Katherine 20
    Michael 2

Location of Hutterites in South Russia

Courtesy of Emil J. Waltner, Freeman, South Dakota

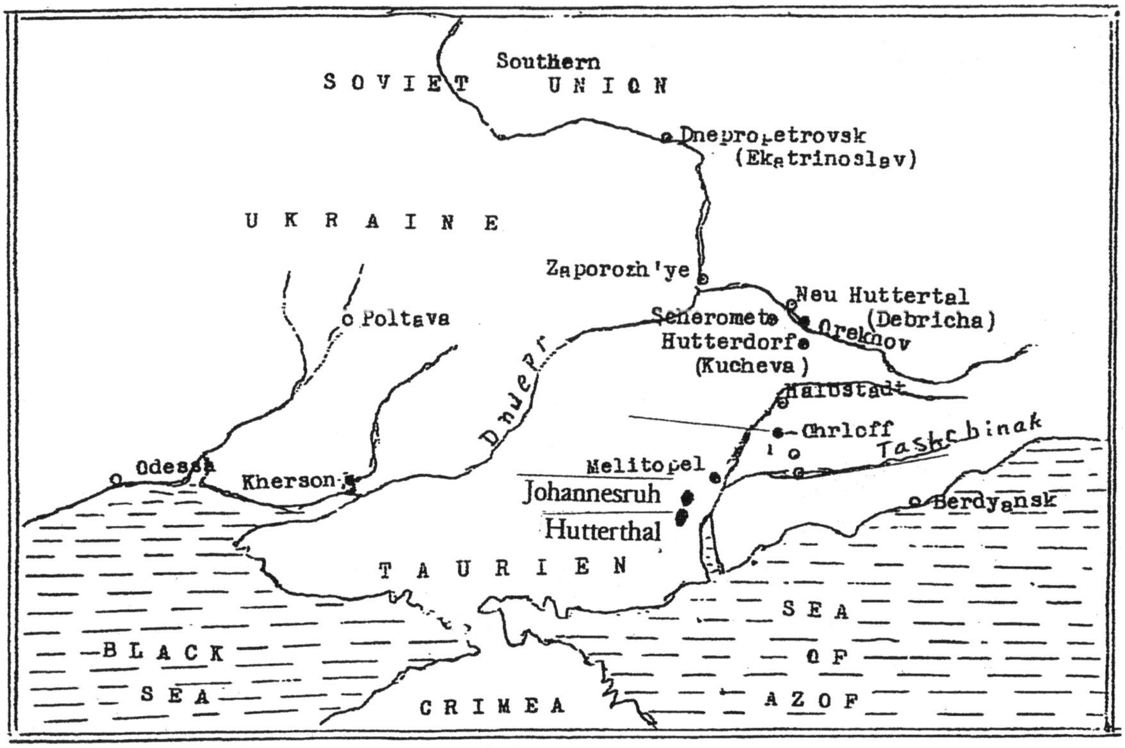

Since the first printing of this Centennial Publication, a detailed map of Russia has been found that shows all the Hutterite dorfs. This map shows Hutterthal as being 12 miles southwest of Melitopel and Neu Hutterthal as northeast of Zaporoshje, about 30 miles northwest of Hutterdorf. Also Shaermet is about 10 miles southeast of Hutterdorf.

Hutterthal	founded 1843	12 miles southwest of Melitopel
Johannesruh	founded 1853	3 miles north of Hutterthal
Hutterdorf (Kucheva)	founded 1857	near Orekhov, 80 miles north of Hutterthal
Neu Hutterthal (Debricha)	founded 1866	near Hutterdorf
Schaermet	founded 1868	10 miles west of Hutterdorf

Chapter 5

(Translated excerpts from)

Die Hungersnot in Russland und Unsere Reise um Die Welt

(The Famine in Russia and Our Trip Around The World)

By D. M. Hofer
K.M.B. Publishing House, Chicago, 1924.

The author: David M. Hofer was born in Johannesruh, Russia on July 24, 1869 and died in Chicago, Illinois on December 31, 1944. In 1879 he emigrated to the United States with his parents and settled on a farm near Bridgewater, South Dakota. From 1902 to 1914 he was engaged in grain and banking businesses. In 1914 he entered the ministry of the K.M.B. Conference. Together with Joseph W. Tschetter he founded the Lincoln Avenue Gospel Mission in Chicago in 1915 and continued with this work for many years. From 1917 to 1933 he also edited *The Wahrheitsfreund,* the official organ of the K.M.B. Conference.

In the fall of 1922 Rev. Hofer and his wife went to Russia to participate in the relief work of the American Mennonite Relief Administration. This was a special organization set up under the recently organized Mennonite Central Committee. Its function was to organize and carry out relief work in Russia during the famine following the Revolution. During the eight-month period of service with A.M.R.A. the Hofers were headquartered at Halbstadt. Working with local relief committees he administered the relief distribution program of a 60 village unit.

At the end of this period the Hofers traveled inside Russia visiting points of interest in areas where there were or had once been Mennonite or Hutterisch settlements. At several places he also conducted evangelistic services. They also visited Moscow and several other large cities.

After leaving Russia the Hofers began an extended tour around the world which took then through European countries, the Holy Land, India, China, and Japan. After an absence of a year and nine months they returned to Chicago where he continued his publication and city mission work and wrote "Famine in Russia and Our Trip Around the World." (Biographical sources taken from his book and from Vols. I and II of the Mennonite Encyclopedia.)

FAMINE IN RUSSIA AND OUR TRIP AROUND THE WORLD

pages 57 - 59:

Dobrischin (Neu-Hutterthal)

. . . We drove to the village of Neu-Hutterthal which was well known to us from hearsay. The village is probably better known by the name Dobrischin. It was especially important to us because it was the home of my wife's parents, Mr. and Mrs. Joseph Hofer (No. 15) who migrated from here to America in 1874.

Ruins of Jak Mendel's house in Dobrischin.

Unfortunately we found only two dwellings left from that time. We were told these were the homes of old Jakob Tschetter and of David Tschetter. Because of the war we found only ruins of Jakob Mendel's house. Seven people had been murdered in it. The outer and middle walls were still standing and one could see that it had been a spacious house. A small mound was all that was left to show where the big barn had once stood. The windmill was no longer there. Only ruins were left of the other houses in the village. Seven families numbering 40 people now live here in apparent poverty.

David Tschetter's house in Dobrischin.

My (D. M. Hofer) Birthplace in Johannesruh.

The dam at the lower end of the village is still there and the pond is filled with water. Quite a few trees are still standing and if some of them could speak they might have told us about the Dobrischiners of the '70ties. Of the old inhabitants of that time we found none anymore. The last ones are said to have perished in the war.

Across the dam lies the Russian village of Lubimowka with about 2000 inhabitants living in typical Russian homes. Some of them still remembered Neu-Hutterthal.

. . . Finally we came to the Alt-Kolonie, to Neuendorf where we found a certain Tschetter whose relatives—Isaac, Jakob, Paul and Lohrenz Tschetter and their widowed sister Barbara Glanzer of South Dakota we know well. He was very glad to see us and with tears in his eyes he told us of his and his eight children's sad plight.

Pages. 129 - 137:

Johannesruh

It was a beautiful day, the weather was pleasant and the mercury in the thermometer was above the freezing point. We made the necessary preparations for our expedition, boarded the auto and drove along the Molotschna Valley—through ten Mennonite villages: Neu-Halbstadt, Muntau, Tiegenhagen, Schoenau, Fischau, Lindenau, Lichtenau, Blumenstein, Muensterberg, and Altonau. We went on through the big Russian village of Wosnjeszensk, across the steppe and in three hours we were in Johannesruh.

Johannesruh is the village where my cradle stood. It is a splendid model village in which our fathers with their Mennonite character could live in peace. With industrious labor and God's help and blessing they made their living. On arriving at our former residence I recognized our house at once. We found that August Vogel who had bought our place had moved away. Two families were living there now. We introduced ourselves and were invited to enter the house. We went through the entrance room into the living room and I recognized the walnut-faced glass cupboard at once. My late father, Michael Hofer (Household Number 10) had made it with his own hands.

In fantasy pictures of my childhood passed before my eyes. It was as though I saw my father walking up and down the room. I saw mother with her busy hands doing the housework. Thoughts of my two sisters, Maria and Elisabeth who have since died, came to me. I saw myself as a child playing with my brothers Micheal, Paul and Peter. Sister Susanna appeared before me as a baby. All this passed before my mind's eye in a few minutes. Strange feelings overcame me and I had to give reign to my tears . . . Soon I noticed that others of those present were also crying. When I was able to compose myself again the room was quiet and I said that I felt the urge to pray. We knelt down and I had to give heartfelt thanks to God for his wonderful guidance. After 43 years, once more I had the privilege of being in the house where our parents went in and out and shared life's joys and sorrows.

Apricot tree in my father's garden.

I felt the urge to see all the other rooms in the house, even the cellar and the upstairs. The kitchen and the big chimney were still there too. Of special interest was the fact that during the war a neighbor saved his life by hiding in this chimney for two weeks. The barn was still attached to the house. In the yard across from the house was a wine cellar which the villagers had used commerically before the war. The threshing-floor we used to use was still there, but in the orchard we found only an apricot tree which I could remember. The large mulberry tree was no longer there. In the woodlot beyond the garden only traces of oak stumps remained. After we had photographed the house, the brick gateway at the entrance to the yard, and the old apricot tree we wanted to go to the house of my uncle Johann D. Hofer, but found that it no longer existed. Accompanied by two brothers, August and Friedrich Bischlar, we went from house to house. With good reason this walk through the village was of intense interest to me, for it took me back to my childhood years.

Of the original purchasers from the '70ties only five were still living. Among them was Michael Blank whom I remembered well. He remembered me too and knew my father. We had a lively conversation in which we recalled many past events. We also met the former shepherd and his wife. They lived on the old Joseph Waldner (Hafner place, household No. 14). A widow Keller was living on the Joseph Wipf place (No. 13). Wipf now lives near Doland, South Dakota. This woman sent greetings to Wipf and his family in America. Old Mrs. Ott living in the house of Michael Hofer (No. 17) is also alive and sent greetings to old "Rotschild" and his family. I recognized the flower decorated stove in this house immediately, also the beautiful wardrobe with the initials M.H. and the date 1869. It was just as old as I.

The row of village houses stand in the same sequence as they did in 1879. Every yard was familiar and made me feel young again. It took me back 43 years. In the schoolhouse I found the same pulpit and felt as if I were seeing my teacher, Johann L. Wipf, standing behind it and hearing him relate stories from the Bible. The schoolyard where we pupils and our teacher often played was still the same. The same community well below the school still furnishes good water today as it did then.

At my grandfather's place the old blacksmith shop was still standing. In the house almost everything remained as it was then. We went into the room where my Aunt Barbara died and lay on her bier. I remembered the boiled eggs which my grandmother often gave me and the other grandchildren. With me I had the official Johannesruh family register which I had gotten from my father. It was from the year 1872—51 years old now. In the house of my grandfather Paul Gross, I found a document from the year 1850—73 years old. It contained the following list: Magistrate—Christian Gross; Councilmen—Paul Maendel and Elias Wipf; Overseers—Jakob Zetter, David Hofer and Michael Hofer. This was very interesting to me.

The old mill which had been on the Matthias and Paul Glanzer place had been moved to the old Paul Mendel place. We looked at it and I remembered the

Old windmill at Johannesruh.

accident in which it had crushed the head of my cousin Paul Glanzer so that he died suddenly and was brought to an early grave.

On the Jeremias Wollman place there is quite a large modern steam mill which is nationalized and not in operation. The old windmill below the Andreas and Jakob Kleinsasser brothers' place is still standing and doing its duty for the village.

The three rent houses at the south end of the village are still there. Even the old house of old shoemaker Schiller still stands on the side street. The old shepherd house had been moved from the upper side of the village to the lower end near the brick kiln. Of the old brick sheds only the ruins remain. The graveyard on the middle street is still there and is still used for the same purpose by the present villagers.

The whole village with its well planned layout, its beautiful brick fences, and its adjoining land complex made a good impression on us. The village consists of 38 large units and eight smaller units with a total population of 408 people. In the whole village there are presently only 37 horses, 121 cows, 103 sheep and two oxen. There are very few fruit trees, mulberry or shade trees along the alley.

In the afternoon we drove to the less familiar village of Huttertal.

Huttertal

On our arrival there our chauffeur asked, "Where shall I stop?" I answered, "At Mr. Schwitzgebel's place (Household No. 10) where our relative Michael Wollman (my aunt Katharina) once lived." We were lucky, although old Schwitzgebel had died his son Albert had a vivid recollection of the Wollman family. He asked about David, Anna, Jakob, Elisabeth, Andreas and Johann. He remembered that on the day of their departure Johann had hidden and had not wanted to go along to America.

When we had looked around in the house we went into the barn and saw the same well which the Wollmans had left at the time of their departure. When we had photographed the house we drove to a Mr. Eduart Hoffmann (Household No. 18). Here the family of Elias Wipf (my aunt Justina) had lived. When I showed Hoffmann the photograph of my father he said, "Why that is Michael Hofer the chief magistrate of Johannesruh!" "Well, yes," I said, "I am his son." Thereupon another lively discussion of that good old time followed. Since then they have had very good harvests in Huttertal. The sad concern he related to us about his own family was the fact that his wife had been sick and bedfast for the past 37 years. We visited this unfortunate woman in her room and had to think of the man who had been sick for 38 years when Jesus healed him. The house on this place had been rebuilt, but the barn and the wells in the barn as well as on the yard were still the same.

The consequences of the war are not as noticeable in Johannesruh and Huttertal as in the villages of the Molotschna, therefore the people here are not as discouraged.

The wonderful day that had greeted us that morning was drawing to a close and we drove back to Johannesruh. Through the telescope we saw the beautiful shade tree adorned village of Darmstadt. As we left Johannesruh the view through our telescope showed us the Russian village of Schilhofka, a place where our parents used to buy ducks and geese. A large orthodox church with its high steeple seemed to be the dominating building in the village. Our path led diagonally across the steppe over the Taschtschenak not far from where the sheep farm of Johannes Kornis had been and soon we were in Melitopel.

An old Colony house in Kuschtschewa (Hutterdorf).

Pages 143 - 144:

Kuschtschewa

. . . To our pleasant surprise the road led past the old Hutterisch-Mennonite settlement of Kuschtschewa. Here about a dozen of the typical old houses from some fifty years ago are still standing. We made inquiry of an old man of 76 years who well remembered the time when Mennonite Brotherhoods practicing community of goods lived here. A lovely little stream bordered by trees winds its way through the region. The area seemed to be very fertile and we saw many sheaves of gain in the fields.

Chapter 6
Pictures of Days Gone By

Main street of Freeman looking North

East side of main street looking south, May 13, 1916. Notice the Sugar Bowl, later destroyed by fire.

Andrew Hofer and John Tschetter's Grocery Store, located in the vacant lot between the old lumberyard and the creamery repair shop.

Kleinsasser Roller Mill destroyed by fire, Sept. 15, 1911; was run and owned by Isaac Kleinsasser.

Left side of the People's Store. Owned by Michael Wollman (Stur-Michael).

Right side of the Peoples Store. Picture was taken about 1908.

J. J. Pullman's Drug Store in Freeman located in the present Walter Furniture Store.

John A. Wipf's Gambles Store in 1936. Notice prices of pans on left wall.

Jake T. Gross's first cream buying station located in the elevator east of The Depot.

Freeman Telephone office owned by J. J. Mendel at left, Barbara Miller operator, and Jake T. Gross, repairman.

Freeman Telephone office located west of Schamber Bros. Store.

Behind the teller's window at the Merchants State Bank in the early 20's with Jacob J. Wollman and Reinhold Dewald.

Merchants State Bank with Jacob J. Wollman at your service.

Advertising their merchandise are Bob Wipf, Freeman and David J. (Kaiser) Wipf, Menno.

Jake T. Gross in his creamery in Freeman in 1924.

Freeman Rural Mail Carriers in 1913. Alex Wipf, Jacob A. Gering, Andrew W. Gross, and Jacob W. Gross.

City Service Station built in 1929, by Jacob J. Pullman at the location of the present Nutra Flo Fertilizer tanks west of the Farmers Co-op Elevator. Standing is a 1929 Chevy delivery truck. Gas price on sign is $.19 and $.22 per gal.

Printer J. J. Mendel owned and operated the Freeman Courier Office from 1902, till 1960. Katie Gross was his assistant for many years.

John K. Hofer druggest in Freeman for many years.

New 1928 Reo Speedwagon owned by Jacob A. Kleinsasser of Freeman. His White Eagle, later Mobile station was located east of what is now the AMPI Creamery.

Pollman and Wipf Elevator. Location was the first Elevator east of the Depot. Was dismantled in 1928.

The Merchants State Bank was built in 1913. Note the Laundry Bath and Barber Shop in the basement.

"Come in without knocking—
Go out the same way."

Jacob J. Mendel's slogan by his office was "Come in without knocking, go out the same way."

Freeman Depot

Dolton Elevators: front, Meyer & Tschetter Elevator; Middle, A. A. Wollman Elevator; Rear, Shandard Elevator.

Paul J. Gross, the blacksmith man in Hitchcock, South Dakota for many years.

John T. Gross Cream buying station at Bridgewater in 1922.

Joe T. Gross cream buying station at Viborg.

The Gross Brothers, Joe, Jake, and John started with cream buying and went into the hatching business. They had Gross Hatchery's located at Freeman, Marion, Menno, Armour, Viborg, Canistota, Bridgewater, Emery, and Yankton.

A Look at the Country Life

Homestead shack now standing on the Raymond D. Hofer farm. Shack was used by Mathias Waldner to homestead, two miles west and one north of Freeman.

Homestead of David Gross, (Schultzel David) South of Olivet

Joseph C. Kleinsasser sod house built about 1875, which is located 3 miles west and 1 south of Freeman.

A common site, a house and barn combination. This house was built with Johann J. Gering's home-made bricks. The barn was later removed and the house remodeled, and is still used today, on the Raymond D. Hofer farm.

Home of Darius Hofer, 3 miles west and 1 north of Menno. Note house was built on the side of a hill.

Home of Andrew Hofer. Located 6 miles west and 4½ north of Freeman.

Taking down the old stone barn on the Joe D. Hofer farm.

Josua Hofer and his sons out plowing. One way to get a lot done in a day.

Breaking Sod in North Dakota

Thrashing with horse power was a common site many years ago.

A Big Machine

This was the way to make hay on the Joseph C. Kleinsasser farm.

Thrashing at Andrew Pullman

Thrashing Rig at W. W. Gross in 1910

When our forefathers came to America they used oxen like this.

Paul Kleinsasser family chasing train car load of hogs to Market in Freeman, about 1912.

MMmmm good watermelon, but look at all those stacks of grain still to thrash.

A farm auction sale on a cold day. Look at all those warm coats.

What a car, a Studebaker. License plate dates it at 1913.

Homesteading near Wall, South Dakota, John I. Walter and Wm. Hofer, about 1910.

Scarecrow plagued with grasshoppers in the drought years of the 1930's.

Jacob and David Wollman homesteading in Montana, in 1915.

The Old School Days

Early picture of the Summit School District 51, located 6 miles north and 1 mile west of Freeman.

Diamond Valley School District No. 56 in 1905. Teacher was Wm. Borman.

The Riverside School District No. 29

Freeman High School in 1911

Summit School District 51 about 1918. Teacher was Mrs. Jacob L. Hofer.

Steaming up for a days work at Gross School District 54.

Progressive School District No. 20 located beside Hutterdorf Church. The teacher was Peter J. Stahl.

Cottonwood School District No. 96 located across from Silver Lake, 6½ miles north of Freeman.

Pupils of Gross School District No. 54 located 3 miles west and 3 north of Freeman. The teacher was Dave P. Gross about 1928.

Foster School District No. 59. Teacher was Dave P. Gross in 1936. Most of the pupils were from New Elm Spring Colony.

Antelope School District No. 52, located 3 miles west and 1 south of La Delle, South Dakota.

Apple Grove School District No. 49 in 1936-37, located 1 mile north and 2½ west of Freeman.

The New Elm Spring Colony children were hauled to school in a hayrack at Foster School District No. 59.

Dave P. Gross didn't worry about the gas shortage in 1926 as he was leaving home tc teach school for another week.

Churches and Church Activities

Old Neu Hutterthal Church in 1947. A day of Bible School just beginning.

Hutterthal Church located 1 mile west and 3 north of Freeman.

Old Salem K. M. B. Church about 1942

Bethany Mennonite Church. It was destroyed by fire, Nov. 4, 1945.

Baptism in the creek at Chasley, North Dakota.

Neu Hutterthal Church choir in 1935

Jacob H. Mendel gave evening singing lessons in country schools during the winter months.

Funeral wagon of J. J. Kleinsasser of Freeman

A card like this was made for relatives to remember loved ones. They were written in English and some in the German language.

A Look at the Colony

Dining Hall and Meeting House of the Old Wolf Creek Colony, west of Freeman.

Homes at the old Wolf Creek Colony

Old Wolf Creek dam about 1922

Milltown Mill

The art of making combs was brought to America from Russia. The Bon Homme Colony still have the machine and knowledge to make combs.

Machine used to thin the edges of a piece of steer horn for making an old Hutterite comb.

Machine used to cut the teeth into the old Hutterite comb.

Wolf Creek Colony Mill west of Freeman

Rock Port Colony Mill

This clock brought from Russia is still in use at the home of the Minister Jacob Waldner of Bon Homme Colony.

MENNONITE AID PLAN CONFERENCE AT THE BETHANY MENNONITE CHURCH, FREEMAN, IN 1907

1. Peter Mendel
2. Sam Z. Wipf
3. George W. Tschetter
4. John L. Hofer
5. Sam Walter
6. Joe K. Schrag
7. D. S. Weldy
8. Paul Kleinsasser, Sr.
9. George B. Neufeld
10. David Goertz
11. A. A. Wael
12. John Regier
13. Isaac Walter
14. Jacob J. B. Walter
15. Paul M. Hofer
16.
17. Paul Tschetter (Sap Paula)
18.
19. Elias M. Wipf
20.
21. George Rupp
22. Joseph Tschetter (Silver Fox)
23. George D. Hofer
24. David Ewert
25. Peter G. Hofer
26. David J. Mendel
27. John C. Mueller
28. Joe L. Hofer
29.
30. Jacob L. Hofer
31. David Hofer
32. Tom Kaufman
33. Peter J. Graber (Sturi)
34. Andrew R. M. Hofer
35. David J. Wipf
36. Peter Graber (Graber Hons)
37. Andrew C. Gross

Michael R. Hofer 100-Year Birthday Anniversary — August 4, 1829-1929

GUESTS AS LISTED BY JOHN K. HOFER

1. Frank F. Walter
2. Sam J. Hofer, Beadle Co.
3. Mrs. Sam J. Hofer
4. Paul J. Hofer, Beadle Co.
5.
6. Math Kleinsasser
7.
8. Mrs. Paul M. Hofer
9. Sam A. Hofer
10. Joseph F. Walter
11. Jacob L. Hofer
12. Paul M. Hofer
13. John L. Hofer
14.
15. Ben J. Kleinsasser
16.
17.
18. Joe K. Hofer
19. Theresa Hofer now Mrs. David S. Tschetter
20. Rebecca Hofer daughter of Michael R. Hofer
21.
22. Mrs. Arnold Hofer
23. Edward A. Hofer
24. Matilda Hofer now Mrs. John Nachtigal
25.
26.
27. Margorie Hofer now Mrs. Sam A. Hofer
28. Mrs. Peter A. Hofer (Pearl)
29. Mrs. Dr. E. J. Hofer
30. Amelia Hofer now Mrs. John S. Gross
31. Anna Gross (Puller)
32. Joe R. Hofer
33. Alice Nachtigal now Mrs. Ulrickson
34.
35. Alfred Nachtigal
36.
37. John B. Wollman
38. Eliz. Hofer now Mrs. Arthur Erck
39. Andrew R. M. Hofer
40. Jacob M. Hofer
41. Paul Hofer Father Jacob M. Hofer
42.
43. Anna Mrs. Paul E. Hofer
44. David D. Hofer
45. Martin Hofer son of Dr. M. M. Hofer
46. Mrs. Jacob M. Hofer
47. Jacob J. Kleinsasser
48. Eliz. Mrs. Christ Freeman daughter of Jacob M. Hofer
49. Sarah Hofer daughter of Jacob M. Hofer
50.
51.
52.
53.
54. Paul D. Hofer
55. Dr. M. M. Hofer
56. John R. Hofer
57. Robert W. Hofer son of Dr. M. M. Hofer
58. Peter J. S. Hofer
59. Adina Mrs. Peter J. S. Hofer
60. Annie, Mrs. Wm. S. Glanzer
61.
62. Maggie, Mrs. Geo. M. Hofer
63. Mrs. John R. Hofer
64. Mrs. Joe R. Hofer
65. Abe L. Kleinsasser
66. Lavina Hofer daughter of John R. Hofer
67. Ruth Hofer
68.
69. Mrs. Jacob J. Gross (Puller)
70. Viola, Mrs. Joe Mendle
71.
72.
73. Eliz. Tschetter, Mrs. Herman Fluth
74. Jacob L. Hofer
75.
76. Mrs. Jacob L. Hofer, Sr.
77. Jacob J. Gross (Puller)
78. MICHAEL R. HOFER
79.
80.
81.
82. Mrs. Michael R. Hofer
83. Mr. Will M. Hofer
84. Joe Hofer, R. Ph. of Bridgewater, S.D.
85.
86. Joe P. Glanzer is holding Aaron
87. Michael M. Hofer, Jr.
88.
89.
90.
91.
92. Mrs. Paul Tschetter No. 34
93. Joshua R. M. Hofer
94. Clara Kleinsasser now Mrs. Clifford Rockwell
95. Eliz. Hofer now Mrs. Dr. M. M. Hofer
96. John P. Kleinsasser (Morgan)
97. Andrew A. Hofer
98. Anna Hofer daughter of Will M. Hofer
99. Mrs. Joe H. Hofer
100. Mrs. Paul Tschetter Sr.
101.
102. Enoch Hofer next to him is Mrs. Enoch Hofer
103. Paul Tschetter, Sr.
104. Paul Glanzer (Joe P. Glanzer) Freeman, S.D.
105. Alma Mrs. Joe E. Hofer Joe P. Glanzer
106. Mary Ruth Glanzer, Mrs. Joe Hofman. Her father Joe P. Glanzer
107.
108.
109.
110.
111. Mary E. Mrs. Joshua Hofer
112.
113.
114. Mrs. John M. Wollman
115. Moses Glanzer
116.
117.
118.
119. Paul M. Tschetter
120.
121. Susanna Hofer daughter of Michael R. Hofer (Mrs. John M. Wollman)
122. John M. Wollman, Bridgewater, S.D.
123. David R. M. Hofer
124. David R. M. Hofer's daughter
125. Mary Jansen married to Erwin Schmidt
126. Ruth Tschetter
127. Paul A. Tschetter
128. Mrs. Jacob J. Kleinsasser
129. Mrs. David R. M. Hofer
130. Mrs. Paul J. Hofer
131. Luella Schmeichel
133. Jacob B. Tschetter
134.
135.
136. Paul L. Hofer
137. Mrs. J. S. P. Hofer
138. Mrs. Will M. Hofer
139.
140.
141.
142.
143. Robert Bauerle
144.
145. George M. Hofer, Freeman
146.
147. Mrs. Geo. J. Janzen
148. Mrs. Robert Bauerle, Parkston
149.
150. Mrs. D. M. Hofer
151. Jacob J. Kleinsasser Jr.
152. Peter Gross
153. Rev. David M. Hofer
154. Mrs. George J. Hofer
155.
156
157.
158.

A reunion of the descendents of Rev. Joseph and Anna (Walter) Hofer of near Olivet. He died August 28, 1905. Reunion was held at the Huron fairgrounds Sunday, July 9, 1950.

First Tornado Ever Photographed?

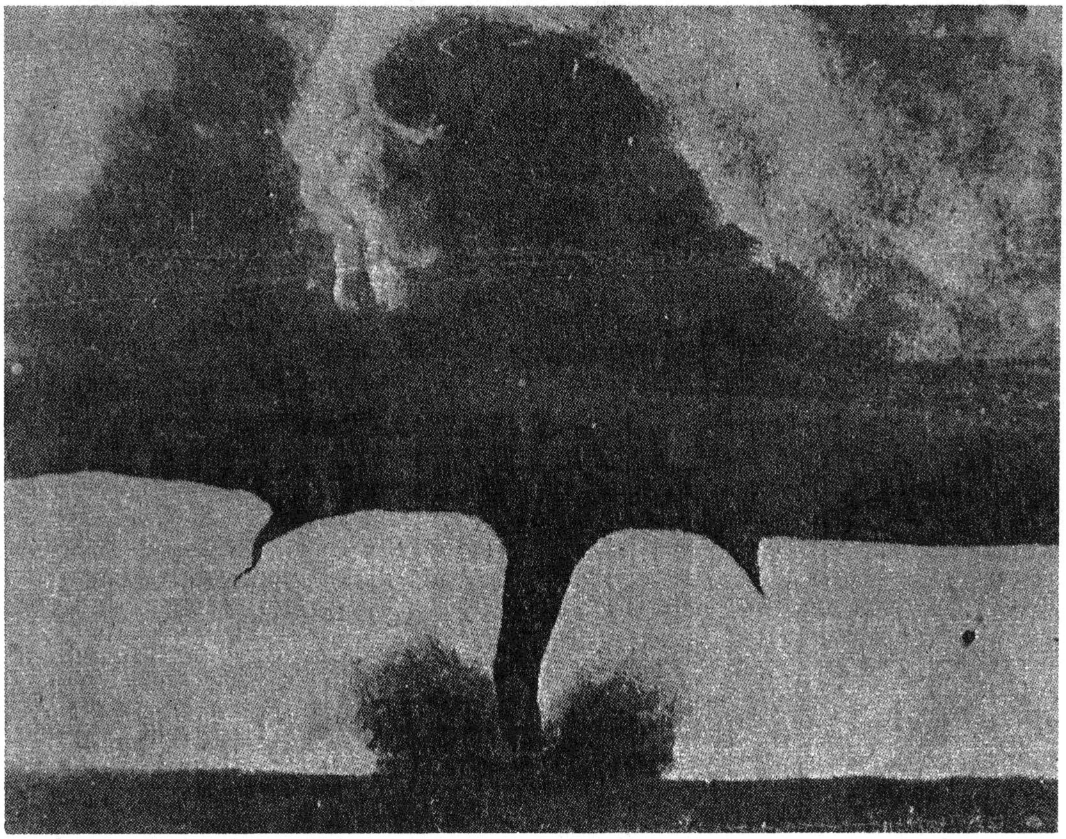

The clouds in the upper part of this photo, taken of the Aug. 28, 1884 cyclone near Forestburg and believed to be one of the first ever photographed, are much like any that may be seen in any community on the approach of a thunder storm. The lower part shows the funnel-shaped "twister." Also seen are two embryos or baby tornadoes in the making. Observers say they saw from seven to nine of these baby "twisters" at one time. Only one hit the earth, doing considerable damage.

Picture copied from an issue of the Daily Argus-Leader, used from a collection of articles compiled by the Sanborn County Historical Society.

From *Der Wahrheitsfruend*

Freeman, Hutchinson County, South Dakota
August 30, 1884

Dear ''Rundschau'',

It's been a long time since I wrote, so now I will endeavor to make up for my neglect in letting you know of the terrible misfortune that happened in our settlement. I want to share this experience with the readers of ''Rundschau.'' On the 28 A.M. the sun shone real hot, the wind, from the South was oppressive and sultry so that it was hard to breathe and people, like the animals, could hardly work. At 2:30 a black, omminous storm cloud came from the North which made the oppressive heat go even high for a terrible storm to take place.

Toward 3:30 a whirl wind started to form in the West, first small, but in a few seconds with great force it turned toward the North where it connected with that rolling storm cloud, where it suddenly turned itself into a double funnel.

Suddenly a bolt of lightning with a terrible crash of thunder, which seemed to shake the earth, came down. It was as though this was the signal for the devastation to start, for immediately the tornado struck the earth and moved from the North to the Southeast. Anything that was in it's path was carried away. From my farm I could see everything for about 10 or 12 miles and with fear and trembling see it come toward us. It is impossible to describe how terrible it was, as in the twinkling of an eye the clouds and earth transformed itself as it rolled about. I haven't figured out yet how wide and long the tail of the tornado was, because I'm busy threshing. It didn't reach far and wide, but wherever it struck it left a lot of misery and damage.

It did the worst damage on the Elias Wipf farm, who lived in Wolf Creek, and was busy cutting hay. His father, a man of 74 years, his son Elias, wife and a son, 7 years old, loaded up the hay when the tornado struck. Young Wipf motioned for them to follow him and hurried to the house, but it was impossible for him to help them, since everything was crashing, quivering and breaking. Doors and windows were pressed inward and everything in the yard was carried away. Wipf quickly grabbed his half dead mother and took her to the cellar, also his three children and he stayed in the cellar till the crashing, roaring and noise eased up a little he went out but what a sight he saw. The big wooden barn which adjoined the house was gone except a part of the side wall lay there. The kitchen which was built on to the house, the shingles and most of the boards were all gone. The hay had disappeared. The pig barn and the feeder pigs were nowhere to be seen. The horses, machines, besides the binder were gone, the sheepbarn had no roof, just the bare walls. In one word everything was destroyed.

Where were father, mother and son, oxen and wagons? Finally everything was found but in what condition: naked, disfigured corpses. One ox had its head torn off and the other one was also killed. The wagon was broken in pieces, not a spoke in the hub, the rim of the wheel was also in pieces.

The young woman (she was Wipf's second wife) was married to Wipf for 1½ years. Her name was Maria Hofer. She and the boy took refuge behind a wheat stack, but with all the rest of the grain you couldn't see where the stacks had stood. The terrible disfigured corpses were buried the following day in the cool lap of the earth. May their ashes rest in peace.

After the tornado did it's damage on the Elias Wipf place it suddenly lifted itself and moved quick as lightening in a Southeasterly direction toward Freeman where it again came down to the ground. Like a snake, it was terrible to see how it flew here and there and blew all the flax around as it lay in the field. But the storm wasn't as bad as it was at Wolf Creek and no lives were lost. It only lasted a few minutes at Freeman and then it vanished as quickly as it came.

One farmer, Andrew Dekker, tried to hurry home when he saw the storm coming, but the storm caught him and lifted him up high, but he came down unharmed. The roof was torn off of his house and his threshed grain swept away. Wipf's neighbor, Jacob Tschetter, lost both his barns in the storm. Wipf lost four splendid horses and two pair of oxen and all his horned cattle. Only his sheep which were grazing in the distance, and three colts were saved. Poor man.

Those concerned will no doubt have a hard time to get over the terrible shock of these deaths. May the Lord our God have mercy on all of them.

Jakob Janzen

This letter was sent to Der Wahrheitsfruend years later by D. J. Mendel.

Chapter 7

Chronological History of Hutterite Mennonite Churches

The venture of compiling a history of churches of the community with a certain ethnic background is a rather difficult undertaking. Some people are very helpful in revealing information, others are rather reluctant. We will not guarantee that all dates will be 100% accurate because some are mere common sense estimates. In order to have every date exactly as it should be, one would have to do much more checking in many more records than was feasibly possible for this report. Then also many of the old church records were written in the German language which made things rather complicated for today's generation. The following are brief histories as we were able to find information:

NEU HUTTERTHAL
(rural Bridgewater)

The first minister of this congregation was Paul Tschetter who was elected to this position in Russia at the age of 21. He was one of the delegates along with Lorenz Tschetter, sent to Dakota Territory to investigate the possibility for migration and settlement. After their migration in 1874 the families conducted church services in their homes. Between 1880-1888 the services were moved to the schools. In 1888 the first church building was erected just 10 rods south of the present site. The name of the church was copied from a village in South Russia from whence the migration originated. The first church building was 30x48 feet and cost $1300. Later benches and other improvements were added for a cost of $600.

Some of the members of this church lived in the Menno area. Since transportation created a problem for these members, they met in schools and later Rev. Joseph Hofer was chosen to minister to this group.

Other members lived north of Bridgewater and felt they couldn't travel this distance so they too met in schools until a church building could be erected northeast of Bridgewater. This congregation was served by Rev. Michael J. Hofer. Later they moved to Bridgewater, and this is the congregation known as the Zion Mennonite Church today.

In 1952 the original church was moved 10 rods north, remodeled, two additions and a full basement were added and today serves the congregation quite adequately.

The ministers of this congregation have been as follows:

Paul Tschetter	1874-1919
John D. Hofer	1884-1914
David J. Wipf	1910-1937
Paul J. Tschetter	1910-1945
Albert Ewert	1947-1963
Peter Tschetter	1965-1974
Paul Kliewer	1974-(elect)

ZION MENNONITE (Bridgewater)

The Zion Church began with about ten families meeting in homes. (Check the Neu Hutterthal history.) Later a small church building was erected northeast of Bridgewater. Michael J. Hofer taught Sunday School and was later elected to serve as pastor.

In 1920 the group purchased the former Methodist Church building in Bridgewater which had been built in 1883. Rev. Michael Hofer served as pastor until 1950. Rev. Paul Quenzer filled this position until 1954. Rev. Paul Dahlenburg served from 1954 to 1960. He was succeeded by Rev. Abraham Friesen who served the congregation until 1964. Rev. Melvin Koehn served this congregation from 1964 to 1974.

Ground breaking services took place on the north end of Bridgewater on August 27, 1972 for a new facility. This was completed and dedicated on July 22, 1973. The total cost of this facility was approximately $110,000.

Hutterdorf Church and Progessive School Dist. 20

HUTTERDORF (rural Freeman)

Hutterdorf, as many of the other Hutterish background Mennonite churches, was the name of a village in Russia from whence our people migrated in 1874. To begin with eleven families constituted this congregation and the worship services were held in the homes. In 1880 the first school house was built in the community and from that time on worship services were conducted in the school house. Among the first families that came were two ministers, namely: Rev. William Tschetter and Rev. David Waldner. Rev. Tschetter was born Nov. 30, 1830 and died near Freeman on May 30, 1913, at the age of 83. He ministered a total of 32 years including some years in Russia.

In 1901 a church building was erected two miles south and three west of Freeman at a cost of $1700.

In 1879 Rev. John Hofer and Rev. Elias Wipf were elected to serve as ministers. Rev. Hofer was born Dec. 18, 1844 and died Oct. 31, 1916. He served the church for 37 years. Elias Wipf was born Jan. 1, 1852 and died July 27, 1910. Rev. Elias Wipf's grandmother was Anna Schrag Waldner. Anna Schrag and Professor Benj. P. Waltner's grandmother were sisters. Anna Schrag also was Mrs. J. J. Mendel's great grandmother, and retired banker John J. Tschetter's great grandmother.

The Hutterdorf Sunday School was organized in 1912 by David J. Mendel.

Rev. Peter J. Stahl served the congregation from 1916 until it was dissolved in 1961. All ministers before Rev. Stahl received no salaries. Even Rev. Stahl for many years received very little pay but depended upon his farming operation for financial support. In the later years of his ministry he received a reasonable monetary remuneration.

The majority of the church members joined the Bethany Church in Freeman when the church was dissolved and the building was sold and dismantled.

HUTTERTHAL (rural Freeman)

The history of this congregation really had its beginning in Russia in 1877, according to the old church record book. John L. Wipf and John Waldner were elected to serve as ministers at that time and then continued here in the Dakota Territory. Some families migrated in 1874, and some came as late as 1879. For the first few years the worship services were held in the homes. In 1882 the first church building was built on the southwest corner of section 15, township 99, range 56, which is approximately one mile west and two miles north of Freeman. This original building still stands today on the Roy Ensz farm near Silver Lake, 6 miles north of Freeman. The cost of the original building was $412. Twelve families constituted the total membership of this congregation. From this number it grew to 118 families today. In 1889 a second church building was built at the present site, one mile west and 3¼ miles north of Freeman, at a cost of $1720.82.

In 1952 the present brick structure was built with an educational wing added in 1967 at a total cost of approximately $140,000. In 1956 a new parsonage was built in Freeman.

In the early years of the church the ministers were actually lay people of the congregation and elected by the members. It was not until Rev. P. P. Tschetter was hired in 1921 that a salary was paid. All of the ministers except the last five were of our own Hutterish people. We could also mention that the first eight have passed to their eternal reward and the last seven are still living. Sermons were preached in the German language until the 1930's during Rev. Jacob B. Hofer's term as minister when English services were held one Sunday per month. There was no piano to accompany the singing until 1936.

The ministers that served this congregation are as follows:

John Kleinsasser	1879-1898
John Waldner	1879-1899
Paul Hofer	1879-1908

John L. Wipf 1879-1909
Joseph Hofer 1903-1906
John P. Hofer 1908-1925
P. P. Kleinsasser 1909-1914
J. W. Kleinsasser 1917-1919
P. P. Tschetter 1921-1937
Jacob B. Hofer 1926-1954
Ronald Von Riesen 1955-1956
Abe M. Wiebe 1956-1963
Harold Graber 1963-1964
Gerhard Peters 1964-1970
Vernon Lohrentz 1970-

SALEM M. B. (rural Bridgewater)

This congregation dates its beginning to 1886. The first minister was Rev. John Tschetter who served some 20 years and then moved to near Huron, S. Dak., and continued his ministry for another 30 years. The founders had no building to worship in, therefore, they as many others during their early years met in homes. In 1894 the services were moved to a sod school house. An addition was added to the school house to provide space to serve the noon meal because services continued all day. Families took turns in providing "Zwieback and Kaffee." This practice continued until the later 20's. In 1900, a church building was erected at the present site. In 1917 a full basement was added and in 1941 the building was remodeled and enlarged. In 1952 a parsonage was purchased in the city of Bridgewater.

During its history this congregation admitted over 700 members. Some families moved to Canada where they founded the Emmanuel Church at Langham, Sask., and assisted in the organization of the Salem Church near Waldheim, Sask. Some families moved to Beadle County, to the Bethel Church vicinity. Some moved to Spink County and established the Ebenezer Church near Doland. In Sully County the Emmanuel Church was established. Later people moved from Beadle County to California and the Zion Church came into being. The Bethesda Church in Huron is an off-spring of the Bethel Church in Beadle County.

On July 25, 1965, a ground breaking service was held for a new edifice and construction started shortly. On July 10, 1966 dedication services were held. The total cost of this beautiful structure was approximately $137,000 with 10,360 square feet of floor space including the educational wing.

In 1973 ground breaking services were held in Freeman for a new parsonage, and this lovely structure was dedicated the later part of February, 1974 with an open house observance.

Ministers that have served the congregation since 1886 are as follows:

Henry Goosen 1885-1899
John Tschetter 1886-1908
Dietrich Goosen 1895-1905
John Z. Kleinsasser 1895-1902
Jacob J. Hofer 1903-1919
Joseph W. Tschetter 1909-1911
Joseph J. Glanzer 1909-1922
David W. Tschetter 1911-1952
Jacob I. Walter 1920-1950
John J. Kleinsasser 1952-1959
Kenneth Ontjes 1960-1961
Franklyn Jost 1961-1971
Carl Carlisle 1971-1974

BETHANY MENNONITE (Freeman)

The origin of this congregation is of Swiss Mennonites and Hutterish backgrounds within and surrounding the municipality of Freeman. The organization of this group grew out of a concern for the spiritual welfare of the Mennonites in the area for whom congregational fellowship was not easily accessible. Sunday School fellowship had been functioning in town since 1896 or 1897. Meetings were held in the public school building then located on the site of the present city park.

In 1898 a building 28x48 was built on the present site. In 1905 an independent congregation was organized and a constitution adopted.

By 1924 the original building had outgrown its usefulness. The building was remodeled with an addition added. On November 4, 1945, fire totally destroyed that building. Plans were underway shortly for a new structure. During the time this congregation was without a house of worship, their worship services were conducted in the Freeman College chapel until February of 1950 when the present edifice was in an advanced stage so that services could be conducted in it. This new structure is 102 feet long and 38 feet wide at one end and 55 at the east end. The total cost of the structure including pews, stained glass windows, and pipe organ was approximately $80,500. In 1964 an educational wind was added which really helped to enhance the Sunday School services. It was dedicated on April 12th of that year.

The following is a list of ministers that served the congregation:

H. A. Bachman	1902-1915
J. M. Regier	1915-1918
Elmer Basinger	1918-1920
John C. Peters	1920-1922
S. P. Preheim	1922-1923
P. P. Kleinsasser	1923-1924
Elmer Basinger	1924-1927
David E. Harder	1927-1930
P. N. Hiebert	1930-1932
Walter Gering	1932-1937
Harold H. Gross	1937-1938
Louis H. Linscheid	1938-1945
Hugo J. Mierau	1945-1951
Lester Hostetler	1952-1957
William Unrau	1958-1968
Levi H. Koehn	1968-

HOPE MENNONITE
(rural Chaseley, N. Dak.)

In the late 1890's some of the Hutterish Mennonite families left the Hutchinson County area of South Dakota and moved to the Chaseley, N. Dakota vicinity because land could be bought here more cheaply and some was still available for homesteading.

Christ C. Kleinsasser moved to this area in 1895 and made the entire trip with horse and wagon. Paul Tschetter moved to the Bowden area. As a layman he was chosen to serve as minister and he served until 1908.

The KMB Church on the left. The school and Hope Mennonite on the right.

In 1899 Paul Wollman ventured forth to this new area and his family arrived one year later. In 1904 the Paul F. Gross family moved to the Chaseley area. Paul F. Gross was Erwin R. Gross's maternal grandfather.

Joseph C. Kleinsasser, Peter J. Kleinsasser, and John G. Kleinsasser also moved north. In 1900 a school house was erected which was used for worship on Sunday. Prior to that time services were conducted in a sod house on the Paul Wollman farm.

In 1908 some old grandma Fast died and Paul F. Gross preached the funeral sermon. He then served the church until 1919. John G. Kleinsasser was elected to serve as minister in 1913. In 1914, both Gross and Kleinsasser were ordained to the ministry by Rev. Paul Tschetter from Bridgewater, S. Dakota.

In the fall of 1919 the Krimmer Mennonite Brethern group began a building program northwest of Chaseley and completed the church building in 1920. It was at this time that Rev. Paul F. Gross joined the KMB conference and was the first minister at this church. After he retired Rev. Sam J. R. Hofer served the church until it was dissolved.

In 1947 the Hope congregation under the leadership of Rev. John G. Kleinsasser purchased this KMB church and used it for worship instead of the school house across the road. Rev. Kleinsasser served here until he died in 1955. After that time Rev. Paul Swarstrom served for several years until it closed its doors.

Others that moved to this area that some people might remember were William Kleinsasser, Mike J. Hofer, Jacob B. Hofer, Andrew J. M. Kleinsasser, and Joe Z. Wipf. In 1932 the Joe D. M. Gross family moved north of Chaseley and a few years later also the Jacob J. C. Gross family. These last two families moved back to Freeman and Huron respectively. Many others have also moved away and today only very few Mennonites are left in this vicinity.

HUTTERTHAL MENNONITE
(rural Carpenter)

The Hutterthal church of Carpenter was first organized in 1906 under the leadership of Joseph M. Hofer. The original building was purchased from the Methodists. A new building was completed in 1948 at the present site, 1½ miles east of the first structure. A Sunday School wing was added in 1964. In addition to Joseph M. Hofer, the congregation has had the following ministers: Elias J. Wipf, Joseph J. Hofer, Paul J. R. Hofer, Edward Duerksen, Paul F. Goosen, and Menno Pullman.

In recent years a lovely parsonage was built just across the road from the church and a little east.

Not much history could be found, but the majority of the original members moved to the Beadle and Spink County area from the Hutchinson and McCook County vicinity.

BETHEL MENNONITE BRETHERN
(rural Yale)

This church was organized in Milford Township of Beadle County in 1902. Rev. John Z. Kleinsasser moved to Beadle County from Hutchinson County, and started a new settlement. He had been a member and minister of the Salem KMB Church of Bridgewater. He was the first minister of this congregation and served until 1910.

The first church building was completed in 1904. It was located 2½ miles north of the present site and was known as the Kleinsasser Church. On October 8, 1922 this property was sold to the then newly formed Ebenezer congregation of rural Doland.

The first Sunday School was organized on March 6, 1904, with John A. Kleinsasser as teacher.

On May 29, 1904, the first baptismal service was conducted by Rev. Henry Wiebe of Hillsboro, Kansas.

A second church building was constructed in 1910, 2½ miles south of the original church. This building is the west section of the present sanctuary. Articles of Incorporation were drawn up on September 12, of the same year.

As the congregation grew more room was needed. It was thus decided to add to the existing structure in 1919. This new building was completed on April 12, 1920 at a cost of $40,527. Dedication of this structure was observed on June 13, 1920 with Rev. D. M. Hofer of the Chicago Mission as the main speaker.

In 1960 a new addition was built on the north end of the sanctuary providing additional Sunday School rooms, pastor's study, and library.

New windows were installed in the sanctuary in 1963, and new pews were dedicated on August 8, 1965.

Rev. and Mrs. A. K. Wiens occupied the first parsonage during his 1944-1947 ministry. On September 14, 1969, a new parsonage was dedicated. New modern facilities were installed in the church kitchen in 1970.

Ministers that have served this congregation are as follows:

John Z. Kleinsasser	1902-1910
John Tschetter	1910-1912
J. M. Tschetter	1912-1941
W. W. Martens	?
J. P. Glanzer	1916-?
Zack Wipf	1940-1943
Henry Epp	1940-1943
Sam J. R. Hofer	1941-1944
A. K. Wiens	1944-1947
Eli L. Hofer	1947 interim
J. J. Kleinsasser	1947-1952
Paul Bartel	1952 interim
George Classen	1953-1960
LaVerne W. Hofer	1960-1965
Menno Pullman	1965 interim
John Guenter	1966-1969
Ronald Seibel	1969-

EBENEZER M. B. (rural Doland)

On November 23, 1919 the first church service was held in what was known as the Irving Church, a community church located just two miles from the present site. Rev. Jacob J. Hofer who had been elder and leader in the Salem KMB Church near Bridgewater and had just moved from there was responsible for organizing this congregation with seven families as its make-up. In March of 1920 several more families from Freeman moved into the community. The Sunday School was organized during this year. It was also at this time that the church was named according to I Samuel 7:12.

On October 8, 1922, a church building was bought for $1000 from the Bethel Church. This building was moved from the Joseph B. Walter farm to its present location, unto a foundation and basement that cost $888.

After some remodeling and repair it was dedicated on June 17, 1922. The basement was and still is used for Sunday School and lunch room. Sunday School was conducted in the afternoon and turns were taken by different families in serving lunch. In 1950 the present church was remodeled and enlarged.

Ministers that served the church are as follows:

Jacob J. Hofer	1919-1929
Mathias E. Kleinsasser	1920-1926
Jacob P. Glanzer	1929-1933
David J. S. Mendel	1935-1946
Paul H. Glanzer	1946-1950
Franklin Wiebe	1950-1954
Duwane Decker	1954 (interim)
Menno Pullman	1954-1957
C. F. Plett	1957-1963
Rueben Dirks	1963-1964
J. J. Kleinsasser	1964 (interim)
M. A. Schellenberg	1964-1970
Luke Miller	1970-1971 (interim)
Edwin Goosen	1971-

EMMANUEL MENNONITE (rural Doland)

In 1921 the Hutterthal Church, Beadle County decided to concentrate their efforts in three areas rather than to remain a single church serving a vast area. One church was to be organized in Spink County, namely Emmanuel; one close to the Fairfield School, ten miles north and two miles west of Huron; and those remaining at Hutterthal were to relocate east of the old church building. The Emmanuel Church was thus organized with 36 members under the leadership of Rev. J. W. Kleinsasser. Property, including land for a cemetery, was purchased, a building constructed, and the dedication services were held on June 11, 1922.

In 1946, a young couple, the Edward Tschetters were accepted by the Gospel Missionary Union to do mission work in Africa. They are still serving in Mali, Africa.

In 1962 the congregation decided to build a new parsonage beside the church property. In 1968 plans got underway for a new sanctuary. On September 12, 1971 dedication services of the new facilities were observed.

Ministers that have served this congregation are as follows:

J. W. Kleinsasser	1922-1936
Jacob A. Friesen	1936-1945
Elmer Dick	1945 (interim)
Frank Loewen	1945-1949
Lyman W. Sprunger	1949-1953
Paul Quenzer	1954-1958
Albert Wipf	1957 (summer)
Wilbur Schmidt	1958-1965
Johnny J. Hofer	1965-

FAIRFIELD-BETHEL (rural Hitchcock)

The writer had great difficulty in finding information concerning this small congregation, partially because it is already dissolved. According to some scant records it was decided in 1921 to break the Hutterthal Church, (rural Carpenter), into three segments, one of which was to be located near the Fairfield School because of the distance that people had to travel to church. Check the history of the Emmanuel Church immediately before this.

From what we could find, this congregation was organized on July 13, 1927, and was dissolved in 1963. We found no record of ministers that served full time until 1939. Seemingly laymen and supply pastors filled in until then. Rev. P. P. Tschetter served part time at the beginning of its organization.

The balance of the ministers that served are as follows:

Jake Friesen	1939-1940
Frank Harder	1941-1946
Issac Derksen	1947-1951
William H. Dahlenburg	1952-1961
Menno Pullman	1962-1963

MOUNT OLIVET MENNONITE (Huron)

In 1942, Rev. J. W. Kleinsasser presented the need to the Northern District Conference, for a General Conference Mennonite Church in Huron. Steps were then taken to follow through on this suggestion. In 1944 the foundation and basement was completed and in March of 1945, a church building was moved to this site at Second and Ohio S. W. from Frankfort, S. Dak. On June 17, 1945, this relocated and remodeled church was dedicated and Rev. Jacob Friesen was installed as pastor. In 1946, a house was purchased at 1154 Frank Street S.E. to be used for a parsonage. It was during this year that Rev. Alfred Regier was installed as pastor.

By 1947, the church discontinued the financial help it was receiving from the Evangelization Board of the Northern District Conference. That same year a cemetery plot was purchased in the Ideal Cemetery.

In January of 1955, the congregation decided to begin a building program. It was agreed to enlarge the existing structure, but on June 27th, the congregation voted to scrap the remodeling plans and build a new structure instead. Lots were purchased on the corner of Sixth and Lincoln on October 6th.

On April 1, 1956, ground breaking services were held at the new site. By August 8th the old building was vacated, and the first service was held in the new church basement.

The parsonage at this time was planned as part of the church building to be later changed to Sunday School rooms as the need may arise. On June 14, 1959, the completed building was dedicated. Since then a new separate parsonage has been built.

The ministers that have served this congregation are as follows:

Alfred Regier 1945-1949
B. J. Nickel 1949-1954
Vernon Buller 1954-1961
Edward Wiebe 1961-1969
Melvin Friesen 1969-

BETHESDA CHURCH (Huron)

On February 21, 1943, ten members of the Krimmer Mennonite Brethern Conference met to organize a church to serve the city and vicinity of Huron. It was also at this time that the decision was made for giving the church its present name. At first the Wednesday prayer meetings were held in the homes of interested families. The first business meeting was held on April 4, 1943, and Mike Glanzer was chosen as the first deacon.

On January 2, 1944, the group decided to buy lots for a church building. A building was purchased and plans were made to construct the basement for this building. On September 1, 1944, Rev. J. M. Tschetter was asked to be the leader of the church services. In October of 1944, at the annual conference of the Krimmer Mennonite Brethren Churches which convened in Lehigh, Kansas, the Bethesda Church of Huron was officially accepted into the conference because of the efforts of Rev. D. J. Mendel who had been working with the Home Mission Board. On November 7, 1944 it was decided that Rev. D. J. Mendel serve as church leader.

The first services in the newly acquired church facility were held on July 1, 1945.

On August 25, 1946, a call was extended to Rev. A. M. Schmidt to be the pastor of this congregation. He was ordained into the ministry in the Bethel Church on September 22, 1946. In the fall of 1946, a parsonage was purchased.

At the conference in Reedly, California in 1960 the merger of the Krimmer Mennonite Brethren and Mennonite Brethern was agreed upon and is now known as the M. B. Conference.

The ministers that have served this congregation are as follows:

A. M. Schmidt 1946-1949
(passed away in 1956)
Peter G. Hofer Jr. 1949-1954
(passed away in 1973)
Rueben Dirks 1954-1962
A. J. Sawatsky 1962-1966
(passed away in 1966)
Menno Pullman 1966-1967
Arthur Willms 1967-1969
LaVerne W. Hofer 1970-

Chapter 8

A Century of Change

(The Prairieleut 1874-1974)

For 350 years in Europe there were periods of time when the Hutterites were harrassed, raided, persecuted, jailed, killed and driven from place to place, sometimes leaving all their possessions behind, but they remained a people who believed in a God who didn't change, and they were determined not to change. They clung to the same Articles of Faith (contained in "The Rechenschaft"), the same customs, the same language and for nearly all of this time to communal ownership and living. They resisted all efforts by the Church and State to make them conform, and this very characteristic, refusing to conform, caused the entire group to leave Russia and settle in the new land. Their loyalty was to God and The Word as they understood and interpreted it.

For the last 50 some years in Russia, communal ownership and living had broken down. But they continued to use the sermons written by their forefathers and the founders of this faith. This resulted in several attempts to reestablish this system. This became an internal issue and a cause of contention. The move to America offered them an excellent opportunity to choose which path they wanted to take. As the report in our Centennial publication verifies, about 800 chose private ownership and about 400 chose communal ownership and living.

This report will concern itself with the 800 in private ownership commonly called the prairieleut or prairie people. They are so distinguished because they settled mostly on level prairie land whereas the 400 in communal ownership settled along rivers in bruderhofs which translated literally is brother yard, meaning a yard where brotherhood is practiced. The latter are commonly called colony people or officially as Hutterian Brethren.

In some circles the prairieleut are best known as Hutters. Usually this term is used to distinguish them from Swiss or Low German Mennonites; consequently, the name, "The Hutterite Mennonites." They adopted names for the churches they established that identified with both the Hutterites and the Mennonites: the Hutterthal Mennonite Church, the Neu Hutterthal Mennonite Church and the Hutterdorf Mennonite Church.

To cover 100 years of history briefly is quite a task. I felt that it could best be done by entitling this as "A Century of Change." The evaluation whether these changes are good or bad, whether they are progression or regression, is left to the hearer or the reader, and for time to manifest.

All of the Hutterites who chose private ownership settled in the Freeman area, almost totally in eastern Hutchinson County with a little spilling over into Turner and McCook Counties.

The resettling brought with it some immediate, drastic changes. They needed to adjust to a new language, a new weight and measure system, new money, a democratic system of government, a new culture, new neighbors, a much more variable climate and a new frontier which challenged them to conquer it. The grasshoppers, the prairie fires, the tornadoes and the South Dakota blizzards were obstacles that they were unacquainted with, and these proved to be troublesome and costly. Lives were lost because of some of these hazards. In order to survive, priority was given to breaking the sod, often with oxen for draft power, to clearing the land of rocks, to digging wells and to building houses for living which were referred to as "similankis."

The relocating in America meant a change from dorf or village living with its outlying farm ground and a communal pasture, to scattered farm living. While this was not by choice, it was necessary under the circumstances. Those that bought land, bought from someone that had homesteaded and had established the farm according to homesteading requirements. Those who homesteaded, of necessity, followed the same pattern. They usually managed to arrange their farms so that they had some close neighbors. This helped cushion this great adjustment, but it didn't prevent other changes from occurring.

PAROCHIAL SCHOOL, GERMAN LANGUAGE

It was not difficult to have parochial schools for their children using the German language in a village style of living. However, now distances made this impractical, especially with the limited means of transportation. In time they resorted to the public school. This eventually meant an end of teaching German. In order to maintain this language, parents sometimes taught it in the homes. A month or six weeks of German school during the summer months was a common practice at one time, but this too was a losing battle. Later the Sunday School hour was used for this purpose for certain age groups, but the handwriting was on the wall, and German became a foreign language to those of the third and fourth generation.

CHURCH

Scattered living brought changes in their church life. In village living the school doubled as a meeting place for business and for church meetings. Everyone was within walking distance. Now distance as well as adequate facilities were a problem. Homes were first used as meeting places and later the small school houses. Churches were built in time, but it was not until 1901 that all church bodies had a building. The Olivet community never did build a church. The diary of Rev. Joseph Hofer of that community reveals that he conducted services in various homes every other Sunday during the 1880's. Later they met in a school house. With the coming of the automobile and the exodus away from the community, the services ceased.

Dr. Unruh's book, "A Century of Mennonites in Dakota," reveals that visiting Mennonite missionaries found the spiritual life and church attendance in the late 1870's among the Hutterian people who had left the colony as very lax, using the term as "sehr verkommen" spiritually. I will not relate in detail what and how change has come about in this century but give a comparison between 1874 conditions and 1974 conditions.

1. Generally, today we have large functional church facilities with educational wings, kitchen facilities, a fellowship hall for the occasional use of fellowship meals for special meetings versus the simple church service held in homes.
2. Today a trained, paid minister who usually comes from outside the Hutterite people versus a lay minister who was elected from the group and served gratis.
3. Now we have a sympathy with dispensationalism rather than the covenant theology.
4. Today there is an acceptance of premillennualism versus ammillennualism.
5. In 1974, the layman involvement in the church attempts to enlist all individuals for the service in music, teaching, youth work, etc., as well as an involvement in visitation outreach and extension work. This compares to a service in 1874 in which the minister and his assistant were the only ones involved.
6. Today we have a conference affiliation for ministries that can best be carried out by a group of churches such as mission work, relief and Christian Higher Education versus no conference organization affiliation.
7. The stewardship emphasis today results in regular and systematic sharing of the Lord's material blessings with the unfortunate, the needy and the underprivileged versus little effort or teaching about sharing with those outside of the group.
8. Today a strong emphasis is placed on the new birth and an identity with Evangelicalism versus a formalism that identified Christians with Cathechism, baptism, plainness in all things and the German language.
9. In 1974 we freely accept musical instruments, gospel singing, choirs, special musical groups versus congregational singing only and without instruments. The minister would recite a line and then the congregation would sing, continuing in this manner until it was felt that there had been enough singing. Most songs were to long to be sung at one time. Some illiteracy and shortage of songbooks probably was the reason for this system.
10. The use of the English language versus the German. In 1874 German was thought of as the language that God used. The 1930's and 40's brought the change to English.
11. Today we have a growing concern to fulfill the last Commission of Christ, Matthew 28:19,20. During their stay in Russia, there was concern for the salvation of their kin and friends back in Austria, as well as a desire to win Mennonites over to communal ownership, but one cannot help but sense a lack of concern for Russian neighbors as well as the heathen in other parts of the world. Since the turn of the century, a growing concern among prairie Hutterites first manifested itself in individuals offering themselves as missionaries to the blacks in North Carolina as well as to the lost of the city of Chicago. This resulted in increased giving for missionary endeavors.

    In just a few minutes, 16 persons have come to my mind who have been commissioned or ordained as foreign missionaries in the last fifty years. No doubt there have been a number of others. Besides this there have been many domestic missionaries, evangelists and an abundance of ministers serving in other denominations.

    Missionary Conventions, Harvest-Mission festivals and Mission sections in denominational publications have inspired giving, praying and going.
12. Today a position against the use of alcoholic beverages stands because of the many attendant evils versus the general use of them by all in 1874. Drunkenness was denounced but was commonly evident. Even ministers were occasionally overindulging at weddings, for instance.

EDUCATION

Of the 1254 who came to this country, only two are known to have attended school beyond the village school. These were sent to the Mennonite High School at Halbstadt to prepare them for the teaching profession. The saying "ye gelehnter, ye verkehrter," (The more learned, the more confused) was an oft repeated remark. Basically, they believed that advanced education was unnecessary and harmful, especially to one's faith.

As early as 1902, there were promoters among the Hutterites to have a part in the founding of Freeman College, and there has been an active interest and support ever since.

There have been two efforts at higher education for which the Hutterite Mennonites alone were responsible. The first was Bethel College near Yale, South Dakota, which was founded in 1908 and started with 49 students, continuing in 1909 with an increased enrollment. It closed after two years of operation. The second effort was in the same community when James Valley Christian High School was organized in 1957 and is still in operation. A more detailed report of both schools is found in our Centennial publication.

Because of the change in attitude toward education, nearly every boy or girl today attends high school and many go on for further advanced training. This has resulted in many teachers, dentists, doctors, engineers, lawyers, nurses, etc. serving mankind today in all parts of the United States and Canada.

PUBLIC OFFICE

To our knowledge, no one held public office before coming to America, and they probably would have been excommunicated if they had. Today no less than ten of their descendents have served in the State Legislature. Another descendent is now serving on the Supreme Court of South Dakota and at this writing the governor of South Dakota who is seeking reelection is asking for one of the descendents of these people to be his running mate.

As early as before the turn of the century, one of these Russian born men served as deputy United States Marshall and in the early 1900's, the people of South Dakota elected a Secretary of State who was a Russian born Hutterite. About 20 years ago, the Democratic Party of South Dakota nominated for the United States Senate a Hutterite descendent, but he failed to be elected.

While not everyone of the above mentioned people has been affiliated with a Hutterite Church while seeking public office, there have been no problems, especially in the last 50 years, for any of those that were so affiliated.

MILITARY SERVICE

This was the issue among others that prompted quick action when the Russian government adopted a Russianization policy for the German people in South Russia.

In the autobiography of D. J. Mendel, part of which is printed in our Centennial publication, he states that the dorf of Neu Hutterthal consisting of 20 families voted unanimously to move to America basically because of the above mentioned reason.

This village, founded in 1866, was only eight years old, which meant much hard labor had been so recently spent to establish farmsteads, orchards and the accompanying small businesses. They were especially prosperous there. Yet because of their belief regarding military service, they voted to sell out at a fraction of the value and go through the hardship of reestablishing themselves in a strange land. This tells us how firm they were in this belief.

One hundred years later in 1974, our Hutterite Churches affiliate with Mennonite Conferences that have an article in their constitution affirming nonresistance and no doubt, most if not all churches have it in their constitutions, yet practice among the members and preaching from some of the pulpits shows little regard for this position. I refer again to Dr. Unruh's book in which statistics show that among all South Dakota Mennonites, 28% took the alternate service position during World War II, 30 years ago. While Hutterite Churches are among those included in the above statistics, I would question if the Hutterite Churches were singled out whether the percentage would be that high. In the matter of swearing an oath, the statistics are almost exactly the same. In Hutchinson County, less than 30% affirmed of those signing the assessment tax forms according to a study by Dr. Unruh.

MARRIAGE

During the 100 year stay in Russia, there was not a single recorded instance of intermarriage with Russian neighbors. Only occasionally were there marriages with neighboring Low-German and Swiss Mennonites. These were tolerated but not encouraged. After a century in America, a study of the church records of a rural South Dakota church reveals that of the 20 marriages since 1969 not a single one is an ''ethnically pure'' Hutterite marriage. In seven both parties were Mennonites but of different ethnic groups and in the other thirteen, one party was of a different faith and culture.

It isn't hard to see what will happen after another generation. Foreseeing the result of this amalgamation, a motivating force is being put forth now during the centennial year to locate all valuable historic articles for identification and perservation while it is still possible.

Something needs to be said about the change in attitude toward the sanctity of marriage. Divorce and especially remarriage after divorce were unheard of among our forefathers before 1874. Today most families need not search much to find such an experience among themselves or their relatives. Obviously it is happening with reoccurring frequency.

SPORTS

Participants once were disciplined and even excommunicated if anyone dared to become involved in sports. Today churches in their socials for youth, sponsor rollerskating, bowling, ice skating and basketball. The heros among the young and old are the sports pros. The Hall of Fame register for the Howard Wood Field Relays in Sioux Falls, South Dakota, has two Hutters on the list. This is without any problems regarding church standing or fellowship in this present day.

COMMUNITY LIVING

It is interesting to note what has happened to the growth over a 200 year period. In 1770, 123 moved from Rumania to Wishenka, Russia. In 1842, 415 moved to Hutterthal, South Russia, and in 1874-1879, about 1250 arrived in New York to make their home in America. It is not difficult to determine the growth of the 400 who were in Communal Bruderhofs in 1880. They have remained ethnically pure with few losses and few additions. Statistics in 1974 find the four Bruderhofs of 1880 with 400 individuals has grown to over 200 Bruderhofs in the United States and Canada, totaling over 20,000 people.

It is hard to determine to what numbers the 800 prairieleut have grown due to intermarriage with others and to the scattering throughout the United States and Canada. Even though they are not as prolific, they should easily also total 20,000 or more. In 1974, there were Hutterite settlements of prairieleut in South Dakota, near Freeman, north of Huron and near Onida. North Dakota has a settlement south of Harvey, and in California there is a settlement in the Dinuba area. In Canada there is a fair sized group in the Langham, Sask., area.

A calculated estimate of the total number of Hutterites in these settlements would find one hard pressed to locate more than 3500. This indicates to what extent the "Hutter Community" has been given up for other places, mostly the cities of the United States and Canada.

SUMMARY

In summary and review, we surmise Paul Tschetter's petition to President Grant as a request for the privilege of:

1. Freedom from involvement in the military and war.
2. Freedom to live in our own communities with our own local government.
3. Freedom to have our own schools and to teach German.
4. Being exempt for jury service and from public office.
5. Being exempt from taking the oath.
6. Leaving the United States should we so desire.

While these privileges were never officially granted by the government to Rev. Tschetter and his followers, they have been the privileges that the United States has granted to its citizens.

This report shows that for the most part they are not very important to the descendents of the Prairieleut. Even to those who live in the Hutter communities of Freeman, Huron, Dinuba, etc. there is merely a remnant who consider some of these privileges important enough to take advantage of them.

I repeat what I said at the beginning. I will not evaluate whether these changes are good or bad, progression or regression. This is left for the reader to decide. Certainly time will be the true judge.

Time has shown us some of the errors of the 100 years in Russia. An example: in the 1810-1820 period, the sign of the zodiac was listed with the birth record of the child in the original church record book. But a people that read and studied God's word come to the light and abandoned this practice. May we today not be so self-righteous as to believe that we do not have our sins to which we are indifferent or blind, nor that we do not need the admonition and correction of God's Word, nor that we are any more than sinners whose hope is in the grace of God through Christ.

Arnold M. Hofer

History of Bethel College

A school named Bethel College located two and one-half miles north of the present Bethel Church, Yale, South Dakota, was located on the prairies of Milford Township, Beadle County. With Rev. John Z. Kleinsasser as founder, it was started in 1908 offering an eight month school term.

Rev. Peter Wiebe from Kansas (brother of the late Rev. Frank V. Wiebe) served as teacher. His wife managed as cook for the dorm students. A rather large two story building provided class room space, dorm facilities and living quarters for the teacher and family. With an enrollment of 48 pupils the first year, it offered learning opportunities to people from grade school to adult age who came to learn the German language and study the Bible, which included "Bible Stories" and Church History. Besides the three R's, other courses included English, physiology, history, geography, spelling, German grammar and penmanship both in German and English script. Choral singing played an important part for the extra-curricular activity. The athletic program included playing ball, ice skating and other games.

For the second school term (which was a nine month term) Dr. John S. Tschetter served as teacher. To gain outreach and support for the school some changes were made and as a result an increase in enrollment occurred. The older students contributed to the cause by helping the teacher recite some of the classes of the underclassmates. Some of the pupils who attended the school at the time were:

Mrs. Jake S. (Katie) Tschetter
Mrs. Andrew A. (Anna) Hofer
Mr. and Mrs. Dave Fast
Steve Waldner

George Waldner
Eli Walter (deceased)
Jake S. Glanzer (Carpenter, S.D.)
Jake Decker (Carpenter, S.D.)
Mrs. Joe G. (Maggie) Hofer (deceased)
Mrs. Sam S. (Susie) Hofer (deceased)
Barbara Glanzer (Huron, S.D.)
Mike M. Glanzer (Huron, S.D.) and sisters Rebecca and Barbara
Dave Glanzer
Mrs. Rev. Jake P. (Barbara) Glanzer
Mrs. Frank F. (Susie) Walter
Mrs. Dave P. (Katie) Glanzer
Mrs. Henry (Rebecca) Wedel
John Stahl
Mrs. John L. (Mary) Hofer (Dinuba, Calif.)
Mrs. Zack Z. (Ann) Kleinsasser
Zack Stahl (deceased)
Mrs. Jake (Lydia) Hofer
Ann Kleinsasser (killed in car accident)
Joe A. Kleinsasser
Mrs. Frank (Anna) Klassen
Dave S. Tschetter (deceased)
Mrs. Albert (Barbara) Hohm
John M. Tschetter (deceased)
John McNeil
Jake and Wilhelm Martin
Dave Warkentin
Elmo Elischman
Reuben Davis
Clifford York

This school served the community for two school terms. Even though the building was first dismantled a few years ago, no photograph could be located to portray the school for this publication.

Contributed by Sam Wollman

History of James Valley Christian High School

James Valley Christian High School, sponsored by the Hutterite Mennonites of the Huron area, is located about 15 miles north east of Huron, along the James River, on grounds that are shared with Lake Byron Bible Camp.

This shows the wooden structure which was destroyed by fire on Feb. 4, 1972.

A new steel framed structure was then built.

In the providence of God, Rev. and Mrs. Paul H. Bartel came to the Huron area in 1952 for one year as interim pastor. While here Rev. Bartel saw the need in the area for a Christian school and became extremely burdened about the lack of spiritual training for our youth. Before he left, he shared this burden with some laymen of the community and convincingly urged them to build a classroom building to be used by Sunshine Bible Academy which was then operating their school in the area. Rev. Bartel's strong emphasis was on the need for a Christian school in the vicinity. This also was the burden of others who had a firm and growing conviction for years that such a school was needed in the community.

The original classroom building was erected in the fall of 1953 with dedication services conducted on December 13, 1953. Rev. Paul H. Bartel served as speaker.

In the fall of 1954, a three room house was donated and moved on the campus. Here it was repaired and used for a teacherage.

The James Valley Christian High School Corporation was not formed until May 16, 1956. September

3, 1957 marked the opening day of James Valley Christian High School with an enrollment of 19 students from the community.

In June of 1958, another donated house was moved to the location. In July of that year, Golden Rule Construction Company commensed to build a new community and school auditorium (54 x 138). Later is was decided to include an additional structure (32 x 28) which had shower rooms, corridor and an office. The facilities were dedicated on October 18, 1959.

The school was spared from the flooding James River in 1962. Another flood threatened the school in 1969. Much prayer and ten days of continuous work saved the building from damage.

On February 4, 1972, fire destroyed the entire school building in a matter of hours. It is believed that an oil furnace exploded. Due to the intense heat, nothing could be saved.

On February 7, 1972, the school board met at Bethel Church and decided to finish the school year in the Byron Bible camp facilities. Many schools and individuals offered help in getting started again.

A public meeting was held on February 28, 1972, to discuss the future of the school. After an open forum, people voted their support for rebuilding James Valley Christian High School by pledging $80,051.00 over a three year period of time.

By August 1972, Huron Steel Structures began construction of the new building. School commenced in the new classrooms on January 31, 1973. The first graduation exercises in the new school building were held May 15, 1973.

Sixty students were enrolled during the 1973-74 school term with a faculty of five. Thirteen graduates received their diplomas which concluded the 17th year for the school.

The school is sponsored and operated by the Hutterite Mennonite people of the Huron area.

Contributed by Sam Wollman

Chapter 9
Traditional Recipes Used by the Hutterites

Our forefathers had a limited diet. Only vegetables and fruits that could be used over winter were used. They had no refrigerators so they dug earthen cellars to store potatoes, onions, cabbage, carrots, beets and their dried fruits. I am awe struck how these women used their ingenuity to cook many different and delicious foods. They used dill, parsley, chives, etc. to help flavor and brighten the looks of their dishes.

Hutterische people were known as meat eaters. They had meat at practically every meal. The women, like the men, had a hard life. There were the cows to milk, the garden to plant and hoe, children to tend to, house to keep, wash day was much work, preserving foods, cooking, spinning the yarn, and sewing all the clothes for the family.

They taught their children to work early. As they worked together with their children they would tell them stories (Bible, etc.) and sing with them.

These recipes are without names. Each family may have varied a little and we couldn't have 15 different versions of the same recipe. These recipes show what our forefathers ate. I marvel at these women and I am proud to be one of their granddaughters.

BREADS

Zwieback

3 cups scalded milk
¾ cup shortening, lard if possible
1 cake yeast
2 eggs
½ cup sugar
2 Tblsp. salt
flour to make soft dough

Mix well. The dough should be slightly softer than bread dough. Let rise until doubled. Form dough into small balls size of a walnut. Place these balls on top of a slightly larger one. Let rise about 1 hour. Bake in 400 degree oven 20-25 min.

Variation: Use 2 cakes yeast.

Geraschta Zwieback
(Roasted Zwieback)

When buns begin to get old, cut in half and put on cookie sheet. Have oven on a low heat and roast till dry. This is good to dunk in coffee.

When our forefathers were preparing their voyage to America, the women spent weeks making this and drying fruit to eat on the journey.

Biscuits

3 cups water
1 Tblsp. quick yeast
3 cups milk and ½ cup sweet cream
Bring to boil
1 Tblsp. sugar
1 Tblsp. salt
1½ cup lard
4 cans flour

White Bread

Mix together in large mixing bowl
4½ cups lukewarm water, milk or potato water
6 Tblsp. sugar
2 Tblsp. salt

Crumble into mixture 2 cakes compressed yeast. Stir until yeast is well dissolved, add 4 Tblsp. soft shortening. Mix in with spoon, then with hand
14-14½ cups flour

Add the flour in two additions using the amount necessary to make easy to handle. Knead until it's smooth and elastic and doesn't stick to board. Place in greased bowl, turning once to bring greased side up. Cover with damp cloth and let rise in warm place until double in bulk, about 1½-2 hours. Punch down and let rise again until almost double in bulk (30-45 minutes). Shape into 4 loaves, place in greased pans and let rise until sides of dough reach top of pan and center is well rounded (50-60 minutes). Bake until brown. About 1 hour.

Rye Bread

Rye bread was made much the same way as white bread. Stone ground rye was used in place of all the white flour depending on how dark you wanted the rye bread. The more rye flour used the darker the bread would be.

—o—

Milch Brekla: bread dunked in milk or cream.

—o—

Early settlers many times made a supper of radishes, onions, homemade butter and bread.

Everlasting Yeast

Boil 4 or 5 potatoes. Then mash the potatoes and put them in a kettle with 2 quarts of warm water (some potato water). Add 1 cake of yeast and 1 cup of sugar. Let it stand overnight in a warm place. In the morning take 1 quart out and use it for bread. Set the quart that is left over in the refrigerator until the next baking. Then again boil potatoes and add them to a quart of water and a cup of sugar. Put the fresh mixture in with the leftover mixture. Always put in as much as you take out. If you take good care of it, it will last for weeks. Keep in the refrigerator.

Everlasting Yeast

Boil 2 med. potatoes in salted water. Drain. Mash. Take 2 cups of potato liquid; add 1 T. sugar. When lukewarm add 1 pkg. dry yeast. Then add mashed potatoes and 2 c. flour. Let rise in big crock or jar. When ready to bake stir up yeast. 1 cup will be enough for 4 loaves of bread. To rest of the yeast, add 1 c. lukewarm potato liquid, little mashed potatoes and 1 c. flour. Keep in cool place.

STRITZEL, KUCHENS, ETC.

Rullkuchen

½ cup shortening
4 eggs
½ cup milk
5 cups flour
1 tsp. salt
1 tsp. baking powder

Mix and roll out thin. Cut into 2''x4'' rectangles. Slit in middle and turn one end through slit. Fry in deep fat until light brown. Serve with watermelon.

Rullkuchen
(Salty Doughnuts)

3 eggs, 1½ cups milk, 1 cup cream (if sour cream is used add ½ t. soda), 1½ tsp. baking powder, 2 tsp. salt. Enough flour to make a soft dough that can be rolled out. Cut into 2''x4'' pieces (or any size desired). Fry in deep fat. Good eaten with watermelon.

Long Johns

Mix:

2 cups water and 1 cake yeast
set and let rise till light
2 cups warm milk
4 eggs
½ cup sugar
a little baking powder
raisins
6 cups flour or a little more

Let dough rise till double in bulk. Roll out cut in strips. Cut a slit in each strip. Pull one end through the slit. Fry in deep fat. Sugar.

Wuchdich

Cut small pieces of bread dough and roll and lay on floured board to rise. Put in iron kettle to which a little water and lard has been added. Bring to steaming until you begin to hear spatter sound. About 25 minutes. Don't uncover while cooking. Make a medium white sauce and pour over dumplings on your plate.

Schneki

1 cup cream
2 eggs
1 Tblsp. sugar
½ tsp. salt
3 tsp. baking powder sifted with
1½ cups flour

Mix in order given, add enough flour for a very soft dough. Roll out ¾ in. thick. Cut into 4'' sq. and bake 10-12 minutes at 375°.

Coffee Cake
(Honkelich)

Use a basic sweet dough. Spread a very thin layer of dough in a pan 12x16x2 inches. Sprinkle ½ cup chopped nuts on top of dough. Mix together well:

2/3 cup brown sugar
1/3 cup white sugar
1/3 cup shortening
1 cup flour
¼ tsp. cinnamon
Pinch of salt
Pinch of nutmeg

Spread mixture over nuts and dough. Sprinkle cream over top to moisten. Let rise about an hour or until double in bulk. Bake in moderate oven.

Honkelich

Make a sweet dough with 2 pkgs. yeast softened in ½ cup water, 2 cups milk, ½ cup sugar, 3 eggs and ½ cup oil. Mix with flour to make a soft dough and let rise. Roll out until about ½ inch thick and put in greased pan. Spread dough with heavy cream (use about ½ cup thick cream on 9x13 inch pan) and sprinkle with sugar (about 1 cup) and sprinkle lightly with cinnamon. Let rise and bake at 350° for about 20 minutes.

Sugar Kuchen

½'' dough in round cake pan. Cover with the following: 1/3 c. sugar, ¼ c. flour, cinnamon and 1 T. butter. Bake 350° for 45 min.

*Can peel and quarter 2 apples and put on before topping. Then top with 3 T. heavy cream.

Honkelich

Use a basic sweet dough recipe. Spread a thin layer of dough in a 9x12 cake pan. Coat the top of dough with a thin coating of sweet cream. Sprinkle the following crumbly mixture over the cream:

½ or more egg yolk
1/3 cup soft butter
¾ cup flour
½ cup sugar
Then dust with cinnamon

Let rise about ½ hour. Bake about 30 min. at 350°.

Cottage Cheese Kuchen

2 cups cottage cheese
1 cup sugar
Little flour
2 eggs
salt
Thin with cream
Put on biscuit dough
Sprinkle top with sugar and cinnamon. Bake.

Poppy Seed Krofflen

1 cup poppy seed cooked in 2 cups cream. Cool. Add 2 eggs beaten, 1 cup sugar to sweeten, little flour, cinnamon and 2 cups raisins, vanilla. Put in sweet roll dough which has been rolled out and cut in squares. Pinch edges together. Put seam side down on pan and sprinkle with sugar and cinnamon. Let rise and bake.

Kroffeln
(Dried Fruit)

Cook until done, drain and mash

1 box dried apricots
1 box dried peaches
1 cup prunes
1 cup dried apples
1 cup raisins

Mix together and add to dried fruit

1 cup heavy sweet cream
1½ cups sugar
6 eggs

Add enough cracker crumbs to make mixture stiff as cake dough. Let this mixture set for at least 2 hours, overnight if possible.

Prepare sweet roll or zwieback dough. Proceed as for buns, roll out each bun with rolling pin. Put a tablespoon of the dried fruit mixture in the center of the piece of dough. Fold over and press edges together. Put on baking sheet with sealed edge downward. Do not let them rise but bake immediately at 350 degrees until brown. Do not over bake because the fruit mixture need only be heated enough to take out rawness of eggs. Brush with shortening after removing from oven. Makes 50.

Variations:

1. Letting rise at least 15-20 minutes, then bake.

2. Use any combination of dried fruit you have on hand. Even home grown plums, fresh or canned may be used with dried fruit.

3. Roll out portion of dough in square, cut into 3 or 4 inch squares, then proceed to put as much fruit on the dough as you are able to enclose without having it come out. The less dough—the more fruit—the tastier the roll.

Fruit Pockets

Filling:

8 oz. pkg. dried apricots
2 cups water
1½ cups sugar
2 Tblsp. flour
10 crackers (soda or graham)

Method:

Cook dried apricots in water until very soft. Add sugar and flour. Cook 5 min., stir to prevent scorching. Remove from heat and beat with beater. Add finely crushed crackers. Cool.

Note: Dried peaches or any dried mixed fruit may be used in place of apricots. May be made the day before.

Dough:

Dissolve 1 pkg. yeast in ½ cup lukewarm water. Place ¾ cup sugar and 1 T. salt in bowl. Scald 1 cup milk and 1 cup water. Pour over sugar and salt mixture and stir until dissolved. Cool to lukewarm. Add yeast, 2 beaten eggs, and ½ cup melted butter. Add 3 cups flour and beat until very smooth. Add enough flour (3 cups), one cup at a time, to make a soft dough.

Turn onto floured board, knead lightly. Place in greased bowl and cover. Let rise in warm place until double in size, about 1 hour. Punch down; let rise again until almost double, about ¾ hour.

Pockets or Kroffeln:

Cut off small pieces and shape into 3½ inch rounds, thinner around the edge. Place a rounded teaspoon of filling on the round; fold up the edge and seal firmly. Place on cookie sheet; let rise 10-15 minutes. Bake in 350 degree oven, 20 minutes until golden brown.

May frost with the following:
2 T. butter melted with 3 T. cream.
Add powdered sugar.

Stritzel
(Coffee Cake)

Batter:
¼ c. butter
¾ c. sugar
1 egg
¼ tsp. salt
1½ c. flour
3 tsp. baking powder
2/3 c. milk
1 tsp. vanilla

Cream shortening and sugar, add egg and beat well. Add milk and dry ingredients. Pour half of batter into a greased pan and sprinkle with half of stritzel mixture. Add remaining batter and top with the other half of stritzel mix. Bake at 350° for 35 min. or until done.

Stritzel mix:
½ c. brown sugar
2 T. butter (room temperature)
2 T. flour
1 tsp. cinnamon
½ c. broken nutmeats.

Stritzel

Roll out sweet roll dough in an oblong 10x12 and ¼ inch thick. Spread with filling and roll like jelly roll. Seal edges well.

Filling:
2 cups sugar
½ cup mild molasses
½ tsp. salt
½ tsp. nutmeg
1 tsp. cinnamon
1 tsp. vanilla
1 tsp. soda
1 cup sour cream
3 eggs
2 cups softened raisins

Add 4-5 cups flour to make batter the consistency of a thick cake batter. Place roll on greased pans and bake at 350° about 50 minutes or until golden brown. If rolled yeast dough is allowed to rise about 5-10 min. before spreading with filling and rolling, the roll will be light when baked.

Dark filling:
2 eggs
1 cup sugar
1 cup sour cream
1 cup flour (or more)
¾ c. black molasses
1 tsp. soda
¼ tsp. salt

Beat eggs, add sugar, mix well, add cream, molasses, and sifted flour, soda and salt. Don't make it too soft or it will run out. Spread on sweet roll dough rolled out thin, and roll up. Bake at 350 for 50 minutes.

—o—

Poppy seed or raisins were added to the stritzel as a special treat for company.

Stritzel

½ c. sugar
2 tsp. baking powder
2 c. flour
3 T. lard
2/3 c. milk

Mix as you would for baking powder biscuits. Roll out and spread filling over; roll up and bake.

Filling:
Mix in order:
2 c. sour cream
1 c. (scant) jam
¼ c. molasses
1 c. sugar
2 eggs
½ tsp. baking soda
2 tsp. baking powder
1/3 c. poppy seed

OR:
1 egg
½ c. brown sugar
2 T. jam
2 T. molasses
2 T. cocoa
1 c. sour cream
½ tsp. baking soda
1 tsp. baking powder
1/3 c. poppy seed

Rhubarb Kuchen

2 c. rhubarb and water
sugar to taste
flour for thickening
cream
cinnamon or nutmeg

Cook diced rhubarb in water to soften. Add sugar, ¼ c. cream or more, enough flour to thicken. Pour into a sweet dough filled round pan. Sprinkle cinnamon or nutmeg on top, or mix in-which ever way you prefer. Bake 400° for 20 min. or until edges of dough is nicely brown.

SOUPS

Noodle Soup

1 cut up stewing hen. Simmer slowly about 3 hours or until tender in 3 quarts water to which 2 tsp. salt has been added. Strain broth and bring to boil again. Add noodles (about one pound) and cook about 5 minutes or until noodles are tender. Serve. Chicken may be served with the soup if desired. Other traditions leave the chicken pieces in the soup and skim off fat.

Noodles

2 cups whole eggs
¾ cup egg yolks (Save the whites for angel food cake)
7 cups flour

Beat eggs together and add flour all at once and knead well. Put under a bowl and knead often till dough is smooth. Cut fist size pieces of dough and roll thin with rolling pin. Dry slightly till not sticky. Roll up and slice very thin. Dry thoroughly and package or use immediately in soup.

Noodles

½ cup whole eggs
1 1/3 cup flour

Add flour to beaten eggs. Mix thoroughly. Work until smooth and blisters appear in dough. Roll thin. Dry until no longer sticky. Roll up and slice width desired.

Nook a La Soup

¼ cup butter
2 large eggs
½ tsp. salt

Enough flour to make a stiff dough that can be mixed with a spoon. Drop rounded teaspoons of dough into boiling broth, either chicken or beef. Cook for about 5-10 minutes depending on the size of the nook a la.

When making nook a la soup one can figure about one egg per person.

Women had to heat water on the stove and pour it into a pan on the table to wash dishes.

Gashtel

(Fine Dumplings)

¾ cup flour
1 medium egg

Mix together well. Grate with grater and put into boiling broth.

Gashtel

¼ cup egg
1 egg yolk
1 cup flour
¼ tsp. salt

Work dough and grate into fine pieces.

Milch Soup

Heat milk and add either noodles or gashtel. Cook until tender. Serve. Eat with sugar.

Gritz Soup

Cook 1 old hen or other soup meat until tender. Remove meat. Stir in 1 cup gritz mixed with 2 egg yolks, salt and pepper to taste. Stir gritz mixture constantly while adding to hot broth. Cook about 15 minutes.

Potato Soup

Cook the bone of a ham (with some meat on it) in about 1½ quarts of water. Add 4 large potatoes peeled and cut in little pieces, 1 small onion put in whole. Cook this until potatoes are soft. Mix 1 Tblsp. flour with ½ cup cream and add to the soup.

Green Bean Soup

Ham bone with some meat on it
1 quart green beans
5-6 potatoes cubed

Boil ham bone in plenty of water till done. Add beans and potatoes. Need not add salt because of the ham. Just before serving add ½-1 cup sour cream.

Borscht

Cook hock of pork in 1½ quarts water to make soup. Take soup and add 1 small head cabbage, cut up, 1 large beet, cut in small pieces, 1 medium onion, sliced, 1 cup peas, 1 cup carrots, 1 cup corn, 1 pint tomatoes. Add 1 Tblsp. sugar. Any kind of vegetables can be added. Just before serving add about ¼ cup cream.

Russian Borscht

4 cups raw potatoes, diced
2 cups cooked navy beans
1 cup pickled beets with juice
salt to taste
½ cup sour cream

Cook potatoes in salted water until tender. Add beans and beets. Bring to boil. Add sour cream and serve. If you use 2 medium sized beets, raw add 1 tsp. vinegar and 1 Tblsp. sugar. Can add a ham bone to the beans while cooking.

Milch Rice

Cook about ¾ cup rice in enough water to make rice soft. Add to about 1 quart of milk which has been made hot. Serve with sugar.

Borscht

Cook 2 pounds beef soup meat in 1½ quarts of water until almost done. Season with salt, pepper and garlic salt. Add:

small head cabbage, shredded
1 can beans
1 can peas
sliced carrots
3 potatoes, cubed
1 small onion
1 pint tomatoes

Simmer. Just before serving add ½ cup cream. Heat to boiling point. Serve.

MAIN DISHES

Stewed Beef
(Dampffleisch)

Bring to boil, simmer slowly
½ c. lard
3 lbs. stewing meat
1 c. water
1 onion cut into quarters
salt and pepper to taste

Simmer slowly for 2 hours or until tender. Serves about 6 depending on how much bone is with the meat.

Roast- Pork or Beef

5 lb. roast, brown roast in 2 T. lard, season with salt and pepper. Add ½ c. water. Put in oven. When half done add carrots, onions, peeled potatoes. Have covered and bake until done. Use meat juice for gravy.

Anten
(Duck)

Take a cleaned duck, rub salt all over skin and add filling. Place in roaster. Add water to bottom, place in not too hot oven. Baste with grease once or twice. An hour and half before done add sliced peeled potatoes to grease and leave roaster uncovered so potatoes and duck get brown.

Filling for Duck

Boil about ½ c. rice
Soak 2 c. bread crumbs in milk
1 egg
1 small onion
salt and pepper to taste
grind heart, liver and gizzard

Jellied Pigs Feet
(Zitala)

Cover pigs feet with water. Cook very slowly with onion, a carrot and stick of celery if desired. When meat is tender enough so it falls from bones, remove from heat. Take out large bones, pour into bowl, refrigerate. May be eaten with vinegar or lemon juice. Use for breakfast meat or for supper with fried potatoes. May also be made with chicken feet, gizzard and liver.

Fleisch Kroffeln

After the head of a hog is cleaned, cut it into small pieces and boil it in salted water until it is tender. If the head of a hog is not available boil two pork hocks (knees knuckles). When the meat is cooled remove it from bones and grind it with a meat grinder. Season with salt and pepper to suit your taste. If meat is quite fat add about a half a cup or more of bread crumbs.

Dough: 2 c. flour, 1 egg, ½ c. milk. Mix well. Knead dough till smooth. Then cut pieces of dough the size of a bun and with a rolling pin about ¼ '' thick. Place a tablespoon full of above meat mixture in center of each piece of rolled dough. Fold dough and seal edges tightly with fingers. Drop into salted boiling water and boil for about 20 min. Drain and brown each kroffeln in a little shortening on both sides.

Sauer Fleisch
(Pickled feet and pork)

2 c. water
1 c. vinegar
⅛ c. salt

Bring to boil. Cool. Pour over cold meat (which has previously been cooked). Feet, hocks, tongue and heart are good pickled.

White Sauce

Thin:
1 T. butter or fat
1 T. flour
1 c. milk

Medium:
2 T. butter or fat
2 T. flour
1 c. milk

Thick:
3. T. butter or fat
4 T. flour
1 c. milk

Melt butter in a skillet on high approx. 2 minutes. Turn switch to med. low. Stir in flour, ¼ t. salt and pepper. Blend well. Add milk stirring constantly and cook until smooth. Yields: ½ pint.

Shooten Kroffeln
(Cottage Cheese Pockets)

2 big cups full of cottage cheese
½ c. dried bread crumbs
1 T. fried onions
1 tsp. salt
½ c. cream, sweet (if home made cheese is used)
2 eggs

Mix all in a bowl with spoon so it is evenly mixed.

Dough:
2 c. flour
1 egg
½ c. milk

Mix well. Knead dough till smooth. Roll dough in a roll about 1½ '' in diameter. Cut off ¾'' pieces and flatten out (roll with rolling pin) about 4'' in diameter. Put on a rounded tablespoon of cottage cheese mixture. Fold over and seal tight. Cook in salt water about 15 minutes slowly, about 12 at a time in 3 qts. of water (if it is cooked too rapidly it will cook out). Drain water off or take out with draining spoon. Fry light brown on both sides and serve with melted butter poured over or good sour cream with brown syrup added. This makes about 2 dozen pockets.

Cottage Cheese—Shooten

1½ gallons sour milk
1 t. salt
½ c. cream

Heat milk slowly until it is too hot to stick your finger in it. Put in cloth bag and drain thoroughly overnight. When dry, crumble the cheese curds and add salt. Mix with sweet cream at serving time and eat.

Cheese Pockets

Dough: 2 eggs, 2 c. milk, ½ t. salt, 5½ c. flour. Beat eggs and add to the rest of the mixture.

Cheese Mixture: 2 lb. dry cottage cheese, 3 eggs, 1 c. chopped onions, ½ c. dried bread crumbs, 1 t. salt, pepper to taste.

Fry onions until soft and a little brown. Add to the rest of mixture. Roll out dough and cut into squares. Put in 1 T. cottage cheese mixture. Fold over and cut in half moon shapes. Pinch edges. Cook in salted water for 10 min. Fry in butter until brown. These can be served with sour cream or white sauce.

Cottage Cheese Knnatul

2 c. cottage cheese
2 - 3 eggs
salt
½ c. bread crumbs
Flour enough to make a roll

Cook 20 minutes and put into boiling cream.

Knnatul mit Kartoffel

4 c. milk
5 eggs
flour for a med. soft dough

Cook in salt water. 1 qt. cubed potatoes and 1 qt. sour cream. (Must be country sour cream.) Cook about 10-15 minutes. This serves a large number of people.

Knnatul

1 egg
½ c. water
Flour to make a soft dough

Drop by spoons in salt water and cook about 10-15 minutes. This is eaten with a white sauce and topped with syrup.

Potato Dumplings

Grate 2 cups potatoes, and squeeze the juice out with a cloth sack. Then add 1 c. flour, 1 egg, 2 T. sour cream in which ¼ t. soda has been dissolved and salt to taste. Mix well. Then form into small balls with wet hands and put in boiling water and boil for 20 min. Drain. These may be eaten with the following white sauce: Bring to boil 1 c. cream, salt and 1 t. flour.

* Another recipe suggests to omit the sour cream and soda.

Kartoffel Knnatul
(Potato Dumplings)

Mix together: 6 cups grated potatoes, 6 T. sweet cream, 1 tsp. baking powder, 1 tsp. salt, and ½ c. flour. Roll by hand to about the size of a walnut. Drop each dumpling in boiling salt water. Boil until done. Drain. Pour white sauce over dumplings and serve.

Multochen

Filling:
- Crumble, fine, 8-10 rolls (bread crumbs may be used)

Add, mix well:
- 1 tsp. salt
- enough cream to dampen (not wet)
- 2 eggs

Mince and fry until lightly browned:
- 2 medium sized onions in
- 5 spoons of lard

Add and stir well until done
- 5 eggs

Combine the two mixtures.

Dough:

Make a dough of ¾ c. water, pinch of salt and enough flour to make a soft dough. Roll out quite thin, in oblong shape (roll dough into long narrow roll and then roll with rolling pin). Spread filling. Roll up as for jelly roll. Close ends. Cut crosswise into 1-1½'' pieces. Close up both ends of each piece. When all are made, put into boiling water and cook from 5-10 min. Dip out of water and serve. Leftovers may be fried for later meal or you may lightly brown in fat and serve.

Multochen

Take bread crumbs, soak in milk to make 1 cup of bread crumb mixture when squeezed out. Fry a medium sized onion until brown. Add 1 egg, salt to taste, mix with bread crumbs and set aside. Mix 1 c. flour, 1 egg and enough water to make a soft dough. Roll out for cookies, take the bread crumb mixture and spread on dough. Cut into 2 inch wide rolls. Cook in salt water about 20 min. Drain, and fry in a little lard in a frying pan until brown. This may be eaten this way or make a cream gravy and pour it over the multochen.

Gebratene Kartofflen
(Fried Potatoes)

Peel raw potatoes, slice fine. Rinse with cold water. Add several tablespoons shortening in skillet and heat to hot. Add potatoes, salt and pepper and fry until brown on one side. Turn and fry until brown on other side. Fry slowly until done. To make cooked fried potatoes cook potatoes with skins on. Cool and peel. Slice with slicer and fry in lard or oil until lightly browned. Season to taste with salt and pepper.

Kraut
(Cooked Cabbage)

Cook cabbage in salt water till done. Drain water and add sugar. Put lard in pan and heat till quite warm, add flour and brown. Add to cabbage and mix.

Kooch kraut in solz voser. Wen es fertig iss, schitz voser ob. Doo zuker ins kraut, nehm schmolz and mehl und hiets in fona bis schan braun, und schit uber kraut und rier.

Sies Solat
(Sweet Salad)

Clean lettuce and wash. Cut up lettuce and add cut up onion tops. Add sliced hard boiled eggs.

Take sour cream and add a little vinegar, salt and pepper and mix together with lettuce and onion tops. Add some hard boiled (sliced) eggs on top and a little paprika.

Schnide solat in kleina schtiker und das grana vona zwiefel. Nehm souren rahm und hart gehoochta ahlen, solz, pfeffer und essich. Rier und schiter uber solat. Schneid ahle uben uber.

Essich Solat
(Vinegar Salad)

Cut enough leafy lettuce from garden. Wash and place in bowl with a few green onion tips, and bacon bits. Take small soup ladle of bacon grease, put in skillet, add about half a ladle of vinegar, sweeten with a little sugar. Make hot. Add to lettuce mixture and stir. Lettuce will wilt a little. It is very tasty.

Cabbage

Cook the cabbage not too soft. Drain. Put ¼ c. vinegar, pepper and a little salt and an onion in. Let simmer a few minutes.

Sauerkraut

1 qt. sauerkraut
1 c. water
¼ c. sugar (about)
2 T. lard
2 T. flour

If kraut is very sour, pour on hot water and drain well. Put into saucepan, add water and sugar. Boil until soft. Make a sauce by heating lard until very hot, adding flour and browning. Add to kraut, mix well. Serve.

Sauerkraut mit Fleisch

Cook 3 lb. pork ribs or pork sausage in about 1 c. boiling water till tender. Add 1 qt. drained sauerkraut and sugar to taste. Cook an additional ½ hour.

Cucumber Salad

Wash, peel and slice enough cucumbers for your family. Sprinkle salt on them and serve with meal.

Cucumber Salad

Wash, peel and slice enough cucumbers for your family. Add a small onion sliced. Take sour cream, and 2 T. sweet cream, a little vinegar, salt and pepper and mix together. Pour over cucumbers and serve.

Fried Apples

2 T. butter in skillet
Add enough sliced apples for your family.
Add sugar to taste and cinnamon.
Serve warm. Add cream if desired.

CAKES AND COOKIES

Angel Food Cake

White of 11 large eggs
1 c. cake flour
1 c. white sugar
1 tsp. cream of tartar
1 tsp. vanilla
Salt

Sift flour once, measure and sift six times. Measure and sift sugar the same way. Break eggs into gal. size crock. Add small pinch of salt. With wire beater whisk to a froth. Add cream of tartar and continue beating until you can turn your crock over and eggs will not slip out. Add vanilla. Fold in sugar, a sift at a time. Then the flour the same way. Never stir; just lift and fold under. Bake slowly in an ungreased tube pan ½ hour; increase heat and bake ½ hour longer. Turn upside down and let cool before removing from the pan.

Angel Food Cake

12 egg whites left from making noodles
Whip whites till peaks but not stiff
Add 1½ tsp. cream of tartar, keep beating.
1 1/3 c. sugar sifted together several times with 1¼ c. sifted flour.

Put in before adding the sugar-flour mixture: ½ c. sugar, 1 tsp. almond and 1 tsp. vanilla. Bake 350° for 45 min.

Topping for Cake

2 c. powdered sugar (more or less)
Heaping T. shortening
¼ -1/3 c. milk
¼ tsp. vanilla

Strawberry Shortcake

3 eggs
1 c. sugar
¼ c. cold water
1 tsp. vanilla
2 tsp. baking powder
1 c. sifted flour
½ tsp. salt

Beat eggs till thick and lemon colored. Add sugar gradually. Beat till light and fluffy. Add water and vanilla. Add sifted dry ingredients. Blend till smooth. Pour in greased 15'' pan with sides. Bake 375° 12 min. Cut, serve with fresh strawberries and cream.

Fruit Cake

2 c. brown sugar
1 c. shortening (half butter, half lard)
2 eggs (if there are any, otherwise use ½ c. water)
1 c. buttermilk or sour milk
1 c. raisins, dried apples, plums (prunes) or other dried fruit
1 tsp. cinnamon
1 tsp. nutmeg
½ tsp. salt
1 tsp. soda
4 c. flour (more if coarse ground)
Nuts may be used; dredge in flour before adding to dough

Cream shortening, sugar and eggs. Beat. Add remaining ingredients, mix well to soften batter. Bake in 2 greased bread pans (8x4x3) until a broom straw comes out clean-about 1½ hours at 325° F. If home-dried fruit is used, soak in warm water until soft. Fruit cake stored in 3-gal. stone jar will keep moist. Yields: 2 loaves of fruit cake.

Red Devils Food Cake

¾ c. sugar
2 eggs, well beaten
Add 1 c. thick sour cream
Sift 1½ c. flour with 3 T. cocoa
1 tsp. vanilla
¼ tsp. salt
Last add 1 tsp. soda to ¼ c. hot water.

White Cake

1 c. sweet or sour cream
1 c. sugar
2 eggs
2 c. cake flour
2 tsp. baking powder
Mix together and bake.

Jam Cake

1 c. sugar
1 c. sour cream (can use sweet)
½ c. jelly
3 eggs
1 t. soda
1½ c. flour

Mix and bake. Can use cinnamon, cloves or other spices.

Soft Molasses Cookies

½ c. lard
1 c. brown sugar
½ c. molasses
2 eggs beaten
½ c. sour cream
1 tsp. vanilla
1 tsp. ginger
1 tsp. cinnamon
¼ tsp. cloves
4 c. flour
1 tsp. soda
½ tsp. baking powder
pinch of salt

Cream lard with brown sugar. Then add eggs, which have been beaten. Add molasses. Sift flour with all the dry ingredients and add alternately to the cream mixture with sour cream. Chill dough. Then roll and bake on floured baking sheet for about 10 min. or until done in a 400° oven.

Lizzie Cookies

4 eggs, well beaten
2 c. sugar
½ c. lard
2 c. sour cream
1 tsp. lemon extract
2 tsp. soda
2 tsp. baking powder
2 spoons molasses
Flour, enough to roll out
Put jam in between cookies.

Fluffy Frosted Cookies

Mix together 1 c. sugar and 1 c. sour cream. Sift together and add 3 c. flour, ¾ tsp. soda, 1½ tsp. baking powder, ½ tsp. salt. Beat in 1 tsp. vanilla and 2 eggs. Roll out to ¼'' thickness. If you prefer crisp cooky, roll thinner. For soft cooky thicker. Cut into desired shapes. Bake until lightly brown at 375°. When cool, frost with Fluffy Frosting: Soak 2 envelopes gelatine in ¼ c. cold water. Bring to rapid boil 2 c. sugar, 1 c. hot water. Add dissolved gelatine. Let cool slightly. Beat until stiff. Pile high on cookies and decorate with colored sugar, nuts, coconut or other decorettes. This cookie can be used without frosting, as a plain sugar cookie sprinkled with sugar.

Lebkuchen

1½ lb. granulated sugar
1 c. water

Boil until this spins a thread. Remove syrup from fire and add during constant stirring, 1 pt. honey. Cool to lukewarm.

Add:

⅛ lb. butter
5 well-beaten egg yolks or
2 whole eggs
1 tsp. soda
1-1½ tsp. cinnamon
½-1 tsp. cardamon
6-8 c. flour

Be careful not to add too much flour; dough must be soft enough to handle easy in rolling out.

1-2 c. nuts—walnuts, almonds, or both

Chopped, candied peel may be added if desired. Mix dough, cover, let stand overnight. Roll out, cut with cutter, and bake at 350 degrees from 10-12 min. Cookies should be only lightly browned. Must be stored in airtight container for several weeks to ripen before they are really good. They should be nice and soft. This is a very old German recipe and is still a favorite Christmas Cookie with many German people.

Ma's Raised Pfeffernusse

1 yeast in 2 tsp. sugar
1 c. lukewarm water
2 c. scalded milk
¾ c. shortening
½ tsp. salt
1 c. sugar
3 eggs
¼ tsp. cinnamon
dash pepper
¾ c. molasses
flour to make soft dough (7 cups
or more)

Combine milk, shortening, and molasses. When mixture is cool add eggs. Mix flour and spices, add to above mixture. Knead; if too soft add more flour. Let rise. Cut small pieces and roll with buttered hands. Bake like buns, at 375° for 20 min. or lightly brown.

* This recipe was most likely given to the Hutterische women from the Low-German women when they lived across from each other by the Desna River in Russia.

ICE CREAM

Grandmother's Ice Cream

Beat:

6 eggs with
1½ cup sugar
5 cups cream
1 tsp. vanilla
milk

Enough milk to fill ice cream freezer to within a few inches of top. Use a lot of salt with ice so it freezes quickly.

Vanilla Ice Cream

6 eggs
3½ cups sugar
5 tsp. vanilla
1 tsp. salt
5 pt. half and half
1 pt. whipping cream

Ice Cream

2 cups cream
3 eggs
vanilla
not quite 1 cup sugar
milk

This makes 2 quarts.

Homemade Ice Cream

Scald 7 cups milk. Mix together: 7 round T. flour. Add and beat 2 cups sugar, 4 eggs, dash of salt. Slowly add hot milk into egg mixture stirring constantly. Bring to a boil. Remove from heat and cool thoroughly. Add 2 tsp. vanilla and 3 cups heavy cream or 3½ cups thin cream.

Whip cream a little—not stiff. Mix together milk and egg mixture, and beaten cream.

* For smoother ice cream strain milk and egg mixture after cooking, before adding beaten cream.

Country Vanilla Ice Cream

4 eggs
2¼ cups sugar
5 cups milk
4 cups heavy cream
4½ tsp. vanilla
½ tsp. salt

Add sugar gradually to beaten eggs. Continue to beat until mixture is very stiff. Add remaining ingredients and mix thoroughly. Pour into gallon freezer and freeze as directed.

PIES

Pie Crust

3 cups flour
1 cup lard
dash salt
Ice water

Mix flour, lard and salt until fine. Add water to make a soft dough.

Pie Crust

1 c. lard
3 c. flour
2 T. vinegar
6 T. water
1 egg
Salt

Mix flour, lard and salt until fine; add remaining ingredients.

Rosina
(Raisin Pie)

Wash well, 1 cup seedless raisins and cook in enough water to cover for about 10 minutes or perhaps less. Add ¼ cup sugar. Make a paste of a little cornstarch, maybe 2 tsp. and water. Add to raisins and cook until thickened. Pour into raw pie crust. Top with crust and bake until nicely browned. A bit of salt may be added to raisins.

Fresh Strawberry Pie

Boil until clear:
1 c. crushed berries
1 c. sugar
1 T. corn starch

Put fresh whole berries into bottom of baked pie shell. Pour cooled filling over berries and chill. Serve with whipped cream. Can also use mulberries.

Custard Pie
(Ahla)

3 eggs
½ c. sugar
⅛ tsp. salt
2 c. scalding milk
1 tsp. vanilla
⅛ tsp. nutmeg

Beat eggs until light and foamy. Add the sugar, salt and blend well. Add scalding milk and vanilla. Roll pie crust and line a 9'' pie plate. Brush with melted butter. Pour the custard into the pastry shell, sprinkle with nutmeg on top of the custard.

Place rack on third glide from the bottom, bake at 450° for 10 min., then 325° for approximately 25 min.

Cottage Cheese Pie

3 c. cottage cheese (homemade-dry)
4 eggs
1½ c. sugar
1 tsp. salt
2 c. heavy sweet cream
or 1½ c. milk
4 T. corn starch
1 tsp. vanilla
Nutmeg

Mix the cream, corn starch, eggs, sugar, salt and vanilla until smooth. Add cottage cheese. Pour into unbaked pie shells. Sprinkle with nutmeg. Bake at 350° for 1 hour in two 8'' piepans. Serve while warm.

Epfel
(Apple Pie)

slice thin (6) apples
¾ c. sugar
nutmeg
dabs of butter
flour 1 or 2 T.
Top crust-holes
Sprinkle on Sugar

Bake at 400° for 35 min.

Pumpkin Pie

3 cups raw pumpkin
1½ c. sugar
½ c. molasses or syrup
4 eggs (beat yellow and whites separate)
little salt
1 T. cinnamon
1 T. ginger
Add beaten egg whites last
Enough for 3 pies

Rhubarb Pie

1 unbaked 9'' pie shell
3 egg yolks, slightly beaten
1 c. sugar
¼ tsp. salt
¼ c. milk or cream
4 T. flour
2 T. melted butter
If you use milk use 1 more T. butter
4 c. rhubarb

Bake 45 minutes, at 375°. Beat whites, add 1 / 3 c. sugar and pinch of cream of tartar. Sprinkle on coconuts. Brown 8-10 min.

CANNING

Dill Pickles

Soak pickles in cold water over night.
Bring to a boil:

1 gal. well water
½ c. salt
1 tsp. alum

Put small piece garlic, dill and small red pepper in jar. Pour hot liquid over cukes and seal.

Dill Pickles

Bring to a boil:

17 c. well water
1 c. salt
1 c. vinegar

Put cucumbers, dill and garlic in the jars. Pour hot liquid over cucumbers, but do not seal. The next morning pour off the liquid and reheat. Pour over cucumbers again and seal.

Sweet Pickles

Put pickles in strong salt water overnight. The next day put pickles on the stove with 4 c. water and 2 c. vinegar until they have changed their green color. ½ c. sugar, 1 c. vinegar, 2 c. water, salt and pickling spices. Boil and pour over pickles and seal.

Bread and Butter Pickles

30 med. sized cukes
8 large onions
2 large green peppers
½ c. salt
5 c. vinegar (cider)
5 c. sugar
2 T. mustard seed
1 tsp. tumeric
½ tsp. cloves

Wash cucumbers and slice as thin as possible. Chop onions and peppers, combine with cucumbers and salt. Let stand 3 hrs., drain. In canner combine vinegar, sugar, and spices. Boil. Add drained cukes, heat thoroughly but do not boil. Pour into jars and seal.

Watermelon Pickles

Peel watermelon. Cut into chunks. Sprinkle with pickling salt and let set for 2 hours. Pack into jars with dill and garlic. Use juice that was drained off, add water (if needed) to make 4 cups, add 1 cup sugar and 1 cup vinegar. Mix well. Pour on watermelon. Seal. Put into canner of water. Bring water to a boil and turn off heat.

Sauer Geetsch
(Whole Pickled Watermelon)

Use small or medium sized winter watermelons. Make a brine of 3 gallons of water, 1 c. pickling salt, ½ c. vinegar. Put dill in bottom of crock. Put in watermelon, another layer of dill until crock is as full as you want it. May add horseradish leaves along with the dill, also garlic or chili peppers if wanted. Pour on brine to cover. Weigh down with board and clean rock. Skim off scum every day. Ready in 3 - 4 weeks.

Sauer Kraut

To make sauer kraut remove outside leaves. In a stone crock put finely cut up cabbage. Sprinkle with pickling salt, approximately ¼ - ½ cup. Stomp with feet till it gets juicy. Stomp down good until it is covered with its own juice. Put a clean tea towel over crock. Set in a cool place to ferment, at least 14 days. Every day push down on cabbage, if not enough juice covers add water. Kraut is now ready for canning. Make sauerkraut when a new moon and it won't get moldy.

Sauer Kraut

After cabbage is cut, put in jars loose and use 2 tsp. salt and pour boiling hot water over slowly. Close tightly. Be sure your lids and jars are clean.

Canning Corn

Pack the jar tightly with corn and add 1tsp. salt. Fill jar with hot water. Cook for 4 hours.

Canned Beans

Clean and put cut beans in jars add 1 tsp. salt and add water to top of jar. Can for 3 hours.

Canned Beets

1 c. sugar
1 c. vinegar

Cook beets soft and put in jar. Add above mixture hot and put in oven. Let it get real hot and then seal this.

Canned Beets

Cook beets till soft
Add:

1 c. sugar
1 c. vinegar
1 c. water

Put beets in jar add hot brine. Put jars in hot water. Boil for 5 minutes to seal.

Bocklajohnnie
(Tomato)

Scald tomatoes about ½ minute. Put in a cool dip, peel and quarter. Pack in sterlized jars. Squeeze a few tomatoes on top to make juice, fill to ½'' of rim. Seal and can for 30 minutes.

Canning Chicken

Press jar as full as possible and add 1 tsp. salt. Cook 2 hours.

To Can Duck or Goose

Put in jars raw and put on stove. Let boil 3 hours. Seal tightly.

Brine for Sausage

1 gal. hot water
1 cup brown sugar-not packed
½ c. salt
1 tsp. pepper
1 tsp. saltpetre

Mix altogether and pour on sausage that has been packed in jars. Boil one hour.

MISCELLANEOUS

Moos

Cook together:
1½ c. raisins
2½ c. prunes

Mix together:
1½ c. water
4 c. milk
3 c. day old cream
little cinnamon
6 whole cloves

Heat to boiling point. Mix together, add small amount of hot liquid and add to milk mixture:
¾ c. sugar
½ c. flour
½ tsp. salt

Let come to full boil. Cool at once in cold water and stir often. When cool, add cooked fruit.

Can be made with just plums or with prunes, apricots, and raisins.

Cherry Moos

Bring to boil:
1 qt. water
1 cup sugar

Add 2 cups pitted cherries. Cook until soft, then add thickening which is made of ½ cup sweet cream and 1 heaping Tblsp. of flour. Boil for a few minutes longer.

Gooseberry Moos

Bring to boil:
1 qt. water
1 cup sugar (perhaps more)

Add:
½ cup raisins
2 cups gooseberries

Cook a little to soften. While boiling, mix thickening:
½ c. sweet cream
1 heaping Tblsp. flour

Baked Apples

Core large apples. In each apple put a mixture of brown and white sugar. Bake, cool and serve with cream.

Mother's Rice Pudding

4 c. milk with ½ tsp. salt
¾ c. rice
¾ c. raisins

Cook and stir often. When rice is soft add 1 egg, ½ c. sugar or more, and 2 T. cream. Sprinkle with nutmeg and stir in.

Baked Custard

3 eggs, slightly beaten
¼ tsp. salt
¼ c. sugar
2 c. scalded milk
½ tsp. vanilla
Nutmeg

Combine eggs, salt and sugar. Add milk slowly, stirring constantly. Add vanilla. Pour into custard cups. Sprinkle with nutmeg, place in pan of hot water and bake in moderate oven (325°) 30 minutes or until a knife inserted halfway between center and rim comes out clean. Serves 4.

Boopola Moose

4 T. flour
¾ c. sugar

Make a paste with 2 c. milk, pour milk in gradually so no lumps. Cook over low heat till thick. Take 1 beaten egg yolk and add a little bit at a time-careful not to get lumpy. Add pinch of salt and vanilla. When cool cut in bananas. Pour into pie shell for a Banana Pie, top with whipped cream. Or use this as a filling for cream puffs.

Cream Puffs

½ c. butter add spoon lard
2 c. hot water

Put butter in hot water while still on stove, put in 2 c. flour. Put off stove, add 8 eggs one by one. Put by spoon full on pan and put in stove but do not look in stove for at least 15 minutes.

Egg Pancakes

4 eggs, whip these and put in about ½ c. cream-mix with milk-½ c. flour and salt. Fry in butter.

Russian Pancakes

1 egg
½ tsp. salt
1 c. flour
1 cup milk

Beat egg until light. Measure and sift flour and salt together. Add to beaten egg. Add milk gradually and beat until batter is smooth. This is a very thin batter. Pour some pancake batter into hot, greased frying pan, allowing it to run over the entire surface of the pan in a thin layer. When edges are golden brown, turn and fry on the other side. These may be rolled up or served with butter and sugar, syrup or jam.

Ahle Douchla
(Russian Pancakes)

1 tsp. salt
1 T. oil
3 beaten eggs
2¼ c. milk
1¼ c. flour

Pour 1 / 3 batter into greased skillet. Brown on both sides. Eat with sugar.

Pancakes

Beat with rotary beater 3 egg yolks. Then beat in 1 2 / 3 c. buttermilk, and 1 tsp. soda. Sift together and beat in 1½ c. flour, 1 T. sugar and 1 tsp. salt. Then beat in 3 T. soft butter. Gently fold in 3 stiffly beaten egg whites. Bake on hot griddle.

Fried Corn Meal Mush

3 c. yellow corn meal
2 qt. boiling water
1 tsp. salt
½ c. white flour

Bring water to a boil. Sift together corn meal, white flour and salt. Slowly add dry ingredients to boiling water, stirring constantly to prevent lumps. When well blended, cover and cook slowly in a double boiler for two hours or in a heavy pan on slow heat for 1 hour. Pour into flat pans to mold. Chill thoroughly. Cut in slices ¼'' thick and fry on griddle or in skillet until a golden brown on both sides. Delicious with hot maple syrup or apple butter.

Peanut Brittle at its Best

Mix ¾ c. sugar, ½ c. white syrup and ¼ c. water, and 1 c. raw peanuts. Now cook 12-15 minutes. When peanuts begin to pop take off, add 1 tsp. soda and while foaming pour out on well greased platters. Let cool and break in pieces. This is the best peanut brittle I've ever seen.

Peanut Brittle

1 c. brown sugar
1 T. vinegar
1 c. white syrup
2 T. water

Let this boil good then add 2 T. butter, 1 c. peanuts and 1 tsp. soda.

Beer

6 gal. water, take 1½ gal. of this and bring to a boil
1 can malt
4 c. sugar
1 tsp. salt

Mix this up then take yeast-1 cake soaked. Take scum (or foam) off next day. Bottle after 72 hours; 1 tsp. sugar in every bottle.

Beet Wine

Wash and cut top off from 8 lbs. of beets. Do not peel. Boil until done in 3 qts. water. Take out beets and let juice cool. Add 3 more qts. water, 1 lb. raisins and peel 3 oranges and cut in slices-1 cake compressed yeast.

6 lbs. sugar. Stir once a day for 9 days. Stir and put in jars. Do not tighten jars. You can pickle these beets after you have cooked them.

Wine

1 gal. wild grapes
3 gal. water

For each gal. of water add 5 lbs. sugar. Ferment for 1 week. Take off juice and sieve it 3 or 4 times. Let it age.

Wine

3 gal. dandelion blooms, cook, leave in sac and hang in juice. To each gal. add 2 gal. water and 5 lbs. sugar. Add 2 lemons, sliced and 2 lbs. raisins. Ferment 1 week.

Fona Kass
(Pan Cheese)

Let skim milk sour. Heat to boiling point, it separates by itself—curd comes to top, pour thru sack, hang it up to dry overnight. Put in a pan 1'' thick for a day and night. Add pinch of soda when it's soft dry heat, salt to taste, add (keem) parsley. Cool.

Home-Processed Cheese

Use 2 gallons of clabbered milk. Process in the morning and make cottage cheese. Let stand until evening, then add 1 T. soda to cheese and stir several times. The next morning put in double boiler until melted, then add 2 egg yolks, 1 T. salt, 1 T. sugar, 4 T. rich sour cream and 3 T. melted butter. Cook 15 min., then remove and put to cool in mold.

Granulated Soap

3 qt. cold water
1 can lye
¾ c. borax
4½ lb. melted grease or tallow (or some of each)

Into the cold water empty the lye. Add borax; stir until it is dissolved. Into this lye solution slowly pour the melted (not hot) grease, stirring constantly for 10-15 minutes after last of grease has been added. Stir occasionally for the next 36 hours. The more often it is stirred, the more granulated it becomes. To even the granulation, rub through a ¼'' square wire mesh.

Soap

9 c. water
9 c. lard
½ c. borax
1 can lye

Mix lard, water and borax in order given, then add lye and stir until it thickens. Cut into bars.

BUTCHERING TIME

Smoking Meat

Each farm had a little smoke house. If you wanted your meat smoked, you would take a tin point and make holes to get to the meat bone. Put salted meat in a big barrel. Hang up in the smoke house. Start a small fire at the bottom with hardwood. It was a tight building with a little hole in the top so the smoke would go straight up. The smoke fire was in a pit below and smoked for 2-3 days.

Salting Beef

100 lbs. meat
8 lbs. salt
3 lbs. brown sugar *or* 1 qt. molasses
1 oz. or 1 T. saltpetre
1 T. red pepper
8 gallons water

For ham use 12-14 lbs. of salt according to size, then boil about 10 minutes, then let get cold and pour on the ham or beef.

Uncooked Mincemeat

Three bowls chopped cooked meat, 5 bowls chopped apples, 1 bowl chopped suet, 2 bowls chopped raisins and 1 bowl chopped currants (or 4 of raisins), 1 bowl vinegar, 1 bowl molasses, 5 bowls white sugar, 2 T. each cinnamon, nutmeg, and cloves, 1 T. salt and pepper. Do not cook. Put in jars with a tight cover. It will keep a long time.

Mincemeat

Perhaps you may wish to make just enough mincemeat for a pie or two. Here is a good small one.

2 c. finely chopped lean beef
4 c. chopped apples, tart
2 c. chopped citron
2 c. raisins
2 c. currants
2 t. salt
1 c. suet, chopped
2 c. sugar
1 c. strong coffee or cider or sweet pickle vinegar from melon or peach or crab pickles
1 t. nutmeg
1 t. cloves
1 t. cinnamon
1 c. meat stock

Gritz Wurst
(Buckwheat Sausage)

Cook 1 hog head with a little fat on it until tender, that has been cleaned and cut in pieces. Remove from bones. Grind meat. Fry 2 large onions, chopped, in lard, until tender. Add enough broth from cooked meat to 1 lb. gritz to cover well. Cook this gritz-broth mixture until about tender. Cool and add to ground head meat. Add ½ t. pepper and salt to taste. Put in beef casings and tie ends with string. Cook sausage in boiling water and bring to boil. Remove and hang to cool.

Liver Wurst

Cook 1 hog head with some skin and a little fat on until tender, after head has been cleaned and cut in pieces. Remove from bones. Grind meat. Take 1 hog liver and simmer in boiling water until barely done (don't let it get dry). Grind and add to ground head meat. Fry 2 large onions, chopped, in lard until tender. Add onions, pepper and salt to taste. Put in beef casing and tie ends together with string. Put in hot water and bring to a boil. Remove and cool well.

Fleisch or Braut Wurst
(Pork Sausage)

Use scrap meat from 1 hog (some fat). Put through grinder. Chop 1 head garlic fine. Put in cup and add 1 round t. salt. Pound well. Add ¾ c. warm water. Let set a few hours. To each pound of meat add 1 t. salt and pepper to taste. Add the juice from the garlic only. Mix all together well. Fry a sample to taste for the right amount of seasonings. Put in pork casings and smoke to desired taste the following day.

Gripen Flake
(Crackling Bread)

1 c. milk
2 t. baking powder
2 c. flour or enough to make a soft dough
1 c. cracklings *
dash of salt

Mix and roll out to fit a cookie sheet. Cut slightly (but not completely through) as in serving squares. Bake at 350° till light brown, about 30 minutes.

*Cracklings were made from freshly ground fat from the butchered hog and were fried or rendered till golden brown and then used in this bread.

Gripen mit Ahlen
(Cracklings with Eggs)

Heat or fry slightly enough cracklings for your family. Add 1 egg per person, salt and pepper to taste. Scramble and cook till set. Eat hot. Can also be eaten with catsup.

Gobick

When hog butchering time rolled around Gobick was also prepared by many Hutterische in addition to the different kinds of wurst. Although an exact proportion of ingredients couldn't be found—these were the ingredients used in the makings of it:

About ½ heart, ½ - 1 tongue, 1 lb. lean head meat, some meat from the hocks and lots of skin were cooked and coarsely chopped. Then ½ c. fried chopped onion and salt and pepper to taste were added and mixed well.

A hog's cleaned stomach was used and the meat mixture was put in the stomach with a sausage stuffer. Then it was secured tightly with string and put in boiling water and cooked slowly about 20 minutes. The following day it was smoked along with the braut wurst. Considered very delicious sliced and eaten cold with fried potatoes.

Pork Brains

In frying pan, slowly fry until light brown 3 - 4 finely sliced medium large sized onions with ¼ lb. pork sausage, broken into bits. In sauce pan simmer the pork brains of 1 or 2 hogs in water for a few minutes. Drain, mash with fork until fine, mix with rest of ingredients in pan. Add salt and pepper to taste. Heat only until it begins to fry well. Serve hot on bread like taverns.

Mush or Head Cheese

Clean the head of a hog well, remove brains, ears, eyes, and jaw bones. Cut into pieces; boil for about 2 hours or until tender. Boil the tongue, tail, heart, knee knuckles, and strips of skin from the cleaned hog with the head meat. The skins are very necessary for this dish because of the gelatine content. Care must be taken as the skins scorch easily on bottom of the kettle. It is thick but will form a little fat which rises to the top. Cook until this fat is clear, no longer cloudy. Cool and chop meat with fine blade of meat chopper and then heat meat in a heavy container. Stir constantly to prevent scorching. Season with pepper and salt to taste. About ¼ - ½ c. salt. Remove from fire, pour into pudding pans to store in cold place. To serve slice and place in oven until hot. Serve immediately on bread as a hot sandwich. Yields 2-4 gallons.

THINGS OF INTEREST

Mealtime Prayers

Komm, Herr Jesu, sei unser Gast und segne, was der uns bescheret hast. Amen

—o—

Vater, segne diese Speise uns zur Kroft und dir zum Preise. Amen

—o—

Herr Gott, dir sei Lob und Dank, fur Speis und Trank, und fur alles Gute. Amen

—o—

Vater, loss uns bei dem Essen, deiner Liebe nicht vergessen. Amen

---

The kitchen was the center of activity. The children would hurry downstairs on a cold winter morning to get dressed by the stove which was busy baking food since mother had gotten up early to begin to get food ready for her hungry family.

However limited we think their variety of foods were their children got plenty of vitamins through these foods. The children ate mulberries in season with milk, in pies or fresh off the tree as they picked them for their mother.

Threshing days were busy days for the pioneer mother. She fed as many as 20 men for breakfast which was served at 6:00 a.m., dinner at 12:00 noon and supper around 7:00 p.m. including morning and afternoon lunches.

When coffee was made the coffee grounds were put directly into the water and brought to a boil. Coffee grounds would be found swimming around in the drinking cups.

For a bad cough lemon was added to a spoonful of honey.

Goose fat was applied to wounds.

Chapter 10

Hutterite Dialect

Listed in this chapter are words that are used in the everyday language of the Hutterites. In many of the homes English has taken priority over the Hutteritch language; therefore the younger generation is no longer being exposed to the language of the Hutterites. A list has been made of some of the common words. A complete list would be impossible since this is not a written language; also the spelling of these words may differ because it is not standard.

Also included here are a few Russian words that crept into the Hutterite dialect, a few childrens nursery rhymes, prayers and Hutterite expressions.

RUSSIAN WORDS THAT CREPT INTO EVERYDAY USAGE

Borscht—A vegetable soup
Bocklajohnnie—Tomato
Geetsch—Watermelon
Blitzer—Muskmelon
Kratzavitz—Cucumber
Viexel—Cherry
Gookerootz—Corn
Silshietel—Single tree
Garetz—Dipper
Bobbet—Leading rope for a horse
Teska—A person having the same name e.g. A John meeting another John says "Hello Teska."
Vishudder—Towel
Bastaronka—Tug or part of a harness
Similankis—A house of sod and wood
Mootzie—Puppy

NURSERY RHYMES

Kritzel Kratzel
Baren Datzel
Krumper fusz
Halla moose
Locholla bohn
Und patch gaben

Lauft a meisel ubern heisel
Drogt a backel hubbelshaten
Wast nit voo zu rosten
Do, Do, in den kosten

Nursery Rhymes said while playing with baby's fingers, similar to, "This Little Pig Went to Market."

Dos ist der Daum
Der shittelt de Pflaum
Der klaubt si auf
Der drogt si ham
Der est si auf und bleibt duch so klan.

English—This is the tree (touch the thumb)
This one shakes the plums (touch forefinger)
This one picks them up (touch next finger)
This one carries them home (touch next finger)
This one eats them up but still stays so small.

STORY

Die JoAnn hot ihr schwester di Berta unt ir familya eingloden feer a molezeit. The Berta unt ir familya sien ober a bissel frea cummen. Nor hot de Berta gvelt ir schwester behilflich sien unt hot ongfongen den desch zi setzen. "Vort" sogt the JoAnn, "ich vill asht a deesch decken drauf don." Ober die Bert hot gsogt, "Dos is alreit si nit so hooch-gadrogen ich kum ya von gleichen nest vi du."

JoAnn invited her sister Bertha and family for Supper. Bertha and her family arrived earlier than was expected. Bertha wanting to be helpful began setting the table. However JoAnn said, "Wait I want to put on a table cloth." Then Bertha replied, "That's okay you don't have to be so high class since we are sisters."

PRAYERS

Komm, Herr Yeasu si unzar Gost unt saegne vos du unz basharet host.

Come Lord Jesus be our guest and bless this food thou hast prepared for us.

Vi bitten dich Heer Gut Hemlescher Foter sagnea desa deina goben de vir von deer empfongon unt zu unz nahmen durch yasum kristum. Amen.

We ask thee our God and Heavenly Father bless these thy gifts that we have received of thee and are about to enjoy in the name of Christ our Saviour. Amen.

INVENTORY OF VOCABULARY

PHONETIC SPELLING	STANDARD GERMAN	ENGLISH
Aishoan	Verscharen	to bury
Ala, alan	Ei	egg
Anckela	Grossmutter	grandmother
Anten	Ente	duck
Antrich	Enterich	drake
Anfoltich	Dummkopf einfalt	a stupid person
Aufhengen	Aughangen	to hang up
Ach	Auch	also
Bam	Baum	Tree
Basel	Tante (base)	Aunt; title of respect
Batchala	fliegenklatsche	fly swatter
batchen	beklatschen	to clap
bochen	backen	to bake
bisel	bisschen (bissel)	a little
blachala	bettvorleger	throw rug
blemble blemblen	Plumlein	little flower
blitzer	eine Art Melone	muskmelon
blutchen	blutchen	leaf, bud
bochhouse	bachhous	bakery
bua, bubm	bub	a boy over 15
bichel	buch	book
buchstaveden	buchstabieren	to spell
daust	draussen	outside
dein, dendla	dirne dierne	girl 15 or older
drack	dreck	dirt
dracket	dreckig	dirty
esht	erst	first
etlecha	etliche	many or some
fakal, faklen	ferkel	young pig
pfat	Hand (pheit)	shirt
ferzeichen	verzeihen	to pardon, forgive
ferzeichnerng	verzeihung	pardon, forgiveness
ferbraenan	verbrennen	to burn up
ferspenden	ausgeben (verspenden)	to spend
fetter	onkel (vetter)	uncle, title of respect
fiatich	schurze furtuch	full apron
filala, filalen	fohlen (fullen)	colt
fitigle, fitiglen	kleine schueze	short apron
fuyar	feuer	fire
furich	fuerig	very hot
gonsel, gonslen	gunslein	gosling
geatsch	wassermlone	watermelon
glick	gluck	luck, fortune
goar	gar	complete
goaten	garten	garden

PHONETIC SPELLING	STANDARD GERMAN	ENGLISH
gons, gense	gans	goose
gluat gluatic	gluhend	glowing, burnt to ashes
glust	glut	glow
grossmaner	muher (mahmaschine)	mower
hai	heu	hay
haas	heiss	hot
haisel	hauschen hauslein	little house
haklir, hakliga	sauber (behaglich)	neat clean
hamkoman	heimkommen	to come home
hamsuchen	heimsuchen (heinsulchen)	to visit
handshich	dummkopf (handschue)	a stupid person
hayna, haynan	honne hiehner	chicken
hone, honen	hahn	rooster
honala honalen	huhn	spring chicken
hiaten	huten	to take care, watch
hiats	jetzt	now then
hiats kroad	grade jetzt	right now
hits	hitze	heat
hoar	hoar	hair
hoarhadle	ein einziges hoar	a single hair
honkalich	gabuck	pie, baked goods
hok	hof (hokker)	yard
fichhok	vichhof	corral
misthaufen	mislthaufen	manure pile
shofhok	schafhof	sheep pen
schvainhok	schweinhof	pig pen
hubal	hobel	plane
hublan	hobeln	to plane
hultz	holz	wood
hutchola	fohlen	colt
injain	tractor	tractor (engine)
yanker	jacke (Jangger)	light jacket
yo	ja	yes
kalblen	kulbein	calfing
kolb, kalbela	kalb	calf
kolbfeech	kalbvieh	stock cattle
kalendar	Illustrierte, (kalendar)	magazine
vontkalendar	kalender (wandkalender)	calendar
kartufel	Kartoffel	potatoe
katus	mutze	cap
kemmet	kamin	chimney
klad, klader	kleid	dress clothing
klaubn	klauben	to pick, gather
klutz	klotz	log
kola, krola	nur	only

PHONETIC SPELLING	STANDARD GERMAN	ENGLISH
kola, sufeil	nur ein bisschen	only a little
koribala	kohlrublein	kohlrabi
kraka, krakenen	spinne (krake)	spider
kratzavitz	gurke	cucumber
knufel	knoblauch	garlic
lampel, lamplen	lumlein	lambkin
letzetle, letzetlen	susser keks	cookies
maklich	behaglich	comfortable
mandel, mandlen	munnlein	a boy under 15
maulber	maulbeer	mulberry
maddel	muhre (muhrlein)	carrot
miader	mieder	vest, jacket
malichhouse	milchhaus	milk house
malichkua	milker	milk cow
malichfich	milkvieh	milk cattle
moan	mann	man, husband
moansleit	manner (mannsleute)	men menfalk
moanit	mond	moon
zvaimoaneten	mondfinsternis (zweimonde)	eclipse
moanit	monat	month
naa	nein	no
naidish	neidisch	jealous
nemp	niemand (niempt)	no one
noodle, noodlen	nudel	noodle
nukola, nukalen	knodel (nockerl)	dumpling
orah	ohr	ear
olfeter	grossvater	grandfather
alba	allweil	always
allotog	jeden, tag	every day
allamorgn	jeden morgen	every morning
ondra	andre	other
ondentog	am andren tag	on another day
ondesht	anders	in another way
passen	besen	broom
pasenhaus	besenhaus	broom factory
prate, preter	brett	board plank
rattich rattlicken	rettich (rettichlein)	radish
roan	rote, rube	beet
rister	ruster	elm tree
ruse	pferd (ross)	horse
ruseshtole	pferdestall (rosstall)	barn
a por ruse	gespoann (ein poar ross)	team of horses
settlen	regeln	to settle, handle
untereindander settlen	untereinander regeln	to come to an agreement
soge	suge	saw
bentsoge	bendsuge	band saw
sogmachine	sugemaschine	saw mill
sorgn	sorgen	to take care of

PHONETIC SPELLING	STANDARD GERMAN	ENGLISH
kindsorger	kindersorger	baby sitter
step	field (steppe)	field
aufnstep	auf dem feld	in the field
suna	sonne	sun
schan	schon	beautiful
schunkenfleisch	schinkenfleisch	ham
schapfala	schopfkella	dipper
schepfer	eine grosse kelle	large dipper
schluttisch	schludering (schluttisch)	sloppy
schmont	sahne (smant)	cream
schmeed	schmiod	blacksmith
schmitten	schmiedewerkstutte	blacksmith shop
spadel	sicherheitsnadel (spatel)	safety pin
spichar	speicher	granary
shrutner	mehlmuhle	feed grinder
stempfle	stempel	stamp
schtemple	pfahl (stemper)	post
schtenden	aushalten	to endure, bear
schtickola	stucklein	little piece
schtik	stuck	piece
schtual	stuhl	chair
schtala, schtole	stall	shed, barn
schtrankle	bohnen (strunk)	string,—bean
zuckershtrankle	erbsen, zuckerstruck	pea
schtricken	struken	knit
schtrick	strick	rope, a foolish person
schtuk	stock, etage	story of a house
zvaschtuket	zwei stock	two story
schtumpf, schtimpf	strumpf, strumpf	stocking
schrubber, schubben	kultivator (schuppen)	corn cultivator
schvaser	schweisser	welder
schvonts, schvents	schwanz	tail
zigarkalla	zigerette	cigarette
zont	zahn	tooth
zveefel	zwiebel	onion
zaun	zaum	fence
umpfar	(zufallig (vonugefehr)	accidentally
vaib, vaiber	weib	wife
veixel	kirsche (wihsel)	cherry
vocklajoni, bucklajonnie	tomate	tomato
vulken	wolke	cloud
vu	wo	where
putsen		cob
lieb		love
unlidich		onery person
Traupf		a poor soul
gadult		patience
kinder		children
vatz		wheat

HUTTERITE SAYINGS IN DIALECT AND THE ENGLISH TRANSLATIONS

1. Gsundheit, Grusvoxen—(Said when a child sneezes)
   English—Good health, Grow up
2. Es is noch ka glenter fom Himbel gfoln. (Said when someone finds learning hard.)
   English—No educated person has fallen from heaven as yet.
3. Mit mahnen bendet mer ka kua on.
   English—Just only thinking about it does not tie up the cow.
4. Vos sich zvaht dos draht sich.
   English—Things that occur twice usually occur thrice.
5. Dos is su gvees vi dos Amen in der Lehr.
   English—That is as sure as the Amen in Church.
6. Dos is Matteu om letzten.
   English—When at wits end one says, "That is like the end of Matthew."
7. Der Orma traupf or de orma haut.
   English—If misfortune has befallen someone says, "That poor Soul."
8. Der is orm vi kirchen mouse.
   English—He is poor as a Church mouse.
9. Ver es klana nit erht is es grusa nit veht.
   English—If you don't appreciate the little things you are not worthy of bigger things.
10. Der is flink vi kotz.
    English—He is quick as a cat.
11. Ver huch steight der foldt ach huch.
    English—He who steps up high also falls high.
12. Der orma Lazarus.
    English—A person sick for a long time.
13. Es is nit olles guld vos glizelt.
    English—All that glitters is not gold.
14. A schenkten gual schaut mer nit in maul.
    English—You don't examine the mouth of a gift horse.
15. Orbeit mockt dos laben seease ober faulheit starkt de glieder.
    English—Work makes life a pleasure but laziness strengthens the body.
16. Er sauft vi feesh.
    English—He drinks like a fish.
17. Schleckt foden is baser vi gehn.
    English—A bad ride is better than walking.
18. A hund vos kolbt beist nit leicht.
    English—A barking dog seldom bites.
19. De yager und de feesher sitzen oft bi lara deesher.
    English—Hunters and fisherman often sit by empty tables.
20. Den reichen gleckts uft.
    English—The rich have more luck than sense.
21. Du neuscheriga Efa.
    English—You curious Eve.
22. Folln is leichter vi Aufstain.
    English—It is easier to fall than to get up.
23. Vergase vos hinter dir is.
    English—Forget those things that are in the past.
24. Glick und glose vi bolt zerbrechk dose.
    English—Luck and glass, how quickly it breaks.
25. On sine lochen kent mir in nore.
    English—You can identify a fool by his laugh.
26. Ver Gut vertraut hot guot gabaut.
    English—He who trusts in God does well.
27. Spore in der zeit so host du in der nute.
    English—Save your money and you'll have it when you need it.
28. Heint rute morgn dute.
    English—Today red, tomorrow dead.
29. Ver olles vissen vill, der lebt nit long.
    English—He who wants to know everything does not live long.
30. Er hots gaschriben ober er kons nit lasen, er is a dummer, asel.
    English—He wrote it but can't read it and is a dumb donkey.
31. Vons der gass guot gat, gat si auf den ice.
    English—When a goat feels good she steps out on the ice.
32. Der epfel folt nit vite fon stome.
    English—The apple does not fall far from the trunk of the tree.
33. Heint a gost, morgen a lost.
    English—One day a guest and the next day a burden.
34. Ver frea aufstat der est sich orm ver long shloft left long vorm.
    English—The early riser eats himself into the poorhouse but the long sleeper keeps warm.

35. Der is es dutschlogen nit vat.
English—A worthless person is not worth killing.

36. A blinda hena findet ach-a-mole a kendel vatz.
English—A blind hen sometimes is lucky enough to find a kernel of wheat.

37. Kupf kolt und de fiece vorm mocht in besten Docktor orm.
English—A cool head and warm feet make the best Dr. poor.

38. A yader nor loopt si agnea vor.
English—Every fool praises his own ware.

Health

Ploba'Husten	whooping cough
Rute'Iauf	fever
Reissen	rheumatism
Hendle'Auga	corn on a toe

Farming

Tesi'teen	2½ acre
Dristen	stack
Shubber	cultivator
Tyxle	tongue of wagon
Sitźläter	wagon seat
Aust-box	hay rack
Hŏber	oats
Gŭka'rŭtz	corn
Bŭrjan	weeds
Blemlen	flowers
Kurīe	thistles
Vintle	creeping vine
Aŭst	harvest time
Ver'mit	white sage
Paŭden	manger
Stănōōk	stable

House

Dorf	village
Beach	outdoor oven of bricks
Sammer'Stume	parlor
Shlofe'bonke	davenport
Somma' Väre	tea crock
Plŭtzer	jug
Keeble	butter churn
Shōlne	cup

Behavior

Untlich	well behaved
Shermant	pretty good
Shvĭnke	habit
Karjōōse	queer
Shpitz'bua	crook
Lope	dunce
Kshwiśtrich Kinder	cousins

Numbers

Anse	1
Zvä	2
Driä	3
Ferä	4
Finfa	5
Sexa	6
Sebena	7
Ochta	8
Nina	9
Tzechna	10
Alfa	11
Zvelfa	12
Drizena	13
Fitzena	14
Fuchzena	15
Sechzena	16
Semsena	17
Achzena	18
Nintzena	19
Tzvanzic	20

All numbers from now to a hundred have the ending zic.

Days of the week

Sundich	Sunday
Mondich	Monday
Eitich	Tuesday
Mitvuch	Wednesday
Pfinstich	Thursday
Fritich	Friday
Somstich	Saturday

Colors

Blōōb	blue
Gāāl	yellow
Rut	red
Gran	green

Weather

Tămich	sultry
Virble	tornado

Food

Vashtan	watermelon patch
Geach	watermelon
Plitzer	cantalope
Kratzaŕvits	cucumbers
Bogli'Jonney	tomatoes
Tzetroon'apfle	orange
Viegsélla	cherry
Vorsh	vegetable soup
Nukella	butter dumpling
Stritzel	roll cake
Hongalich	coffee kuchen
Soat	stomach full of food
Fasilla	bean

Carpenter Shop

Stemple	fence post
Klampela	staple
Kriesht	scafold
Puke	saw horse
Pussákle	sledge hammer
Tzangle	pliers
Homer'Shlissel	monkey wrench
Loam	bar
Klachle	latch lift

Animals and harness

Shimble	a white horse
Hutchella	colt
Pobet	tie rope
Fasta'ronka	tug

Clothes

Shlodden	shoes
Yănker	jacket
Fesinater	knit head cover
Fŭss decken	robe

Compiled by Mr. & Mrs. Joe H. Tschetter
Emery, South Dakota

Chapter 11

God With Us Past, Present, Future

SATISFACTION GUARANTEED

Isaiah 55:1-11

"... my word... that goes forth from my mouth; it shall not return to me empty, but it shall accomplish that which I purpose, and prosper in the thing for which I sent it (Isaiah 55:11 RSV)."

The year was 1557, about 425 years ago. Hans Kräl, a Tyrolean Hutterite preacher was seized, thrown into a dungeon, and fastened in the stocks. Kräl himself says (Hostetler and Huntington, 1967, page 8): "My shirt decayed on my body. There was not a single thread left of it except for the collar. I did not see the sun for one and a half years. In the dark and awful dungeon I no longer knew the difference between day and night. All of my clothes rotted so that I was stark naked. The insects and the worms ate my food as soon as they smelled it."

From time to time, Kräl's captors would pull him up from the dungeon with a rope in order to persuade him that he should give up his faith. Coming up out of the dark pit hurt his eyes so much that he was actually glad when they lowered him back down again among the rats.

After remaining steadfast for 23 months, the government issued an edict: "Because you are obdurate and will not accept good advice, you are sent to the sea as a galley slave." Kräl's response was: "I will trust in God my Master who is present on the sea as well as on the land, who gives me aid and patience."

Hans Kräl later escaped from the galleys and became a leader in the colonies of Moravia.

In the year 1918, just 50 years ago, Joseph Hofer, Michael Hofer, David Hofer, and Jacob Wipf, four young Hutterite men from South Dakota, were summoned for military service. They refused to be inducted on grounds of Christian objection to war. Their sentence was pronounced as 37 years in prison at Alcatraz in San Francisco Bay.

At Alcatraz they were forced to remove their outer clothing and given military uniforms. When they refused to wear these uniforms, they were placed in solitary confinement. They slept on the cold, wet concrete wearing nothing but light underwear. They were given half a glass of water every 24 hours but no other food. They were placed so they couldn't speak with one another. They were beaten with clubs. With their arms crossed, they were tied to the ceiling. Each Sunday afternoon they were allowed one hour of outdoor exercise.

After four months at Alcatraz, they were transferred to Fort Leavenworth and further humiliated and tortured. Joseph and Michael Hofer died from their severe treatment (Hostetler and Huntington, page 9).

Testimonies like this, taught our forebears to sing:
Glaube gibt Siegeskraft, (Faith is the Victory)
O glorreiche Siegeskraft (O glorious Victory)
Die alle Welt bezwingt. (That overcomes the world)

The stories of Hans Kräl and of Joseph and Michael Hofer, make us sad about the intolerance of man. But these stories also make us glad. They are evidence of the continuing power and presence of God in our history!

THE DAYS ARE EVIL

We in America have an abundance of possessions. The average individual adult earns between 4-5,000 dollars per year. Even the "Hutter" and Hutterite closets hang packed with extra sets of clothing. Refrigerators are full. Tractors and combines are air-conditioned, not to speak of cars, trucks and houses. Education is a right for everyone.

A European psychiatrist visiting in America, couldn't help but notice all the "things" that Americans have. In addition, he noticed all the amusement and entertainment places.

Surely Americans in all their affluence should be a people both happy and content. But here the visiting psychiatrist was led to comment: "I also notice that your country sells the most books on 'How to Be Happy.' "

Over half of the hospital beds in the U.S. are occupied by people with emotional illness. One out of every ten people in this country will sometime in his life be treated for psychological disturbance.

Less than one out of four first marriages in this country turn out to be lasting and happy. The biggest problems in marriage are boredom and loneliness.

Dishonesty and an ethic of personal convenience have come to dominate both secular and sacred society. Credibility whether in Washington, Rome, Hillsboro or Newton, is nowhere too highly respected.

American youth has gone from the pot-culture, the violence craze, the booze troops, the permissive society, the star-gazers, and the Jesus-freaks; a whole spectrum of counter-activity that has produced nothing of substance.

Those who dared to breathe hope, the Kennedys—Jack and Robert; Martin Luther King; have been shot down by fellow-Americans.

Somehow the 70's of the twentieth century are evil days. The specters of inflation, corruption, pollution, waste, sexual perversion, and alienation, loom darkly and imminently upon the horizon.

Where have we gone wrong? What has happened?

Easy answers are tempting, but they are not likely to be sufficient.

God gave the first man a helpmeet, another person; to combat his loneliness. God gave man things for his use.

Could it be that man has reversed God's intention? Today's man seems more likely to *love things* and to *use people*!

The words of St. Paul are perhaps appropriate: "Look carefully then how you walk, not as unwise men but as wise, making the most of the time, because the days are evil (Ephesians 5:15-16)."

Michael Green in *Man Alive* (1968) suggests that Hollywood is perhaps the clearest demonstration of empty living. It is the richest six square miles in the world. The average house costs about $150,000, they have 2,000 swimming pools and an average family income of about $25,000 per year. But they also need 1,200 lawyers for 34,000 people; 34 private detective agencies; and about 200 psychiatrists!

The Beatles sang about it in the popular song Eleanor Rigby: "All the lonely people. Where do they all come from?" It is a song about a young girl who lives and loves and dies in loneliness. At her funeral Father McKenzie preaches the sermon, but "No one hears, No one is saved."

THE BREAD THAT SATISFIES

This general disillusionment with life is everywhere evident. Bookstores feature horoscopes and almanacs and exorcism books where once the Bible was proudly displayed.

It would be hard to speak a prophetic word of hope and assurance in the 1970's except for one thing—history. Many people resent history. Others neglect it. Some scoff at it.

Frequently, history is associated with museums—a depository for artifacts that are no good any more. And who expects to find exciting and relevant discoveries in a museum?

But it can happen! The ancient Greeks believed that history is cyclical—it simply repeats itself. The biblical Hebrews demonstrate a contrary faith—they see history as moving forward to a goal. That kind of history tells a story; it is packed with lessons!

When Jesus Christ came upon this planet, the "time" was ripe. Scarcely 25 years before His birth, the people were excited about the Pax Romana and Augustus was being hailed as "Savior of the State." In 25 years, Rome became degenerate. Orgies, homosexuality and obscenity flourished (e.g. dance of Salome, feasts described in Revelation 2:13, 20). Horoscopes abounded. Philosophical gymnastics became an art. The rich got richer at the expense of the poor. Some men owned as many as 30,000 slaves on their estates. Death was regarded as "one unbroken night."

And then the unexpected happened. Within a few generations, vast areas of the Roman Empire discovered a new dimension of life.

A new hope, a new zest for living, a new motivation, a new and deep concern for *other* people began to show itself in all parts of the civilized world. It radiated forth in concentric circles from a little insignificant part on the edge of the Roman map—Palestine. This transformation was not initiated by a political edict, not by social movement or cultural renaissance. It was brought about by a practical, living demonstration of the Christian Faith!

In the sixteenth Century, the Christian Church had become lax and weak. Roland Bainton (1950) the Church historian says in *Here I Stand,* page 15: "Nationalism was in process of breaking the political unities . . . the Popes of the Renaissance were secularized, flippant, frivolous, sensual, magnificent, and unscrupulous."

In that climate, a monk, Martin Luther struggled to find a 'gnädiger Gott" (gracious God). He fasted and prayed in the church's tradition, made a special pilgrimage to Rome and climbed Pilate's stairs on hands and knees repeating a Pater Noster for each one and kissing each step for good measure in the hope of delivering a soul from purgatory. But he found no release.

Then in his study of the scriptures, he commenced to lecture on the Psalms in 1513; on Romans in 1515; and on Paul's letter to the Galatians throughout 1516-17. These studies proved to be Luther's "Damascus road" experience. He experienced the personal power and indwelling of Jesus Christ.

This became the touchstone of the Reformation. A new fire of revival and regeneration swept the world. The Protestant church born in the wake of Luther's experience, today numbers over a quarter billion adherents.

Among the followers were the Hutterite forefathers. Only, they committed themselves to a more radical reformation than Luther. The first Bruderhof was established in 1528 at Austerlitz, Moravia and expanded very quickly to 80 colonies with 20,000 members. In 1965, there were 170 colonies with 16,500 adherents in the whole world.

History tells us that the Hutterites have been the target of much senseless persecution. South Dakota's own story shows shameful records of intolerance and abuse.

The world in which we find ourselves today, is once again in disarray. And once again it is in the hands of some people who will boldly commit themselves to a radical discipleship, to ignite the fires for a new Reformation!

The prophet Isaiah many hundreds of years before Christ, admonished his people: "Ho, every one who thirsts, come to the waters; and he who has no money, come, buy and eat . . . Why do you spend your money for that which is not bread, and your labor for that which does not satisfy (Isaiah 55:1-2)?"

The prophetic question that we must face on this historic day is a simple one: "Are we today living on bread that satisfies?" Have we learned from history? Are we sharing in a heritage that we can proudly pass on to the future generations?

TRY IT — YOU'LL LIKE IT

The history of civilization is littered with an epitaph that rings with repetition: "Ancient China rose to great heights, and it fell. Greece was once the highest culture, and it fell. Rome became a word synonymous with power and authority, and it fell. The British boasted that the sun never sets on its empire, and it fell. Germany built the first, second and third Reich, and they all fell." What about Marxist socialism? What about the Western world as we know it?

The history of the Christian Church reads differently. Christianity's influence has been strong and then become weaker. But it has never fallen—and it never will! The Kingdom of God rises, weakens, and becomes strong again.

It happened through the witness of the first apostles. It happened through the Reformation. It will happen again.

But it has always required a fresh hunger and thirst for that "bread of life" which satisfies. It requires a realization that too much effort is spent on that which does not and cannot ever truly satisfy.

Let me illustrate. You can visit Lancaster county in Pennsylvania and see the Amish dressed today like they were 450 years ago. You can visit Sunset Boulevard in Los Angeles, California, and see rebellious youths dressed in an almost identical garb.

Does this mean that if we use too much energy to hang on to the past, that finally our customs and traditions become as eccentric as the ways of those who see it as their primary goal to tear down the "institution?"

What are we as Christians spending our efforts on? Michael Green in *Man Alive* (1968) says: "If one of the uninitiated ventured close enough to listen, he could be pardoned for supposing that the Roman Catholics were primarily concerned with priestly defections, Vatican II and birth control; . . . the Ecumenicals ardent for church mergers; the Radicals devoted to the New Theology and the New Morality; the Orthodox muttering about liturgy; the Pentecostals enthusing about speaking in tongues and the Conservative Evangelicals going on about sin."

In the meantime, the world evidences a growing alienation, a bent to violence, corruptions, etc. Where are those who will once again "turn the world upside down?"

The prophet Isaiah's call was to a people who thirst, a people who desire satisfied living, a people who are willing to taste the goodness of God anew. When Isaiah stepped forth, he spoke to Israelites who had seemingly accepted their situation "as is." They seemed to be ready to live as a part of the wickedness of the Babylonian Empire. But Isaiah knew that his people were not experiencing inner satisfaction. Man can never find this feeling of fulfilment outside of God.

The call of Isaiah to Israel is God's call to us for our second century in America. Let us acknowledge our thirst, our emptiness before God. Let us drink deeply once again of the "water that quenches the eternal longing."

Our forefathers were not content with a partial Reformation, they committed themselves to a radical discipleship. This form of life did precisely what Isaiah prophesies; it served as a witness that drew attention without any professional public relations program. These people found God's thoughts to be higher than theirs as far as the heavens are higher than the earth. And God's Word accomplished its purpose through these faithful vessels. Yes, a revolution can be found in a museum; history can point us to new directions and new hope.

The Kingdom of God will rise again! The challenge to us here today, is whether we shall hasten that rise. Our history tells us that the formula of dedicated Bible Study and committed Discipleship, was successful 450 years ago. Our spirit of Christian sharing (koinonia, community, Bruderschaft / hof) caught the world unprepared and resulted in severe presecution.

From my vantage point, it appears that today's world might be ready for such a demonstration of Christian commitment, if it were to come from a fresh openness to come to the source and there to drink and eat anew of the "living bread."

The advertising slogan says: "try it, you'll like it." Perhaps it wouldn't always be fun, but it would bring inner peace. Isaiah promises it; history bears evidence to it; you and I know it—whenever we have allowed God to share His "living bread" through our lives; purpose and meaning suddenly seemed so sure.

I challenge all of us for the second century to eat of the bread that enables us to live new lives—and along with Isaiah and the pages of history, let me assure you that this process comes with a "satisfaction guaranteed" label. And it has never failed yet!

—Bernie Wiebe

Bibliography

Listed below are references used in the compiling of this book:

Banton, Roland H., *Here I Stand.* 1950. New York: Mentor Books.

Braght, T. J. V., *The Bloody Theatre* or *Martyrs Mirror* of the Defenseless Christians who baptized only upon confession of Faith, and who suffered and died for the testimony of Jesus, their Saviour, from the time of Christ to the year 1660. Translated from the Dutch. Mennonite Publishing House, Scottdale, Pennsylvania.

Daily Press and Dakotan, Yankton, 1874 newspaper article "Rascality Comes to Light."

Friedmann, Robert, *Hutterite Studies.* Harold Press, Scottdale, Pa.

Green, Michael, *Man Alive*, 1968. London: Billings and Sons Lrd.

Gross, Paul S., *The Hutterite Way.* 216 pages. Available from the author whose address is Reardon, Washington. Written by a Hutterite Colony minister who has travelled in Europe visiting former places of settlement as well as archives, studying manuscripts written by Hutterite writers of former days. A very good account "from the inside" of Hutterite life, customs and beliefs. Well illustrated.

Horsch, John., *The Hutterian Brethren.* Mennonite Historical Society, Goshen College, Goshen, Indiana.

Hostetler, John A. and Huntington, Gertrude Enders, *The Hutterites in North America.* 1967. New York: Holt, Rinehart and Winston. 115 pages. Available from Freeman College Bookshop. A case study of cultural anthropology involving the Hutterian Brethren in America and Canada.

Interpreter's Bible. Vol. 5. Ecclesiastes, Isaiah, Song of Songs, Jeremiah.

Lederach, Paul M., *Mennonite Youth.* 1971. Scottdale, Pa.: Herald Press.

Maslow, Abraham H., *Religions, Values, and Peak-Experiences.* 1970. New York: Viking Press.

Mendel, J. J., *History of the People of East Freeman, Silver Lake, and West Freeman.* Pine Hill Press, Freeman, South Dakota. Mendel, J. J., 1528-1961. 300 pages. Our of print and not available. Has many pictures which were compiled during his nearly sixty years as editor of The Freeman Courier. Also contains an account of the main events as they happened year by year starting with 1875. Contains much interesting information about the Hutterites in private ownership.

Mennonite Encyclopedia. The Mennonite Publishing House, Scottdale, Pa.

Mennonite Life. July 1946. March 1973 and June 1973.

Mennonite Quarterly Review. 1929-1930. 1931-1932. 1946. 1949-1950.

Poettcker, Henry and Regehr, Rudy A., eds. *Call to Faithfulness.* 1972. Winnipeg, Manitoba: Canadian Mennonite Bible College.

Sanderson, John W., *Encounter in the Non-Christian Era.* 1970. Grand Rapids, Mich.: Zondervan Publishing House.

Smith, C. Henry, and Bender, Harold S. *Mennonites and Their Heritage.* Herold Press, Scottdale, Pennsylvania.

Smith, C. Henry, *The Coming of the Russian Mennonites.* Mennonite Book Concern. Berne, Indiana, 1941. An episode in the settling of the American frontier. An excellent account of the settling of these people which includes the settlements in South Dakota. Gives one good overall picture of the Mennonite migration of 1874-1880.

Unruh, John D., *A Century of Mennonites in Dakota.* Pine Hill Press, Freeman, S.D. This gives an in depth account of the prairieluet of South Dakota along with other Mennonites. Also has a chapter on the Hutterian Brethren. Available from Freeman College Bookshop.

Waltner, Emil J., *Banished For Faith.* Available from Freeman College Bookshop. A section of this book (134 pages) deals with the Hutterites and is a translation of parts of the *Klein Geschichtbuch* giving one a good English account of the 1770-1874 period.

MANY MORE BOOKS ARE AVAILABLE FOR ADDITIONAL STUDY CONCERNING THE HUTTERITES. A SMALL PORTION OF THESE ARE LISTED BELOW.

Dyck, Cornelius J., *Twelve Becoming.* Faith and Life Press: Newton, Kansas.

Hostetler, John A. *Hutterite Life.* Freeman Press, Goshen, Indiana, 1951.

Krahn, Cornelius, *From the Steppes to the Prairies.* Mennonite Publication office, Newton, Kansas.

Peters, Victor, *All Things Common.* The University of Minnesota Press, Minneapolis, Minn. An excellent study of the history, the organization and the external relations of the communal living Hutterites. Available at some Mennonite book stores.

Zieglschmid, A. J. F., *Die Altesta Chronik der Hutterishen Brüder.* A history of the Hutterian Brethren written by their leaders as history happened in 1528-1665. Two handwritten copies brought from Russia are yet to be found among the Hutterian Colonies. One at Bon Homme, claimed to be the original, and another at Sage Creek Colony, Chester, Montana. This book has been put into print.

Zieglschmid, A. J. F. *Das Klein Geschichtbuch der Hutterishen Brüder.* A chronological continuation of their history as recorded by Johann Waldner and others as it happened until today. This also is in print. The original is in a colony in Manitoba.

Updated Bibliography for the 2011 Reprint Edition

The Chronicle of the Hutterian Brethren I. An English translation of Das Grosse Geschichtbuch der Hutterischen Bruder. An 887 page translation of the original Hutterite Chronicle.Plough Publishing House. ISBN 0-87486-021-0

The Chronicle of the Hutterian Brethren II. An English translation of Das Kleine-Geschichtsbuch der Hutterischen Bruder. An 867 page translation of the "Small Record Book. Crystal Spring Colony, Ste. Agathe, Manitoba, Canada, Copyright # 460767

Banished for Faith by Emil Waltner 1968. Reprinted in 1979 by End-Time Handmaidens, Inc. A 256 page book tracing the history of the Hutterite Brethren and the Swiss Mennonites from Europe to America. End-Time Handmaidens, Inc. P.O. Box 447, Jasper, Arkansas 72641

The Hutterites of North America by Rod Janzen and Max Stanton 2010. A 373 page book tracing the history of the Hutterian Brethren. John Hopkins University Press, Baltimore, ISBN 10:0-8018-9489-1

Hutterite Society by John A. Hostetler 1974, 1997 by John Hopkins University Press. A 400 page book tracing the history of the Hutterian Brethren. ISBN 0-8018-1584-3

The Prairie People Forgotten Anabaptists by Rod Janzen 1999. A 326 page publication tracing the "Prairie People" branch of the Hutterian Brethren. University Press of New England, Hanover, NH 03755. ISBN 0-87451-931-4

Paul Tschetter The Story of a Hutterite Immigrant Leader, Pioneer, and Pastor by Rod Janzen Pickwick Publications, Eugene Oregon. 303 pages ISBN 1:3 978-1-60608-134-1

Mennonite Historical Atlas by William Schroeder and Helmut T. Huebert 1996 Springfield Publishers, 6 Litz Place, Winnipeg, Manitoba ISBN 0-920643-04-3. A 183 page book of maps, charts and data of Mennonite Historical locations throughout Anabaptist history.

The Diaries of Joseph "Yos" Hofer 1997. A 154 page translation by Arnold Hofer of the three diaries of Joseph Hofer (1839-1905) The St. Petersburg Diary, the Wolf Creek Years, and the Prairieleut years, 1880-1905. Hutterite Mennonite Centennial Committee, Freeman, South Dakota 57029

Hutterite CO's in World War One by Patrick Murphy. 1996 A 154 page book of Stories, Diaries, and other accounts from the United States Military Camps. Spring Prairie Printing, 6189-170th St. N. Hawley, MN 56549-9094

The Golden Years of the Hutterites by Leonard Gross. 1980 A 264 page book. The Witness and Thought of the Communal Moravian Anabaptist during the Walpot Era, 1565-1578. Herald Press

JOHANN CORNIES By David A. Epp. 1995 A 137 page book tracing the history of Johann Cornies, the wealthy Mennonite entrepreneur and his many benevolent activities, including the 1842 migration of the Hutterites from Raditschewa to Hutterthal in southern Russia. Published by Canadian Mennonite Bible College & Manitoba Mennonite Historical Society of Winnipeg, Manitoba. Printed by Derksen Printers, Steinbach, Manitoba R0A 2A0

The Hutterian Language. 149 pages 1997 by Walter B. Hoover. An excellent source of Hutterian language, grammar and lexicon compiled by Dr. Walter B. Hoover, Box 1070, Saskatoon, SK S7K 3M4

Hutterian-English Dictionary by Dr. Walter Hoover, Box 1070, Saskatoon, SK 2001. A 165 page dictionary of the "Hutterish" language, translating "Hutterish" words into English.

Hutterite Roots 1985. By Arnold M. Hofer. A 127 page book listing the births, baptisms, marriages, and deaths of the Hutterites 1757-1883. Hutterite Mennonite Centennial Committee, Freeman, South Dakota 57029

Rooted and Grounded in Love The History and Family Records of the Langham Prairie People, Langham, Saskatchewan by Edna Wurtz and Catherine Masuk, Saskatoon, Sask. 2000. A 450 page book tracing the 33 "Prairieleut" families that migrated from South Dakota to Langham, Saskatchewan beginning in 1901.

A Century of God's Blessings. A History of the Neu Hutterthaler Mennonite Church, Bridgewater, South Dakota 1988 A 47 page book tracing the history of this "Prairieleut" church from 1888-1988.

A Century of God's Great Faithfulness Hutterthal Mennonite Church, Carpenter, South Dakota. 2006 An 80 page book tracing this "Prairieleut" church from 1906-2006. Companion publication is the Cemetery Directory Chart.

Our Journey of Faith Hutterthal Mennonite Church, Freeman, South Dakota. 2004 Edited by Norma Hofer. A 107 page book tracing the history of this "Prairieleut" church from 1879-2004. Companion publication is the Cemetery Directory Chart. Pine Hill Press, 4000 West 57th St. Sioux Falls, SD 57106 ISBN: 1-57579-289-3

A History of the Salem Mennonite Brethren Church, Bridgewater, South Dakota. 1986. Edited by Mrs. Paul S. Gross. A 129 page book tracing the history of this "Prairieleut" church from 1886-1986. Pine Hill Press, Freeman, South Dakota.

A History of Bethel Mennonite Brethren Church, Yale, South Dakota by Joseph A. Kleinsasser 1979. A 120 page book tracing the history of this "Prairieleut" congregation from 1902-1979.Pine Hill Press, Freeman, South Dakota.

Index to Mennonite Immigrants on United States Passenger Lists 1872-1904 by David A. Haury. 1986. Mennonite Library and Archives, North Newton, Kansas. 223 page book listing the ship lists of Mennonite & Hutterite immigrants migrating to United States.

Hutterite Colony Family Records. All three groups of Hutterite branches: Schmeidleut, Lehrerleut and Dariusleut keep very accurate family records. Lists are updated each year, including names, births, deaths, baptism, and marriages. A valuable source of data for compiling family trees and genealogical records.